KAIZEN FOR QUICK CHANGEOVER
Going Beyond SMED

Originally published as Zero dandori kaizen tejun ©1987 by Nikkan Kogyo Shimbunsha.

English edition copyright ©1992 by Productivity Press, a division of The Kraus Organization Limited. Translated by Bruce Talbot.

Productivity Press
444 Park Avenue South, 7th Floor
New York, NY 10016
Telephone: 212-686-5900
Fax: 212-686-5411
Email: info@productivitypress.com

Cover design by Gary Ragaglia

Library of Congress Cataloging-in-Publication Data

Sekine, Ken'ichi, 1944–
   [Zero dandori kaiszentejun. English]
   Kaizen for quick changeover : going beyond SMED / Kenichi Sekine, Keisuke Arai.
      p.   cm.
   Translation of: Zero dandori kaizen tejun.
   Includes index.
   ISBN 1-563273-41-1
   1. Assembly-line methods.   I. Arai Keisuke.   II. Title.
TS178.4S4513   1992
658.5'33—dc20   91-41984
                                                        CIP
                                                        Rev.

05 04   13 12 11 10

Contents

Illustrations

Publisher's Message

Mixed-model, one-piece flow manufacturing can become a reality only when setup can happen in seconds. Many companies today are doing mixed-model assembly. Progressive automobile manufacturers use mixed-model assembly methods to customize each vehicle as it comes down the line. The power of the approach presented in *Kaizen for Quick Changeover* is to help make it possible to do mixed modeling in production as well, by making changeovers even faster.

The concept of quick changeover has done more to enhance the manufacturing process than any other improvement approach. An astounding shift in thinking about your process occurs when you realize that you can reduce setup time from 40 hours to 4 hours to under 4 minutes! The next realization that dawns is that you don't need huge dedicated machines to do what you need to do. Smaller machines organized to process "families" of products can do the same work and offer much more flexibility to meet a variety of customer needs. A third important understanding that arises from improvement of your changeover methods is the improvement you will see in quality and scrap rates. As predetermined settings replace post-changeover adjustments, your first piece off after changeover is likely to be the "next good piece."

Many companies in the United States have attempted to use quick changeover for their manufacturing processes. Very few, however, have developed a methodology for approaching changeover improvement in a systematic way. The late Dr. Shigeo Shingo developed a methodology from which others could learn, based on his experience helping Toyota and other companies develop one-piece flow manufacturing.

Dr. Shingo called his changeover improvement work *SMED* — single-minute exchange of dies — changeover in under ten minutes. The very idea of bringing changeover time for huge machines into this range seemed radical to many, but the methodology worked. Dr. Shingo's quick changeover approach became a powerful tool for many companies seeking to achieve wide-variety small-lot production.

Although Dr. Shingo passed away in 1990, others continue the valuable work he began. In *Kaizen for Quick Changeover*, Kenichi Sekine and Keisuke Arai, two experts on manufacturing process improvement, carry changeover improvement forward to a new level: changeover measured not in minutes but in *seconds*. Their approach, called *zero changeover*, aims to shrink changeover times to three minutes — or less.

Again, the suggestion sounds radical. Yet *zero changeover* is an effective set of principles that works in a wide variety of manufacturing industries, as shown in the case studies in Part III of the book.

Kaizen, or continuous improvement, is an unending spiral of activity, building small improvements one on another for a big effect. It is primarily a process rather than a result, but it is driven by basic ideals. These ideals are inherent in the very definition of the problem to be solved. In quick changeover, the ideal, the ultimate time-saver, would be to have no need for changeover. All improvements in quick changeover methodology are based on the awareness that any setup at all means waste. There is always room for improvement.

Kaizen for Quick Changeover begins with "the basics" in Part I, laying out the authors' main principles of changeover improvement. Chapter 1 defines the concept of zero changeover, with examples of how it might be applied for various types of presses. Chapter 2 presents 8 steps on the path toward quicker setup, including

- attaining a practical grasp of your changeover loss time
- gaining top management support and forming a changeover improvement team
- holding changeover demonstrations and using video and other types of operation analysis
- applying the results of your analysis to reduce waste
- using goal-based thinking against waste
- creating wide-participation improvement plans
- implementing improvements

• evaluating results and deploying successful methods horizontally throughout your organization

Chapter 3 of the book describes 9 basic principles that form the heart of the authors' approach to changeover waste elimination. These principles are organized around the three basic phases in which changeover waste occurs:

• setup (preparation)
• replacement (removing and attaching dies, etc.)
• adjustment

Part II of *Kaizen for Quick Changeover* moves to examples that apply the basic principles to improve changeover on a processing line. For Sekine and Arai, the issue of changeover improvement does not occur in isolation from other aspects of production improvement. The efficient production of many different products on one line requires very rapid changeover as well as group technology. Chapters 4, 5, and 6 present an integrated scheme that deals not just with direct setup improvements but also with line layout improvement and visual management aids to eliminate wasteful travel and unnecessary searching and adjusting — principles known as *process razing*, treated in depth in another book by Sekine, *One-Piece Flow* (Productivity Press, 1992). These chapters delve into U-shaped cell design and concerns relating to efficient use of automated equipment. A key issue is reducing wasteful use of employees as mere machine-watchers, streamlining automated operations so that they can be handled by fewer employees.*

Chapter 6 homes in on issues related to incorporating these improvement ideas into new processing lines, using process-route analysis to organize production around families of products with similar processing. It presents the Toyota production system method of line improvement, along with a simplified method developed by the authors.

---

* It should be noted that manufacturers in Japan, facing a labor shortage, are in very different circumstances than many North American manufacturers in the early 1990s, and that Japanese companies tend to retrain and reassign employees whose jobs are eliminated as a result of improvement efforts. Some measure of job security is a basic foundation for any type of companywide improvement effort. Productivity, Inc., encourages management to act responsibly in managing the effects of process improvements by employees.

The knowledge available in *Kaizen for Quick Changeover* is particularly valuable for component suppliers working in a wide variety of industries and processes. The techniques apply to virtually any type of manufacturing work. To help companies adapt the concepts to their type of production, Part III of the book offers a chapter on each of nine different industries that have applied the "zero changeover" method to advantage. The examples involve press line processing, steel forging, transfer machines, process production, circuit board auto-inserters, sheet metal fabrication, plastic-molding machines, and die-cast machines, as well as an assembly line example. Although each industry has unique issues to resolve, the basic principles remain the same, with adaptations for each type of process.

In this significant book Sekine and Arai bring together years of experience in assisting companies analyze and improve their manufacturing operations. It is an honor to work with them in publishing this English edition so that others might benefit from their expertise.

Many people made this book possible. Sincere thanks to Kenichi Sekine and Keisuke Arai for choosing us as their American publisher. I am also grateful to Hajime Kitamura, director of publication for Nikkan Kogyo Shimbun, Ltd., publisher of the original Japanese edition, for permitting us to produce this material in English. I also wish to acknowledge the efforts of Bruce Talbot, translator; Karen Jones, series editor; Dorothy Lohmann, managing editor; Laura St. Clair, editorial assistant; Peter Tietjen, manuscript editor; Maureen Murray, proofreading; Northwind Editorial Services, indexers; Gayle Joyce, Karla Tolbert, and Michele Saar, production, typesetting, and art preparation; and Gary Ragaglia, cover design.

Norman Bodek
Publisher

Preface

Japan's manufacturing industries are moving overseas. Japan is internationalizing, and this trend has included the overseas expansion of Japanese manufacturing facilities. There is only one way for manufacturing plants in Japan to remain competitive: by successfully developing wide-variety small-lot, just-in-time production. Specifically:

- They must achieve zero changeover, defined as changeover that can be completed within 3 minutes, and
- They must improve their production-line layout without incurring large costs. In other words, they must implement "process razing," create zero-defect production lines, and cut their staffing requirements by half.*

The secrets for achieving these objectives are explained in this book. After chapters on the basic principles of changeover improvement, case studies are presented in industry-specific chapters, as listed below. Please give close attention to the chapters that relate most directly to your own industry.

Press processing industry	Chapter 7
Forging industry	Chapter 8
Transfer machines	Chapter 9
Process industry	Chapter 10
Electronics industry (especially changeover of auto-insert devices)	Chapter 11

---

* For a description of process razing, see Chapter 5. See also Kenichi Sekine, *One-Piece Flow*, (Portland, Ore.: Productivity Press, 1992).

Sheet metal industry   Chapter 12
Plastic-molding industry   Chapter 13
Die-cast forging industry   Chapter 14
Assembly line industry   Chapter 15

Readers will benefit from studying the description in each case study that shows what to do and in what sequence to achieve changeover improvements. Even small initial successes in reducing changeover time can create a contagious "can-do" attitude toward changeover improvements. Once such a start has been made, it is time to get a firm grasp of the basics.

Structure of the book

Part I describes the basic principles of zero changeover. Although the changeover examples in this part come from the press industry, readers from other industries should not conclude in haste that it has nothing to do with them. In fact, people from all industries should read this chapter — perhaps several times — until they get a good grasp of these basic principles.

The secrets of successful changeover improvement are rooted in the principle of unwavering processing standards. Therefore:

1. Various types of changeover can be done as die set changeover.
2. Once an improved changeover method is developed, it should be established as a die set changeover. Die set changeovers are the best way to ensure consistency in maintaining standards.
3. When there is deviation from proper standards, it is important to restore the conditions according to these standards and find a way to prevent such deviation from recurring.

Those who understand this principle of unwavering standard conditions have passed the first test. Readers still unclear about it should study Part I of this book again. During the second, third, or fourth reading, the reader will become increasingly familiar with the basic principles of zero changeover. In the process, he or she will develop a better eye for spotting and removing waste from changeover procedures.

Chapter 1 introduces an example of zero changeover and explains the meaning, purpose, and development of zero changeover. We advise readers who are completely unfamiliar with zero changeover to study this chapter before proceeding to the rest of the book.

Chapter 2 describes the steps toward zero changeover. Readers from factories that have attempted changeover improvement with little or no success can rest assured that the improvement steps explained here are reliable if faithfully followed.

Chapter 3 presents a 9-point formula for achieving zero changeover. Readers can dramatically increase their efficiency in making changeover improvements if they learn this formula.

Part II describes changeover improvement methods and case studies pertaining to processing lines. Chapter 4 presents the basic principles of changeover improvement on processing lines. Chapter 5 describes changeover improvements that smaller companies can make without incurring large costs. Chapter 6 describes changeover improvements made using two methods, the orthodox Toyota production system (TPS) method and a simplified method (S method).

Part III presents case studies from a number of companies, organized by industry-specific chapters.

The material in this book is an expansion and revision of material previously published as "The Changeover Improvement Manual" in the August 1987, edition of *Factory Management* magazine (*Kojo Kanri*).

Part I
Basics

This section provides a detailed description of the formula and steps for changeover improvement in stand-alone equipment.

1

Steps in Changeover Improvement

WHAT IS ZERO CHANGEOVER?

Zero changeover is changeover that can be completed within 3 minutes. Changeover itself does not add value to products; it must be viewed as waste. Since waste is something you must always strive to eliminate, you must find ways to minimize changeover. Changeover cannot be eliminated completely. Through a persistent, step-by-step approach, however, you can reduce current changeover times by half, then to within 30 minutes, 9 minutes ("single changeover," or changeover within a single-digit number of minutes), and finally the zero changeover range of 3 minutes. This approach is illustrated in Figure 1-1.

This part of the book presents the knowledge needed to achieve the following five objectives:

1. Reduce the labor hours required for changeover
2. Remove waste in materials and parts used for changeover, thereby improving changeover efficiency
3. Raise the capacity utilization rate for specific devices and large presses
4. Develop changeover methods that prevent deviation from standards and ensure quality control for small lots
5. Implement small-lot production to reduce inventory levels

We will also introduce several case studies showing how such changeover improvement can be done in press factories.

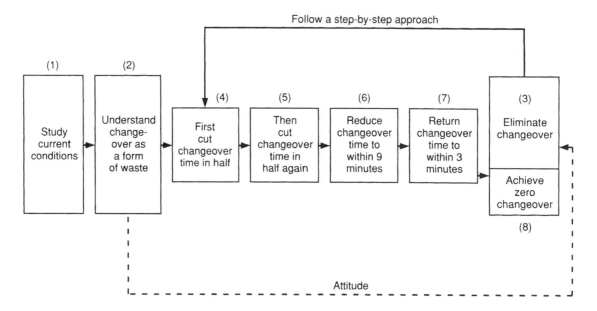

Figure 1-1. Development of Improvements Toward Zero Changeover

ZERO CHANGEOVER FOR SMALL PRESSES

Figure 1-2 illustrates a changeover improvement that Company O made for one of its small presses.* After improvement, part-time workers easily handled the changeover on the small press in just 25 seconds. The press is used for 10-unit lots, and each punch of the press takes about 3 seconds. Therefore, the processing time per lot is 30 seconds which, with the changeover time of 25 seconds, makes a total cycle time per lot of 55 seconds.

Before improvement, changeover for this press was done using a conventional shank-equipped die assembly; the changeover time was close to an hour. It did not take a direct threat from management for the workers to know that jobs would be lost unless the factory could successfully handle small-lot production.

The employees assembled their collective wisdom and devised a drawer-style cassette system (see Figure 1-2). Their starting point in making the improvement was to eliminate the die assembly shanks. This was in keeping with

---

* For further discussion of this improvement, refer to Kenichi Sekine, *One-Piece Flow* (Portland, Ore.: Productivity Press, 1992), Chapter 12 and Figures 12-16 and 12-17.

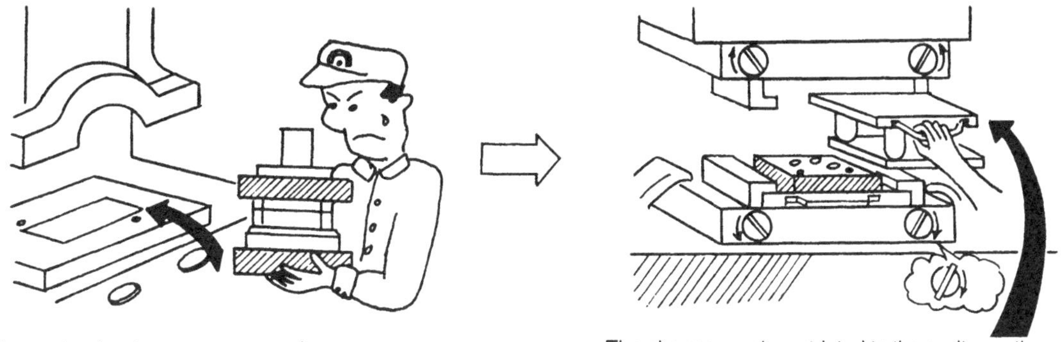

Before improvement (30 minutes)

After improvement (25 seconds)

Currently, the changeover procedure uses large dies that are too heavy for some workers to handle.

The changeover is restricted to the cavity section and the rest of the die assembly is left as is. The changeover procedure is done without bolts and uses simple locking tools that workers can quickly learn to use. Cost: about ¥30,000 ($230) per unit.

Figure 1-2. Zero Changeover for a Small Press

point 7 of the zero changeover formula described in Chapter 3: Eliminate such shanks whenever possible.

ZERO CHANGEOVER IN A LARGE PRESS LINE

At Company T, changeover on the 2,000-ton transfer press line is done within 3 minutes (zero changeover). Figure 1-3 shows the "just push" layout of the press line.

The line consists of six linked presses. Using sequential changeover (see Chapter 4), the entire line's changeover can be done in just 2 minutes and 30 seconds, to which we add the press punching time of 5 seconds per press. Specifically, the press punching time is counted only for presses 2 through 6, since changeover is done after each punch; total punching time is 25 seconds (5 seconds × 5 presses). Therefore, the total time is 2 minutes and 30 seconds + 25 seconds = 2 minutes and 55 seconds — just under the 3-minute range defined as zero changeover. Ten years earlier, it took a full hour to set up this six-press line with new dies.

The "just push" mechanism that makes this zero changeover possible was the brainchild of one of Company T's factory supervisors, Mr. A. When told by his superiors to find a way of reducing changeover time to less than 3 minutes, Mr. A began thinking about it. One day he happened to be looking at a worker's

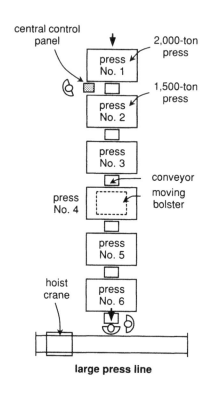

large press line

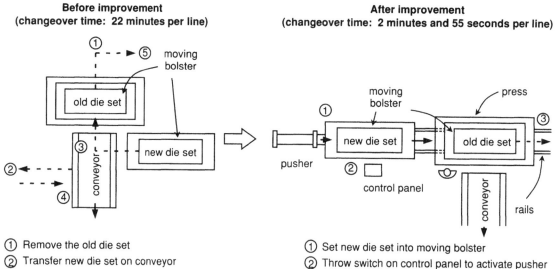

Before improvement
(changeover time: 22 minutes per line)

① Remove the old die set
② Transfer new die set on conveyor
③ Attach new die set
④ Return conveyor to original position
⑤ Take away old die set after resuming operation

After improvement
(changeover time: 2 minutes and 55 seconds per line)

① Set new die set into moving bolster
② Throw switch on control panel to activate pusher in auto-feed and auto-stop mechanism
③ Take away old die set after resuming operation

Figure 1-3. Zero Changeover on Large Press Line

thermos bottle, with a popular-styled lid that did not have to be unscrewed to pour ("just push" was actually the advertising slogan for the thermos). Mr. A thought a similar system could be applied for his press operations, using a pusher that would laterally extract and insert press dies.

The main drawback of this plan was its cost: each pusher mechanism cost about one-fifth as much as the press itself. (Those interested in such mechanisms can contact the press department at Komatsu, Ltd., which makes them to order.)

Before improvement, Company T's press line used a last-in, first-out system, as shown in Figure 1-3. Because the dies could not be changed unless the transfer line's conveyor moved, it took that much more time to make the die change.

The "just push" system is adaptable to various kinds of changeover. For example, changeover for large extruders can be done without having to stop the machine. Naturally, the system can also be used for small presses.

ZERO CHANGEOVER FOR GENERAL-PURPOSE PRESSES

Figure 1-4 shows the first-in, first-out flow of zero changeover layout for general-purpose presses. Before the changeover begins, the new die is put on the roller conveyor on the left side of the press. Previously, a manual lift had been used to bring in the new die. A die lifter was built into the bolster for removing heavy dies; lighter dies are removed by hand and placed on another roller conveyor on the right side of the press. Stoppers are used to simplify the attachment of new dies. A separate clamping tool fastened with only one turn is used to simplify and speed the die-clamping procedure. (See also Figure 3-6 in Chapter 3.)

Three basic conditions had to be established to allow zero changeover for the general-purpose press:

1. *Standardization of dies:* At first, the dies were standardized in four respects:
   • die height
   • die sizes (small, medium, and large)
   • clamp height
   • clamp position

   Other standardization changes were made later, as secondary improvements.

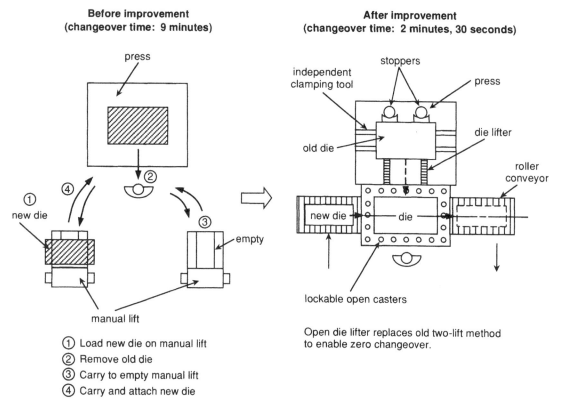

Before improvement
(changeover time: 9 minutes)

press

④ ② ①
new die

③
empty

manual lift

① Load new die on manual lift
② Remove old die
③ Carry to empty manual lift
④ Carry and attach new die

After improvement
(changeover time: 2 minutes, 30 seconds)

independent   stoppers
clamping tool   press

old die   die lifter

roller
conveyor

new die   die

lockable open casters

Open die lifter replaces old two-lift method
to enable zero changeover.

Figure 1-4. Zero Changeover for a General-Purpose Press

2. *Use of independent clamping tools*
3. *Installation of a stopper device to aid positioning (see Figure 1-5)*

These small, inexpensive improvements were sufficient to reduce the general-purpose press's changeover time to less than 3 minutes — zero changeover. Such inexpensive improvements are especially advantageous for smaller companies. If a company has the money to invest, it may want to install a quick die change (QDC) device, such as shown in Figure 1-6.

However, such QDC devices cost about ¥500,000 (approximately $4,000 at ¥125/$1) each, which would mean a total price of about ¥10 million ($80,000) for a 20-press line, a cost that is beyond the means of many small companies. The QDC solution also has the disadvantage of being a prepackaged solution that does not incorporate the ideas of the people who work in the target production line. Factories should not rush to introduce new or remodeled equip-

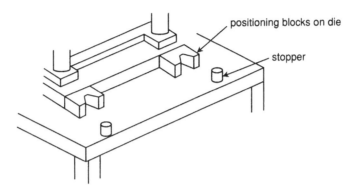

The positioning blocks are set in different positions on each die, depending on die size.

Figure 1-5. Stopper Device to Aid Positioning

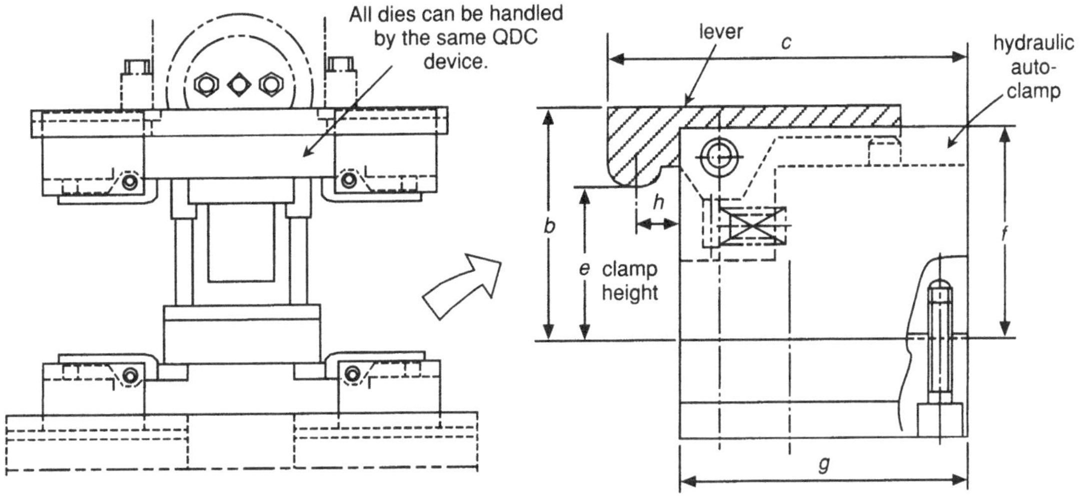

Figure 1-6. QDC (Quick Die Change) Device

ment when the their problem might respond to a much less expensive and more ingenious solution through small improvements made by the people who operate and supervise the target production line.

If possible, it is better to make the kind of zero-changeover improvements shown in Figure 1-2 or Figure 1-4. Such improvements allow factory-floor supervisors to make full use of the expertise and wisdom available to them. The results can be applied to other production lines in the company.

A ROTARY SYSTEM FOR AUTO CHANGEOVER

Zero changeover is one way that suppliers can facilitate the introduction of the Toyota Production System. This system uses cards called *kanban* to convey delivery orders on a just-in-time basis.* For example, if the kanban tells you that the delivery cycle is 1-12-2 (delivery 12 times a day, with parts delivered two times after the order is received), you know that various amounts of products must be delivered every 2 hours. Suppose that this means your press die will require about 40 changeovers per day. The average lot size is 100 units and each press punch takes 6 seconds. The processing time for the lot is therefore 100 units × 6 seconds = 600 seconds (10 minutes).

If you perform a changeover every 10 minutes and the changeover time is 3 minutes, your changeover loss rate is only 30 percent, which is hardly a boost to productivity. In this case, the zero changeover range is 30 seconds instead of 3 minutes.

One solution is an auto-changeover system. Figure 1-7 shows a rotary system for auto-changeover that was developed at Company M. The many dies used during the frequent changeovers are stored nearby in a three-level die storage system. A bar-code reader interprets production instructions from the kanban and the required dies are automatically transported from the storage system. A pusher automatically removes old dies and inserts new ones. This highly automated system can complete each changeover operation in just 10 to 30 seconds.

The main drawback of this system is that, like special QDC devices, its cost is beyond the means of smaller companies. How might a small company approach the same problem and find a solution that it can afford?

TEST YOUR SKILLS

Company S is a subcontractor that supplies parts to its parent company, among others. The parent company makes greater demands on Company S's delivery schedule, even though Company S already completes three deliveries a

---

* For more on kanban and the Toyota Production System, see JMA, ed., *Kanban and Just-in-Time at Toyota* (Portland, Ore.: Productivity Press, 1989), and Giorgio Merli, *Co-Makership: The New Supply Strategy for Manufacturing* (Portland, Ore.: Productivity Press, 1991).

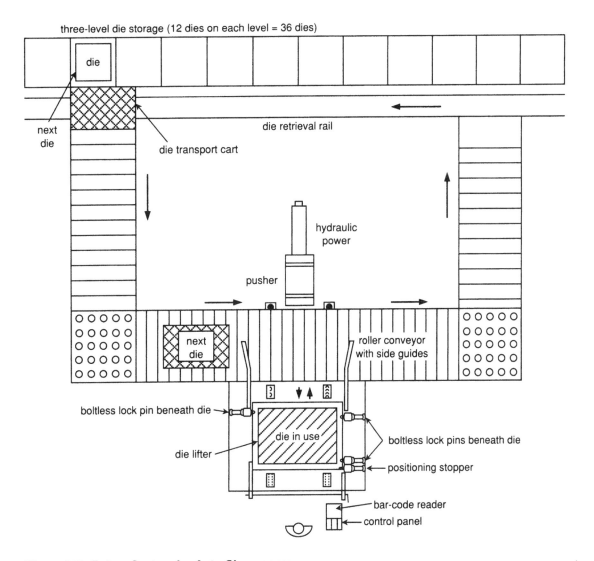

three-level die storage (12 dies on each level = 36 dies)

Figure 1-7. Rotary System for Auto Changeover

day. As a result of trying to meet this rigorous schedule, the company's stocks of defective goods were piling up. The company president decided that the company must solve this difficult situation and should begin by implementing zero changeover.

Company S gets its dies from its parent company. The current changeover time for the production line is 20 minutes. If you were the president of Company S, what would you instruct your factory managers to do?

Solution

The first step: Tell them to organize a changeover improvement team and challenge them to cut the changeover time in half (to 10 minutes), regardless of which company's dies and equipment are used. Remember that prior approval will be necessary from the parent company if the improvement team wants to remodel any of the dies it has received from that company.

Chapter 2 describes the improvement-team approach and the remainder of the book presents approaches the team can use to reach single changeover and zero changeover.

2

Steps Toward Zero Changeover

Although this book focuses primarily on changeover improvement in various types of presses, the principles taught here can be applied in many other manufacturing situations.

The word *press* refers to a wide variety of equipment, including punch presses, forge presses and other forging equipment, die-cast presses, and plastic molding machines. At the large end of the spectrum, there are the 6,500-ton presses used to make automobile bodies; at the small end, there are simple table-top push presses. What all have in common is that they use a die or mold that is moved up and down to help make a product.

The die or mold is what gives shape to the product during press processing. Therefore, different products require different dies or molds. We will restrict our discussion of zero changeover for presses by speaking only in terms of two factors: the press machines and the dies they use.

The focus of this book is on kaizen-type methods of improving changeover — small, inexpensive advances rather than big capital-expense innovations. The steps for achieving zero changeover without incurring substantial costs include the following:

1. Gaining a practical grasp of changeover loss time
2. A declaration of support from top management and formation of the changeover improvement team
3. Open changeover demonstrations and observation, video recording, and analysis of factory operations
4. Applying analysis results to three types of waste
5. Goal-based thinking to remove waste

6. Red-tag strategy (creating wide-participation improvement plans)
7. Implementing improvements
8. Evaluating results and horizontal deployment

GAINING A PRACTICAL GRASP OF CHANGEOVER LOSS TIME

Before beginning an improvement effort, it is important to have a clear picture of your present situation as a baseline. *Changeover loss time* is the measure usually used. To understand the meaning of changeover loss time, consider the economic aspect of changeover loss. The point is to accurately grasp the loss incurred from the wasteful activity that we call changeover. Table 2-1 shows the results of a survey of actual changeover times. We suggest you conduct a similar survey and make a table such as this for your company. Table 2-2 shows capacity utilization rates for various presses.

Since wide-variety small-lot production is a cause of frequent changeover, you should also conduct a product-quantity (P-Q) analysis to understand how product lot sizes affect changeover. Figure 2-1 shows the results of such a P-Q analysis. For a detailed description of how to create P-Q analysis charts, see Chapter 6.

Table 2-1. Table of Actual Changeover Times (Measured over a 7-Day Period)

Process \ Changeover item	(A) Total process time (min.)	(B) Total production time (min.)	(C) Total changeover time (min.)	(D) No. of changeovers
M_1	1,033	1,700	1,151	41
M_2	968	1,370	1,336	56
M_3	1,304	1,454	1,553	72
M_4	880	1,028	1,743	54
M_5	1,429	2,016	631	43
M_6	1,831	2,679	352	83
M_7	1,575	2,323	288	45
M_8	1,956	2,528	374	39
M_{29}	2,365	3,371	90	15

The gist of what these illustrations show is that production of product Group A will be moved overseas, while domestic factories will continue to produce product Groups B and C via small-lot production with short delivery deadlines. This switch to small-lot production was estimated to more than double the frequency of changeovers, and this fact alerted the company to the need to reduce changeover.

Table 2-2. Capacity Utilization in Various Presses over Four Months

Press	A	M	J	J	Average
160-ton press	95%	65%	70%	81%	78%
150	87	59	41	43	58
110-1	76	48	26	30	45
110-2	47	29	15	46	34
60-ton press	39	59	80	57	59
100-2	64	85	79	67	74
100-3	69	41	53	67	58
100-4	59	36	56	61	53
60	87	72	87	88	84
55	61	34	46	39	45
Average	68	53	55	58	59

Target values	High-speed press: 75%
	Large press: 70%

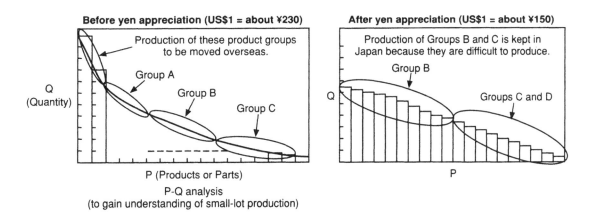

Figure 2-1. A Change in the P-Q Analysis for Predicting Output Due to Yen Appreciation

A DECLARATION OF SUPPORT FROM TOP MANAGEMENT AND FORMATION OF THE CHANGEOVER IMPROVEMENT TEAM

Once you have studied the current changeover loss situation and the change in P-Q factors caused by the company's overseas production shift, you must persuade the top managers to recognize and formally declare that changeover improvement is needed. Improvement efforts will not go far nor will the results last long unless you have the support of the company management.

The company's current changeover loss rate averages 22.5 percent. One reason for this high rate of changeover loss is that managers have been content to use production equipment designed for rapid growth and low-diversity large-lot production without considering the equipment needs of today's wide-variety small-lot production. When the president of the company in this example noticed this, he immediately ordered the formation of a changeover improvement team, which he called a "study group."

A study group must be led by the factory manager, assisted by the head of the production engineering department. The members of the group should be drawn from the factory foremen or technicians who actually perform changeovers. This group of four or five people should meet once a week for about 2 hours, perhaps late Friday afternoon. A good way to begin the first few meetings is to study the 9-point formula for changeover improvement described in Chapter 3.

Next, the study group could take the following approach:

1. Plan and execute weekly demonstrations of changeover at various production lines. Remember: Everyone in the company has something to teach as well as something to learn. Everyone should study the current conditions and contribute toward removing changeover waste.
2. Since the open changeover demonstrations are conducted once a week, the study group must meet beforehand with the line that will conduct the demonstration that week. Each line has to devise procedure improvement ideas; all lines must participate.
3. Once a month, the study group must review the past month's changeover improvements to see whether any of them can be applied on other workshops or production lines. This is vital because lines that achieve improvements — and even those that achieve zero changeover — are often reluctant to invest the time needed for horizontal deployment.

4. Convene plenty of small improvement planning sessions.
5. Once every three months, hold a large-scale open demonstration of changeover.

OPEN CHANGEOVER DEMONSTRATIONS AND OBSERVATION, VIDEO RECORDING, AND ANALYSIS OF FACTORY OPERATIONS

How to carry out an operation analysis

Let us begin by defining our terms.

- *Changeover time* means the time required for removing the old die, attaching a new one, and running the press until it yields a nondefective product.
- *Operation analysis* means an analysis of the operation conditions pertaining to the operator and the machine. The measurement of changeover time is based on a combination of these two types of conditions.
- Table 2-3 shows an example of an *operations analysis chart*. Any ordinary paper can be used for the chart. This analysis is a time study of the press operator's work at the press.
- *Internal changeover* refers to changeover work (such as removing and attaching dies) that cannot be done unless the press is stopped.
- By contrast, *external changeover* is changeover work (such as preparing new dies, transporting required materials, sorting items, etc.) that can be done while the press is in operation. This work may include wasteful motions, such as unnecessary preparations or searching for items, that are repeated throughout the day.

Always keep a pen and notepad on hand to jot down changeover improvement ideas that occur to you as you observe current conditions. It may help to use two people: one to take the time measurements and the other to think about improvement ideas. If a third person is available, he or she can start an operation analysis of the press being observed. In any case, it is good to have an observer who is not the operator, since this increases the objectivity of the study.

Table 2-3. Press Operation Analysis Chart

No.	Work element	Cumulative time	Net time	Internal	External	Waste	Improvement notes
(3)	Throw switch	24.02		O			⎫ Simplify die setting
(4)	Remove air hose	24.12		O			⎬ procedure.
(5)	Put away air hose	24.40				O	⎭
(6)	Remove material from die	25.15		O			
(7)	Lower stroke	25.23		O			
(8)	Loosen bolts	25.43		O			
(9)	Loosen center bolt in upper die	26.08		O			
(10)	Remove counter	26.22		O			
(11)	Remove upper die	26.38		O			
(12)	Loosen bolts in lower die	26.54		O			⎫ Eliminate need to
(13)	Remove lower die	27.19				O	⎭ remove bolts.
(14)	Bring cart over	27.45				O	Convert to two-
(15)	Set cart at bolster	28.07			O		person job.

Observation using video cameras

Video cameras and VCRs have become much more accessible and they are good tools for studying factory conditions. However, if the operations observed are over an hour long, it is generally better to observe them firsthand, since they are likely to involve quite a lot of waste. In other situations, a video recording of the operations offers the advantage of enabling everyone to study current conditions from the same view and to work more closely and easily in identifying waste and developing improvement plans.

Waste elimination based on observation of operations

Although it takes about 20 hours of experience in performing time studies to be able to create operations analysis charts such as the one shown in Table 2-3, it requires no special experience for factory employees to study other factory workers' work and find waste in their work motions. They can quickly learn to spot wasteful motions and then create a waste elimination chart based on their observations.

APPLYING ANALYSIS RESULTS TO THREE TYPES OF WASTE

Divide the observation results (time measurements, etc.) into the operation categories of setup, die removal, die attachment, positioning, standard-setting, inspection, test processing, and adjustments. By standardizing the approach for developing improvement plans for press changeover, anyone can cut change-over time in half. Table 2-4 shows a changeover waste elimination chart created by workers at Company B based on their analysis of changeover operations.

The results of the analysis are eventually applied to three types of waste:

- Setup waste
- Replacement waste
- Adjustment waste

Table 2-5 shows a changeover waste elimination chart that uses these three categories as a framework. It was created simply from observation of operations with no time measurements.

Table 2-4. Changeover Elimination Chart for 150-Ton Press

Category	Internal	External	Total	Improvement ideas
Setup	90	240	330 (13%)	(1) Use specialized changeover carts. (2) Teach standard terms for evaluating change-over.
Remove, attach	Lower 180 Upper 300	Rework 140	620 (24.5%)	(3) Use the same attachment height and attachment jig. (4) Study die dimensions and draw up a chart of die machine correlations. (5) Do a P-Q analysis in which A = die set, B = guide pin, and C = interface jig.
Positioning and standard-setting	80	0	80 (3.2%)	(6) Attach a tapering device (use guide pin method). (7) Get factory workers together to develop a simple position and standard-checking method.
Test processing, adjustment	150	Tapping to adjust, gave up after 1,350 seconds	1,500 (59.3%)	(8) Use a center line for the press attachment site (and for the dies). (9) Create a specialized inspection jig and improve the gauges. (10) Use an address system for organizing die storage sites.
Total	800 (31.6%)	1,730 (68.4%)	2,530 (100%)	

Note: Inspection is included in the "adjustment" category. (Unit: 1 second)

Table 2-5. Changeover Waste Elimination Chart for Red-Tag Strategy

Waste	Activities	Time	Types of waste	
Setup waste	Setup	10%	1. Lining up jigs 2. Transporting inspection jig 3. Transporting dies 4. Layout that makes changeover more difficult	
Changeover waste	Removing and attaching dies, etc.	20%	Dies	1. Bolt fasteners 2. Die changeover 3. Positioning of dies 4. Variation in dies 5. Nonuniformity of fastening tools 6. Use of L-shaped clamp 7. Hoop material changeover 8. Undo hoop strings
Adjustment waste	Positioning, standard-setting, test processing, inspection, and other adjustments	65%	Materials	
			1. Stroke adjustment 2. Feed height 3. Feed amount 4. Waste in moving chutes 5. Inspection waste	
	Other	5%	1. Position of oil supply ports 2. Air (pneumatics, air) 3. Electrical connections 4. Selection of materials	
	Total	32 minutes		

Problem point / Category	Waste elimination plan		
	A (small improvement)	B (medium improvement)	C (large improvement)
Removal of waste from setup work	1. Use tray containing the seven changeover tools 2. Use address system to organize die storage (color-code dies and machines) 3. Use changeover *andon*	1. Use specialized change-over carts with rotating tops	1. Establish U-shaped cells of presses
Waste in removing and attaching	4. Use independent fastening devices (spring-loaded devices, etc.) 5. Standardize male and female fittings 6. Study die dimensions • Width and length • Die height • Attachment height • Upper die dimensions • Feed device height • Width • Feed device centering • Oil supply • Chutes • Check categorization of dies 7. Bunt method	2. Try to reduce fastening tools to two per operation 3. Eliminate the need to remove bolts; use U-shaped washers 4. Develop die standardization plans • Draw up correlation chart for machines and dies 5. Establish external change-over for hoop sets	2. Install auto-clamping devices 3. Remodel equipment for standardization • Standardize die designs • Decide how big the largest press's die must be • Use A, B, C (P-Q) grouping to simplify standardization if necessary
Adjustment waste (waste in flexible standards)	8. Insert shims for die setting 9. Attach chutes to dies so they can slide 10. Make stroke more visible by removing part of cover (and leave a measure scale inside) 11. Build a bin set to enable file drawer-type selection of materials	6. Develop a gauge for stroke standard settings (set up for die) 7. Install oil sprayer for dies 8. Study whether two-person changeover would be better	4. Use "floating die" design (trim shanks) 5. Establish and practice standard operations for one-person changeover 6. Restrict changeover to cavity section

GOAL-BASED THINKING TO REMOVE WASTE

Before you devise an improvement plan, you need to have an improvement target. If your goal is to cut changeover time in half, set a target of 30 minutes for a changeover that now takes an hour. Having a target helps sustain your focus as you progress step by step. Once you have a target, start thinking about the means that will get you there. Then proceed systematically, tackling waste in the three main categories listed in Step 4.

Setup waste

Setup waste is most commonly found in the motions of searching, finding, selecting, lining up, and transporting.

The first question to ask is, "Can we eliminate this process?" One labor-saving solution to the problem of searching for the changeover tools is a specialized changeover cart with a tray that holds the seven changeover tools (see Figure 2-2). This cart corresponds to the first point of the 9-point formula for achieving zero changeover: Make sure everything needed for setup is already organized and on hand (see Chapter 3).

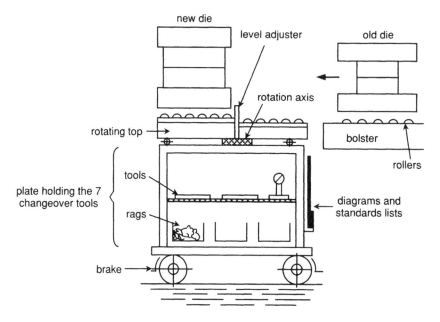

Figure 2-2. Specialized Changeover Cart

Replacement waste

The most common types of replacement waste occur in the acts of removing and fastening bolts. Ask yourself, "Do we really need to remove and fasten bolts?" Boltless fasteners can sometimes be used instead. When bolts are necessary, you can still eliminate bolt-related waste in line with point 3 of the zero changeover formula by using pear-shaped holes and U-shaped washers (see Figure 2-3).

The point of the improvement shown in Figure 2-3 is to loosen the bolt with just one turn. Although the threads on most bolts have 12 to 20 rotations per inch, only the last rotation fastens the bolt tightly. All other rotations are waste. So, the question is how to remove this waste by turning the bolt only once to fasten it.

Starting point: Identification of waste

The bolt's fastening strength is in its final turn.

waste

Improvement plan

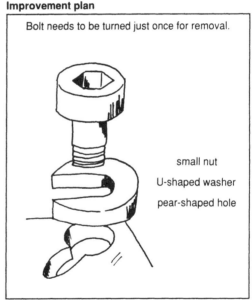

Bolt needs to be turned just once for removal.

small nut
U-shaped washer
pear-shaped hole

Figure 2-3. Eliminating the Need to Remove and Fasten Bolts

Adjustment waste

Adjustment waste is the result of loose adherence to standards during changeover. For example, the operator may need to use a scale to visually set the feed pitch according to very precise standards. Since this is very difficult to do with the required precision, and since no recording is made of actual settings, a calculator must always be used to make the high-precision adjustment.

Figure 2-4 shows how one workshop answered the question, Can we do without this? by devising block gauges for equipment models A and B. These block gauges, made in a U shape to keep them from separating, are laid alongside the scale. For a more detailed description of these block gauges, see Chapter 3.

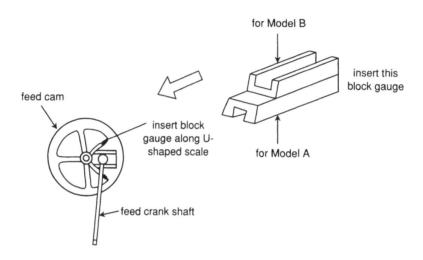

Figure 2-4. Use of Block Gauges for Crank Standard Setting

RED-TAG STRATEGY (CREATING WIDE-PARTICIPATION IMPROVEMENT PLANS)

Wide participation is the key to successful improvement making. The specific waste-removing improvement plans that come of such participation fall into the following categories:

1. Improvements that can be implemented right away: small improvements
2. Improvements that require little time or money: medium improvements
3. Improvements that require equipment remodeling, technical studies, or other time- or expense-consuming elements: large improvements

When scheduling a group of improvements, start with the smallest improvements and work toward the large ones. Quite often, small and medium improvements alone are enough to cut changeover time in half.

Again, the key is wide participation. Through group discussions, you can take what Table 2-5 tells you and develop it into a schedule of improvements, such as shown in Table 2-6. To do this, you must decide as a group who is to do what, by when, and with what means. You must also set your targets and clarify specific implementation plans. The final schedule should be drafted on large poster paper and then posted on a wall in the factory where everyone can see it.

IMPLEMENTING IMPROVEMENTS

When you begin implementing improvements, you start taking down the red tags that were put up to indicate problem areas. The first day of the implementation should be marked in the improvement record book; the factory team leaders should provide a lot of support, commending progress in the removal of red tags.

If the implementation lags behind schedule, establish a rapid-response center to give expert assistance in making the necessary technical aids you need for quicker changeover. Smaller companies that do not have such improvement support centers are advised to hire outside firms that can swiftly fabricate new jigs and tools that are needed. Corporate management and the factory managers bear the chief responsibility for dealing with tardiness in improvement implementation.

EVALUATING RESULTS AND HORIZONTAL DEPLOYMENT

Once zero changeover has been achieved on a model line, the improvements should be horizontally deployed to other lines throughout the company through changeover demonstrations and new changeover operation standards. Chapter 3 details the 9-point formula for achieving zero changeover and shows how those points were applied in several case studies.

TEST YOUR SKILLS

An improvement group at Company A followed the above steps and reduced its changeover time to within 3 minutes. However, its products have very short life cycles and existing dies are wearing out. Since the group must start making new dies, they have decided to standardize the die designs and fabrication methods. How should they approach this task?

Table 2-6. Changeover Improvement Schedule (Red-Tag Strategy)

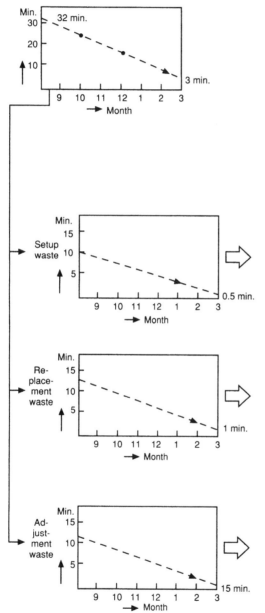

Improvement category	(a) Small improvement			
Type of waste	Improvement item	Cost*	Effect (min.)	Due/ in charge
Setup waste	1. Plate containing 7 changeover tools	0	1	9 / A
	2. Address system for die storage	0	1	10 / A
	3. Color-coding of presses and dies	0	1	10 / A
	4. Use hoop bands	0	0.5	10 / A
Replacement waste	1. Improve unscrewing of bolts	0	2	9 / A
	2. Use independent fastening tools	0	3	9 / A
	3. Use protruding stoppers	0	1	9 / A
	4. Establish and practice standard operations	0	2	9 / A
	5. Devise single-turn screws	0	1	9 / A
Adjustment waste	1. Attach chutes	0	0.5	9 / A
	2. Stroke position marking	0	0.5	9 / A
	3. Use pull strings for materials	0	0.5	9 / A
	4. Standardize die height and width and attachment height	5	5	9 / A

Key: – – – – – – = Target values

——————— = Measured values

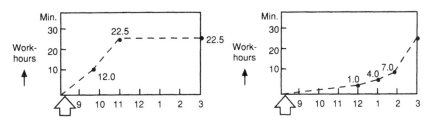

(b) Medium improvement				(c) Large improvement			
Improvement item	Cost*	Effect (min.)	Due/ in charge	Improvement item	Cost*	Effect (min.)	Due/ in charge
1. Specialized changeover carts	10	2	10 / B	1. In-line integration of presses	50	0	3 / C
2. Changeover kanban	0	1	11 / C	2. Improvement of die storage sites	100	3	3 / C
3. Move dies closer to presses	10	1	11 / C	3. Improve accessories and peripheral equipment	30	3	3 / C
1. Reduce fastening tools to two	0	1	11 / B	1. Use double pins for hoop materials	10	1	12 / C
2. Keep bolts in fixed positions	5	2	11 / B	2. Use auto-clamp devices**	50	3	2 / C
3. Simplify correlations between dies and presses	0	0.5	10 / B	3. Redesign dies for greater uniformity**	30	3	3 / C
4. Use small nuts and U-shaped washers	0	1	10 / B	4. Use "floating die" design**	50	3	3 / C
5. Improve inspection tools	10	0.5	10 / B				
1. Use block gauges for setting stroke standards	1	3	10 / B	1. Limit replacement to cavity sections**	5	3	1 / C
2. Install oil sprayer for dies	5	0.5	11 / B	2. Establish file drawer-type selection of materials**	5	5	3 / C
3. Try two-person changeover	0	5	10 / A				
4. Eliminate shank	0	3	11 / B				
5. Use block gauges for scales	5	2	11 / B				

*Cost unit = ¥10,000
**Some of this may be repeated or overlapped until the target labor-hour reduction is reached.

Solution

The group could start with the following steps:

1. Group products into families.
2. Standardize die structures.
   - Establish family groupings of existing die structures.
   - Select the most appropriate of these structures and establish them provisionally as the standard structures.
   - Create standard structures in line with the 9-point zero changeover formula.
   - Determine the required dimensions for each die structure.
3. Standardize the die attachment units.
4. Standardize die parts. Reduce the variety of commercial parts used and establish in-house bolt standards. In so doing, remain as compatible as possible with external standards, such as JIS or outside manufacturers' standards.
5. Clarify the processing standards.
6. Standardize information. Create an in-house handbook of die design and fabrication to ensure that everyone uses the same information.

3

A Formula for Achieving
Zero Changeover

A formula for successful changeover improvement can be learned from one's experience or from the experiences of others. If you attempt 1,000 times to achieve a goal (say, twice a day for about a year and a half), you may discover a formula firsthand. However, the chances of achieving your goal will vastly improve if you know the formula beforehand.

That is a good reason to begin by learning the fundamentals. If you learn the wrong ideas about fundamental matters, you are likely to continue making mistakes later, no matter how much you study the formula and no matter how enthusiastic you are about implementing improvements.

Consider an analogy from golf. The key in golf is to become skilled at hitting the ball consistently to your average distance for each club. The goal is not simply to send the ball flying but rather to judge your own average distances accurately and to be able to send the ball about that far to achieve a consistent, predictable score. To achieve this kind of consistency, a golfer must establish and enforce strict standards for addressing the ball.

One key difference between amateur and professional golfers is the way they move as they hit the ball. If you were to look at a professional golfer's swing in slow motion, you would see that the vertical pivot through the neck and head rotates but does not wobble, and that the shoulders also rotate with no vertical motion. These are the standards that professionals do not allow to vary (see Figure 3-1).

The typical amateur golfer who only plays once a month has little experience, but can still improve his or her game by learning and practicing the correct position for addressing the ball, which is to maintain a rigid vertical pivot without wobbling the shoulders up or down. Amateur golfers who do not

amateur   professional

Figure 3-1. The Vertical Pivot Is the Standard

know or practice this standard try to control their swing from the wrist instead of from the shoulders; they tend to look up just as they hit the ball to see where it is going. The rigid vertical pivot is destroyed by this motion and, as a result, the ball usually flies in some unintended direction.

Fortunately, amateurs regard golf as just a game — they can still enjoy playing and having refreshments at the clubhouse, no matter how bad their score. When it comes to factory changeover operations, however, such a carefree attitude is disastrous.

Changeover work that takes two hours or longer is a real pain; it is psychologically boring and physically tiring. Eventually, workers become apathetic about enforcing standards; this, of course, leads to more rework, defects, and complaints from downstream. The basic principle of quality control for wide-variety small-lot production is to establish zero changeover to help workers maintain unwavering standards.

A 9-point Formula for Changeover Improvement

The formula for achieving zero changeover in press changeover operations has 9 points:

1. Ensure that everything needed for setup is already organized and on hand.

2. It is OK to move the arms, but not the legs.
3. Do not remove bolts completely.
4. Regard bolts as enemies; do whatever you can to get rid of them.
5. Do not allow any deviation from die and jig standards.
6. Adjustment is waste. Do not move the base section. Selecting is OK, but adjustments are simply waste.
7. Cut off shanks if possible. Use the floating-style die instead. Keep only the lower die in a fixed position.
8. Use block gauges for all adjustments currently done visually with scales.
9. Find ways to carry out changeover without having to stop the press. Begin by asking if the changeover operation itself can be eliminated.

We will now look at each of these points individually, describing their starting thresholds, special considerations, and ideas for waste elimination (the general concepts behind concrete waste-elimination plans). The framework for this analysis will be the elimination of the three types of changeover waste mentioned in Chapter 2.

ELIMINATING SETUP WASTE

Because changeover generally includes some setup work, begin by eliminating the "searching" waste that occurs during that stage. If you check your operation analysis data to see what elements are searched for and what other setup waste exists, you are likely to discover the following items:

- Waste in searching for, finding, lining up, and transporting the seven changeover tools
- Standby waste related to materials, especially missing items
- Searching waste related to bolts, nuts, and washers for attaching dies
- Searching for carts and waiting for an available crane
- Searching for dies
- Finding chutes and searching for their bolts
- Searching for block gauges
- Searching for inspection tools
- Searching for clean rags
- Checking the technical drawing or manufacturing specifications (processing conditions)

- Checking personal notes on gauge values
- Searching for pallets
- Searching for product containers
- Searching for a conveyor

This list could go on and on. Setup work is full of searching, finding, selecting, and arranging motions that don't add a cent to the value of the product.

To eliminate this waste, everything you need for the changeover should be already organized and in place. The changeover cart shown in Figure 2-2 is one way to accomplish this. Organizing the setup tools and materials also enables you to see at a glance if anything is missing or in short supply. In addition, it is a good idea to make a checklist and to make sure that everyone is using the same terms to describe the items used in changeover.

Point 1: Ensure that Everything Needed for Setup Is Already Organized and on Hand

Starting point: The goal is to remove waste from setup and cleanup operations.

Special considerations: Organize items to reduce the setup time required.

Waste-elimination ideas:

1. Remove waste in searching, finding, selecting, and transporting
2. Establish well-defined and well-marked storage places for dies, jigs, and other changeover materials and tools
3. Design and build specialized changeover carts
4. Create a checklist and establish standard terminology
5. Develop kanban for changeover
6. Draft a standard operations chart

To add some detail regarding the second item above:

- Assign addresses to the dies
- Arrange the items according to their frequency of use or the process undergoing changeover
- Use color coding and slide values

This means giving more than lip service to the principles of orderliness and organization. All items should be assigned specific storage sites, with both items and sites well marked (see Figure 3-2).

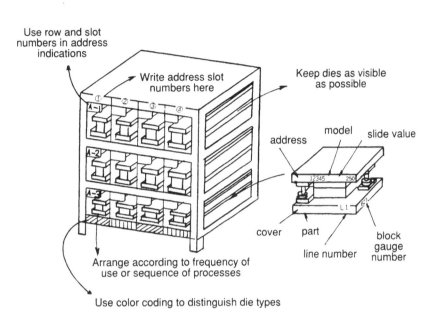

Use row and slot numbers in address indications

Write address slot numbers here

Keep dies as visible as possible

address   model   slide value

cover   part   block gauge number

line number

Arrange according to frequency of use or sequence of processes

Use color coding to distinguish die types

Figure 3-2. Well-marked Storage Sites for Changeover Items (Before Improvement, One-Person Changeover)

With regard to designing and building specialized carts, recall the illustration of such a cart in Figure 2-2. However, this kind of cart is not reliably serviceable for medium-size presses. In such situations, it is generally better to use a rail-mounted changeover cart, such as shown in Figure 3-3. An auto-stop device can also be installed to mechanize the cart and reduce manual work. The seven changeover tools and any other items needed for changeover should be organized into sets on the cart to reduce setup waste.

With regard to drafting a standard operations chart, take a look at three examples of simpler charts: the sequence chart shown in Table 3-1, the joint work operator-machine chart shown in Table 3-2, and Company T's standard-operation combination chart shown in Table 3-3. These three types of charts can be created in much less time than is needed to draw up a full-fledged standard operations chart.

If you have the time to draw a standard operations chart, it still may be wiser to devote that time instead toward achieving zero changeover. Since the current operation conditions are full of waste, standardizing those conditions merely validates the waste they contain and makes it more difficult to abandon certain operations for the sake of reducing waste.

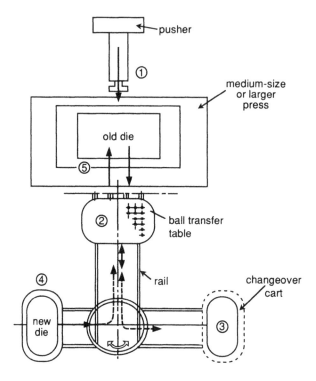

Figure 3-3. Rail-equipped Changeover Cart

Table 3-1. Sequence Chart

Item Sequence	Work element	Time (min.)
1	Lower slide	0.1
2	Unclamp adaptor	0.1
3	Raise slide (150mm)	0.1
4	Unclamp bolster	0.1
5	Move bolster (extract)	0.2
6	Replace bolster cable	0.2
7	Move bolster (insert)	0.2
8	Clamp bolster	0.1
9	Lower slide (150mm)	0.2
10	Clamp adaptor	0.2
11	Move to rear	0.2
12	Set iron hand	0.2
13	Move forward	0.1
14	Raise slide	0.1
	Total:	2.1 min.

Table 3-2. Operator-Machine Chart of Joint Changeover Operations

Person / Time	Leader	Worker A	Worker B
1 min. 2 min.	Raise safety guard, remove scrap, shut cover, remove die coolant hose, use guards to prevent product from falling, lower safety guard	Idle, remove scrap, shut cover, remove die coolant hose, use guards to prevent product from falling, remove air-blower hose	Move finished pallet
	Write data on slip		
3 min.		Feed materials	Prepare finished sample, prepare check sheet, prepare check table
4 min.	Run automatic die changer (4'20")		
5 min.		Set up air-blower hose Check automatic die change operation	Prepare pallet for next operation
6 min.	Raise safety guard	Idle	
	Set up coolant hose	Set up coolant hose	
7 min.	Remove air-blower hose	Open scrap chute, idle	Attach card to pallet
	Lower safety guard		
8 min.	Test processing	Set up conveyor, auto setup of destacker, idle	
9 min.			Clean up peripheral area
	Process workpiece check	Process workpiece check	
10 min.			Idle
	(Lower side)	GO	

Source: Fujisawa Press Factory, Press Dept., Press Industries, Co., Ltd. (see Shigeru Otanaka, "Single Changeover Case Study: Toyoda Steel Co.," *Press Technology*, Vol. 19, No. 3, 1981).

Table 3-3. Standard Operation Combination Chart (Company T)

Standard Operation Combination Chart (After Improvement)

Category	Work element	3	5	8	9
Setup	1. Specialized carts				
	2. Processing standards				
	3. Prepare materials				
	4. Transport materials				
Replacement	5. Turn switch				
	6. Change width				
	7. Set up width jig				
	8. Prepare gauge				
	9. Remove old jig				
	10. Transport old jig				
Adjustment	11. Test processing				
	12. Check width				
	13. Stable operation				
	14. Remove scrap				
	15.				

———— = Worker A   ------ = Worker B

Company T's standard-operation combination chart (Table 3-3) is all that is needed for making improvements, since it serves the main goal of helping to identify waste. Another waste-revealing device is a walking route diagram, such as the one shown in Figure 3-4.

Table 3-4 provides a good example of a press changeover checklist.

Point 2: It Is OK to Move the Arms, but Not the Legs

Starting point: The starting point is walking waste. Draw a walking route analysis chart to help reveal this form of waste.

Special considerations:

1. Change the layout so the walking route follows a U shape.
2. Remove walking waste caused by using a central control panel.

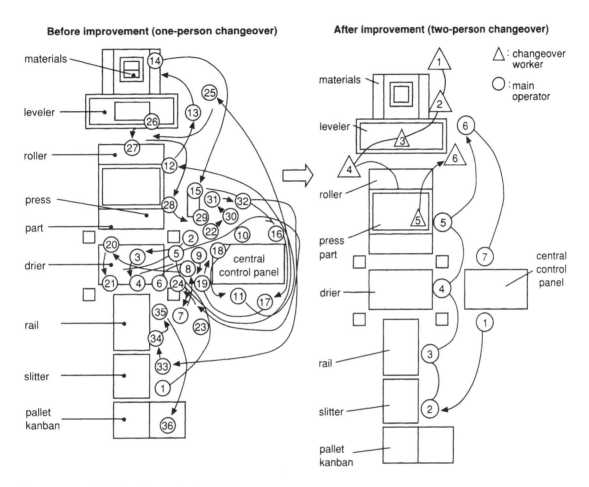

Figure 3-4. Walking Route Analysis Diagram

Waste-elimination ideas:

1. Design and build specialized changeover carts.
2. Establish two-person changeover.
3. Train a changeover worker to work with the regular press operator.
4. Draw up a walking route analysis diagram.

Poor changeover layout causes the changeover worker to waste a lot of time walking around. Some of this walking is related to the common types of setup waste described earlier: searching for, finding, selecting, lining up, and transporting.

Table 3-4. Changeover Checklist

Check item		
Die	1	Is the die in the correct place?
	2	Has each die part been fully checked?
	3	Is the die really clean?
	4	Is the die scratched or otherwise damaged?
Measure-ment tools	1	Are there any micrometer gauges in supply?
	2	Are there any calipers?
	3	Are there tube gauges?
	4	Is there a magnifying glass?
	5	Are there any dial gauges?
	6	Are all of the inspection tools present?
	7	Are there measurement jigs?
	8	Has everything been kept in good repair?
	9	Are the measurement tools all in their correct places?
Tools	1	Are there any wrenches?
	2	Are there screwdrivers?
	3	Are there tweezers?
	4	Are there any clean rags?
	5	Are there any level gauges?
	6	Are there brushes?
	7	Are all of the tools in their correct places?
Other	1	Are all the required materials present?
	2	Has the thickness of materials been checked?
	3	Are all the process workpieces present?
	4	Is there a standard operations chart?
	5	Is there an inspection data sheet?
	6	Are there any projection diagrams?
	7	Are all of the required parts bins there?
	8	Are there carts?
	9	Are there sampling forms?
	10	Is the lighting good?

Source: "Case Study of Company B," *Press Technology*, Vol. 19, No. 3, 1981.

Use of a central control panel, such as shown in Figure 3-4, is another major cause of walking waste, due to the many trips the operator must take to and from the control panel. This becomes clear from operation analysis charts and walking route analysis diagrams. It is not uncommon to find that the operator must walk more than 1,000 meters during a single changeover.

When using a large press or a secondary processing machine that has been integrated into the production line, it is usually better to have two people involved in changeover, one on each side. Table 3-3 shows how two workers function together in such a case. It is not difficult to cut the current changeover time in half by using a trained changeover specialist in addition to the regular press operator.

Implementing these first two points of the 9-point formula for achieving zero changeover in press operations should be enough to reduce setup time by 75 percent. For equipment such as plastic-molding machines, die-cast machines, and extruders, of course, changeover improvement also involves the use of preheater equipment. These first two points, however, do not incur the substantial expense of machine modification; therefore, they should always be implemented first.

ELIMINATING REPLACEMENT WASTE (WASTE IN REMOVING AND ATTACHING ITEMS)

Although it is inevitable that changeover operations include motions such as taking off and putting on fastening tools from dies, most changeover operations include far more of these motions than necessary.

Examples of such unnecessary motions include:

- Loosening, removing, and then refastening bolts
- Inserting and removing nuts and washers
- Removing and inserting braces, blocks, cushions, and spacers
- Removing and attaching chutes
- Removing and attaching air hoses
- Removing and attaching pullout conveyors
- Removing and attaching counters
- Removing and attaching dies

This amounts to a lot of loosening, removing, replacing, and tightening work with parts and tools that are peripheral to the use of dies. No matter how hard you work at this, it adds nothing to the value of the product.

How can you reduce the waste in this work? To begin with, instead of removing a bolt or other fastening tool, simply loosen it. This alone eliminates a lot of work, since it saves you from having to loosen the bolt until it comes off, put the bolt down, and later find the bolt, replace it, and tighten it. Instead, just loosen a little and tighten a little.

If possible, keep the bolt attached to the bolster. If this is impossible, find a way to keep it attached to the die. If even that is not possible, find some way to change the fastening tool, such as by replacing it with another kind of fastening tool or by cutting or grinding it down to reduce the number of motions required.

Work-hours are a reflection of the number of motions needed, and motions are mainly a reflection of waste. Therefore, the key to reducing work-hours is to eliminate wasteful motions.

In the typical press workshop, a list of the tools, jigs, and other items used for die replacement work might include:

- Wrenches
- Washers
- Braces
- Chutes
- The next die to be attached
- Materials
- Pallets
- Spare equipment
- Rags
- Grease
- Product samples
- Drawings
- Bolts
- Nuts
- Blocks
- Various tools
- Gauges
- Air hoses
- A conveyor
- Cushions
- Covers
- Inspection tools
- Process specifications

Obviously, when there are so many items, it is easy to forget something. That is why you should design and build specialized changeover carts with plates designed to carry all of the required items in well-defined locations. Figure 3-5 shows the basic approach to reducing replacement work in changeover operations.

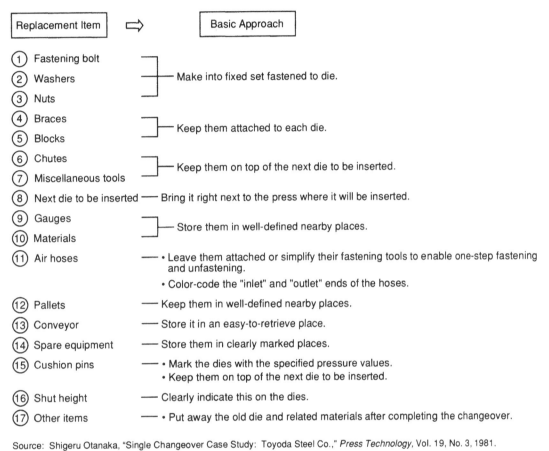

| Replacement Item | ⇨ | Basic Approach |

① Fastening bolt ⎤
② Washers   ⎬— Make into fixed set fastened to die.
③ Nuts   ⎦

④ Braces   ⎤
⑤ Blocks   ⎬— Keep them attached to each die.

⑥ Chutes   ⎤
⑦ Miscellaneous tools ⎬— Keep them on top of the next die to be inserted.

⑧ Next die to be inserted — Bring it right next to the press where it will be inserted.

⑨ Gauges   ⎤
⑩ Materials ⎬— Store them in well-defined nearby places.

⑪ Air hoses — • Leave them attached or simplify their fastening tools to enable one-step fastening and unfastening.
            • Color-code the "inlet" and "outlet" ends of the hoses.

⑫ Pallets — Keep them in well-defined nearby places.

⑬ Conveyor — Store it in an easy-to-retrieve place.

⑭ Spare equipment — Store them in clearly marked places.

⑮ Cushion pins — • Mark the dies with the specified pressure values.
               • Keep them on top of the next die to be inserted.

⑯ Shut height — Clearly indicate this on the dies.

⑰ Other items — • Put away the old die and related materials after completing the changeover.

Source: Shigeru Otanaka, "Single Changeover Case Study: Toyoda Steel Co.," *Press Technology*, Vol. 19, No. 3, 1981.

Figure 3-5. Basic Approach for Replacement Items

Point 3: Do Not Remove Bolts Completely

The point here is to loosen, not remove, bolts. Remember that the fastening strength lies only in the final turn of the bolt or nut; all other turns are pure waste. The goal is to eliminate waste, and one way to do it in this case is through the use of pear-shaped holes and U-shaped washers with hex bolts (see Figure 2-3).

There is another solution: an independent fastening tool (see Figure 3-6). This is a simple, spring-loaded tool that can be used under the condition that the die fastening height has been standardized.

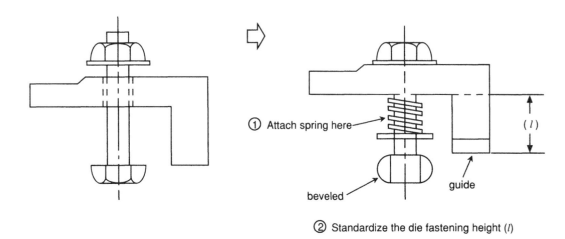

Figure 3-6. The Clamping Method of Fastening

Starting point: Avoid having to remove and replace bolts.

Special considerations: When fastening tools must be replaced, try to devise a boltless fastening tool for the job. If boltless fastening tools are not possible, find a way to do the job by loosening the bolt without removing it.

Waste-elimination ideas:

1. Use wing nuts
2. Use pear-shaped holes and U-shaped washers with hex bolts
3. Use independent fastening tools (such as L clamps)
4. Use hinged bolts with wing nuts
5. Use U-grooves with U-shaped washers
6. Minimize the variety of fastening tools
   - Ratchet wrenches
   - T-head bolts
   - Electric-powered fasteners
7. Reduce the number of fastening points
8. Cut down all screw threads to three turns
9. Use boltless fasteners

Figure 3-7 shows two labor-saving fastening tools. These can be used, for example, with punch presses for plastic nameplates. Figure 3-8 shows a commercially available "easy clamp." When using die fastening heights that are standardized in certain increments, the easy clamp can accommodate a range of fastening heights with a simple adjustment (from 20 to 35 mm in this example). Dies can be changed very quickly with this kind of clamp. This is another example of a quick-replacement fastening tool that costs little to buy and install.

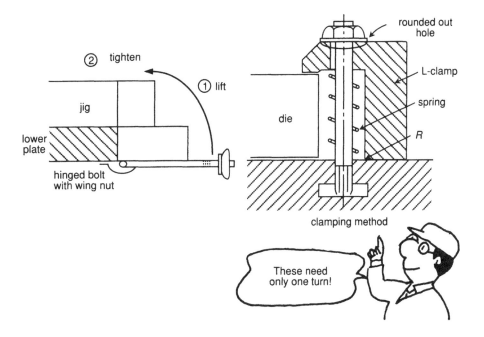

Figure 3-7. Fastening Tools that Enable Single-turn Loosening

If you are a subcontractor using dies on loan from the purchasing company, you obviously cannot remodel the dies to make the die heights into standardized increments, but you can use an adjustable-increment jig and clamping device of the type shown in Figure 3-9.

Point 4: Regard Bolts as Enemies — Do Whatever You Can to Get Rid of Them

The function of bolts is to either fasten or position things. If you need the fastening function, you can instead use levers, cams, or hydraulic or pneumatic devices. For positioning, you can replace bolts with knock pins, protruding stoppers, and index devices.

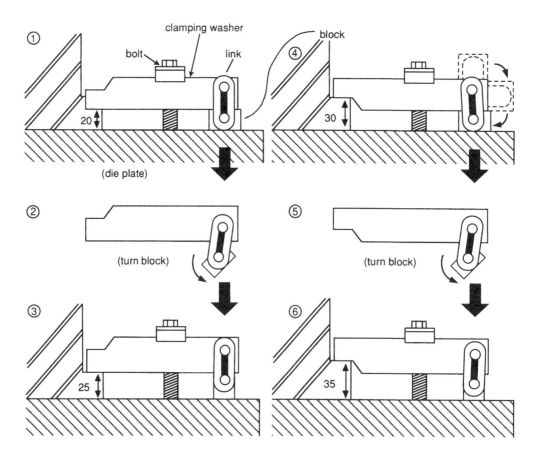

Figure 3-8. A Commercial "Easy Clamp" for Single-turn Clamping

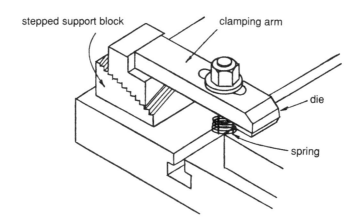

Figure 3-9. Step Clamp

Starting point: Devise boltless fasteners.

Special considerations: Consider using lever-type fasteners (hinge bolts, etc.), auto-clamps, or cassettes.

Waste-elimination ideas:

1. Devise a lever-type fastener
2. Devise a cam-type fastener
3. Devise an auto-clamp device
4. Develop a cassette-type replacement jig (replacing only the cavity section of the die)

Figure 3-10 shows typical examples of boltless fasteners. The operator loosens a hand-operated vise and removes the old die, then inserts the new die and tightens the vise until the lower die reaches the stopper and becomes tightly fastened. This kind of device can usually be built in-house and is safer and more reliable than most commercial QDC devices.

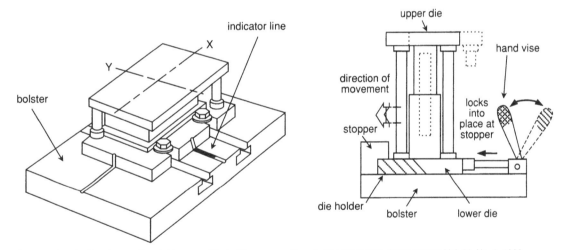

Source: Norihiro Hayakawa, "Special Issue on Single Changeover: Toyoda Gosei," *Factory Management*, Vol. 26, No. 6, 1980.

Figure 3-10. Boltless Fastener Using Hand Vise

A typical hydraulic auto-clamp, as shown in Figure 1-6, is costly. Commercial models cost about ¥500,000 ($4,000); moreover, they leave no room for factory workers to use their experience-based wisdom to devise improvements. (Still, hydraulic auto-clamps can be the best solution when a company must have the problem solved within a month.)

Figure 3-11 shows a die replacement that is done using only the cavity section of the die. This is a very simple and convenient way of replacing dies if you can work it out with the die design engineers.

This method is also attractive because it can reduce the cost of new dies by more than half. At Company O, all die changeovers are done using index-type, cavity-only die cassettes, such as the one shown in Figure 1-2. The use of these die cassettes is not so different from the use of videocassettes — just insert them, press a button, and the work is done!

Figure 3-12 shows another type of boltless fastener; in this case, an inserted wedge pin is used to hold the upper die, while the lower die is secured with hinged stoppers on its left and right sides. Such pin-type devices are appropriate for small table-top presses that do not require a lot of fastening torque.

The use of boltless fasteners, cassette dies (cavity-only replacement), and independent fastening tools such as clamps can reduce changeover waste by as much as 80 percent.

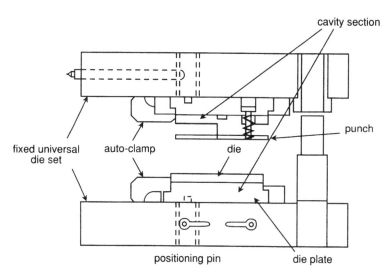

Since only the cavity section needs replacing, changeover can be done in less than one minute – zero changeover!

Figure 3-11. Die Replacement Using Cavity Section Only

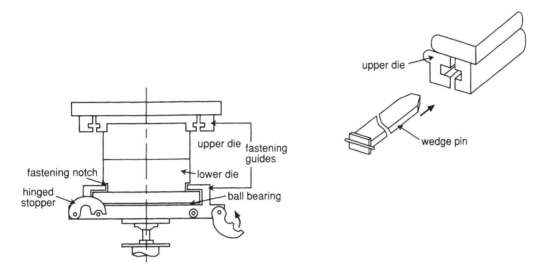

Source: Norihiro Hayakawa, "Special Issue on Single Changeover: Toyoda Gosei," *Factory Management*, Vol. 26, No. 6, 1980.

Figure 3-12. Boltless Fastener Using Wedge Pins

ELIMINATING ADJUSTMENT WASTE

Adjustments are made necessary by changeover settings that do not fully meet relevant standards and specifications. All too often, settings are left to the operator's discretion. Items are therefore not set precisely according to standards, which usually becomes apparent during the test run. So adjustments must be made until the test run produces a nondefective product. Typical adjustments include:

- Adjustment of closing height
- Adjustment of die position
- Adjustment of fastening height
- Adjustment of feed rollers
- Adjustment of chute height

None of this adjustment work adds value to the product. Although "adjustment" might sound like important work, it could be more accurately called wasteful adjustment of inaccurate settings. Point 5 of the 9-point formula is a good principle to follow for eliminating adjustment waste.

Point 5: Do Not Allow Any Deviation from Die and Jig Standards

There are four types of standards to be met concerning press changeover:

1. Centering standards (X and Y axes): Dies must be centered on the middle of the bolster.
2. Die height standards (Z axis): The die height must be set as specified according to the press stroke.
3. Fastening tool location (height) standards.
4. Standards related to alignment of the upper and lower dies, especially the aligning of punch-cutting edges.

Some secondary processing equipment imposes more numerous and more difficult standards than dies and presses. Consider the following types of standards, for example:

• Machine standards (the central shaft in a drilling machine, for instance)
• Fastening tool and jig standards (chuck centering, etc.)
• Blade standards (drill-bit points, etc.)
• Workpiece standards (centering of rod materials, etc.)

When you get sloppy about meeting one of these standards, all others are soon affected, and you spend more and more time on adjustments. Therefore, it is better to meet all of the standards fully. If you can do that, you won't have to align the upper and lower dies separately.

Starting point: Study the current variation in die fastening heights.

Special considerations: Standardize only the fastening height, die height, and die size (length × width).

Waste-elimination ideas:

1. Do an ABC analysis of the frequency of die usage.
2. Standardize the fastening height, die height, and die centering for the most commonly used "Group A" dies only.
3. Set a fixed value for the feed-roller height, and standardize the devices needed for attaching chutes to dies, for cushion heights, and for other required items.

The main focus here will be on the second waste elimination idea.

Do an ABC analysis on frequency of die usage

One of the goals in die replacement is to center the press with the die. Often the operator does not know the precise location of the press center nor the die center, so he or she approximates the centering visually. This often leads to adjustment work later.

Figure 3-13 shows a simple device in which two stopper pins are attached to the bolster to ensure correct centering of the die. The stopper pins are spaced to accommodate the largest of the dies. For smaller dies, V blocks are used to compensate for the size difference and still ensure correct centering. Both ways use the same one-step insertion motion.

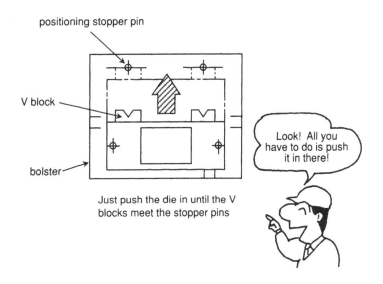

Figure 3-13. Simple Device for Press-die Centering

Standardize the die heights

To set the die height, the operator must find the bottom dead center of the upper ram. To find the bottom dead center, slowly lower the ram and locate the center point visually or by using a scale. Once you have determined the height of this point, you can insert blocks for lowering the ram.

Figure 3-14 shows a spring-back, floating-style die that has a free upper die. In this case, once you have determined the standard center points, you can attach the lower die. This takes only about a minute.

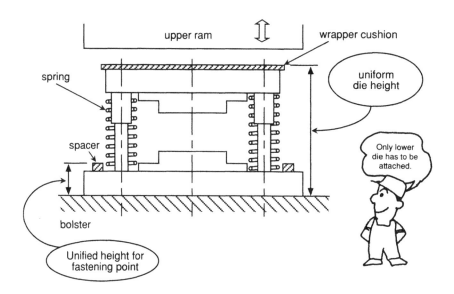

Figure 3-14. Floating Die

Factories that cannot redesign and remodel dies in-house must determine which slide values have served best in the past for each die, and paint these slide values clearly on the sides of the dies (see Figure 3-2). They should also measure and record the gap between the ram center point and the bolster for each die so that they can make block gauges. The numbers of these block gauges should also be painted onto the dies for quick location of the correct block gauges to use for each die.

Table 3-5 shows some improved die height and fastening height standards developed by one company for its Group A dies.

An auto-clamp can be used on the upper die and an inexpensive independent fastening tool on the lower die (see Figure 3-6). This sort of setup has the advantage of being affordable to most smaller companies.

Standardize fasteners

If possible, the fastening height should be made universal. If this is not possible, standardize fastening heights into no more than two or three groups.

Table 3-5. Die Height and Fastening Height Standards

Press		30-ton press		55-ton press	
		Before improvement	After improvement	Before improvement	After improvement
Shut height (mm) (includes adjusted amount)		145 - 200	105 - 160 125 - 180	165 - 225	150 - 210
Die attachment	Upper	fasten shank	hydraulic auto-clamp	fasten shank	hydraulic auto-clamp
	Lower	fasten bolts	hydraulic auto-clamp	fasten bolts	hydraulic auto-clamp
Liner		yes	no	yes	no
Die height distribution		Dimension / Percentage of dies	Dimension / Percentage of dies	Dimension / Percentage of dies	Dimension / Percentage of dies
		0 or less — 1%	154 — 69%	120 - 155 — 2%	170 — 91%
		111 - 155 — 68%			
		156 - 170 — 19%	170 — 23%	156 - 205 — 90%	205
		171 - 205 — 12%	— — 8%		
		206 or more — —	— —	206 or more — 8%	225 — 9%
Total		100%	100%	100%	100%

Die height	New die height	Address
110 - 155	154	30TP
156 - 170	170	30TP, 55TP
171 - 205	205	55TP, 150TP
206 +	225	150TP

Once you have determined these standard heights, cut away or add spacers to each die to achieve standardization (see Figure 3-15). These tasks are simple enough to be done in-house.

Factories that carry out the three types of standardization can expect to reduce off-spec die changeover by about 70 percent. (Other types of standardization are described later in a discussion of secondary processing equipment.)

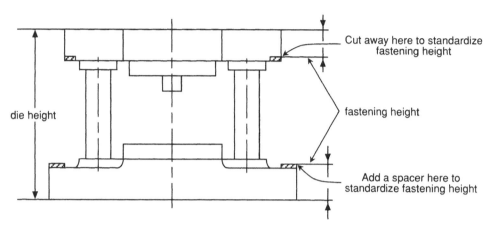

Source: Shigeru Otanaka, "Single Changeover Case Study: Toyoda Steel Co.," *Press Technology*, Vol. 19, No. 3, 1981.

Figure 3-15. Standardization of Die Height and Fastening Height

Point 6: Adjustment Is Waste. Do Not Move the Base Section. Selecting Is OK, but Adjustments Are Simply Waste.

If you have to move something, it should be only the small items at the contact point. Most of these small items, such as spacers, blocks, and braces, can be manually replaced. In presses, the cavity section contains all these small items. "Adjustment" may sound like important work, but it is really just re-work to fix imprecision that should not exist in the first place.

Starting point: The first basic principle is to make the upper and lower dies into a die set of standard dimensions. The other point is to make the cutting edges into an interchangeable cavity section within the die set. The objective is to be able to change only the cavity section, without adjustment.

Special considerations: Whenever you hear the word "adjustment," realize that changeover standards have not been met. Observe the changeover operations to find where this has occurred. Do not accept theoretical technical explanations of the causes. Instead, observe the changeover operations firsthand.

Waste-elimination ideas:

1. Set up guideposts for separate upper and lower dies in a one-shot die. If possible, make it a die set.
2. For odd-shaped dies, create adapter jigs to bring them to standard dimensions that do not require adjustment.

There is a common type of separate upper and lower die with the upper die attached to a shank (see Figure 3-16). This older type of die is used only about once a year. Veteran press operators find these devices easy to use, but less experienced workers tend to have a hard time with them. The following is a summary of the steps in using them.

1. Partially fasten the shank to set up the upper die. Align the upper and lower cutting edges and adjust the center point.
2. Once the die is aligned, fasten the shank securely to the upper die, then check the cutting-edge alignment. Assume in this case that they are not properly aligned.
3. Use the manual handle on the left to adjust the cutting-edge alignment. Clean out any burrs that are produced and recheck the alignment.

In this case, the cutting edges went out of alignment because too much pressure was applied to the upper die when the bolt was tightened, causing the shank to slip about 0.2 mm. This slippage of the upper die translated directly into an off-spec misalignment of the cutting edges. The operator then had to use the handle to adjust the alignment.

This is a very delicate manual operation, which is why many less-experienced press operators have trouble doing it. For a modest expense (about ¥200,000 or $1,600), a simple die set can be made by installing two spring-loaded guideposts. This improvement gets rid of the troublesome shank and instead uses a floating-style die (described in more detail under point 7 of the formula).

As an example of using an adapter jig, Figure 3-17 shows an irregular rectangular die that is difficult to mount correctly. In this case, the adapter jig makes it easier to center the die. It is kept as part of the die set, as shown in the figure. It could even be welded onto the die set. Such intermediary jigs enable you to standardize odd-shaped dies to avoid adjustment.

In the case of secondary processing equipment, the main problem is that the secondary machine or its cutting edges are not compatible with the standardized die sets. To avoid this problem, follow the die-set principle (cassettes) in designing new dies.

For secondary processing equipment, try to set standards for immobilizing the base section of the dies. As stated in point 6, you must limit movement to the contact points in the middle (the cavity section). Figure 1-2, for example,

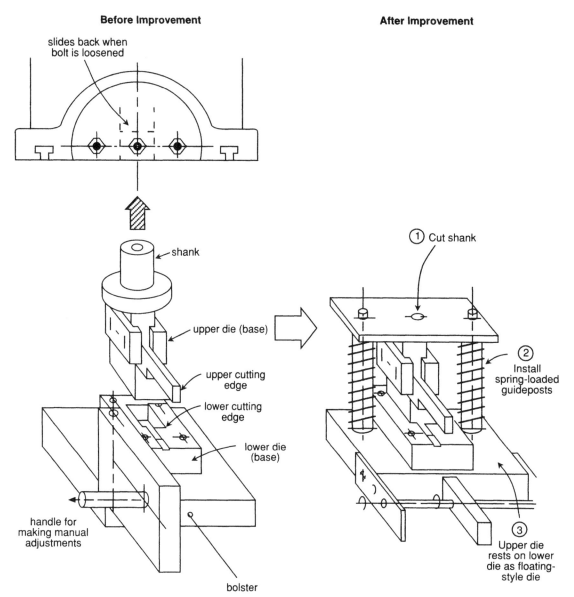

Before Improvement   After Improvement

slides back when
bolt is loosened

shank

upper die (base)

upper cutting
edge

lower cutting
edge

lower die
(base)

handle for
making manual
adjustments

bolster

① Cut shank

② Install
spring-loaded
guideposts

③ Upper die
rests on lower
die as floating-
style die

Source: Yoko Sone, "Prince Development Industries," *Press Technology*, Vol. 24, No. 7, 1986.

Figure 3-16. One-shot Die with Guideposts

shows an example of how Company O devised a cavity-section changeover
method for one of its presses.

An improvement made in a transfer die is shown in Figure 3-18. The operator of the die spent a lot of time adjusting the alignment of the left and

right bases of this die since they were rarely aligned to begin with. Because the base sections are separate, the alignment between them was lost during changeover. To fix this, plates were attached to the top and bottom dies to establish a one-piece set in which the bases remain permanently aligned, as shown in the figure.

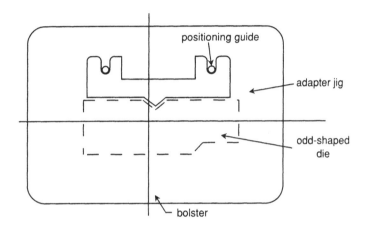

Figure 3-17. Adapter Jig for Odd-shaped Dies

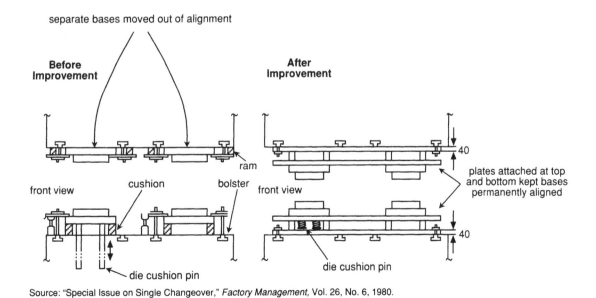

Source: "Special Issue on Single Changeover," *Factory Management*, Vol. 26, No. 6, 1980.

Figure 3-18. Improvement of Base Alignment in Transfer Press

Point 7: Cut Off Shanks if Possible. Use a Floating-style Die Instead. Keep Only the Lower Die in a Fixed Position.

This type of improvement requires people who have reached an advanced level in making zero-changeover improvements. They must be able to redesign and standardize dies. Such people can make the kind of shanked-to-floating die conversion shown in Figure 3-19. To reduce noise and shock, the upper die should be layered with foam bumper pads that prevent direct contact.

With this kind of floating die, even if the stroke adjustment is a little loose, the difference will be absorbed by the bumper pads and the springs. This is also true for the die shown in Figure 3-14.

Starting point: Check to see if tightening the shank bolt causes the die to go off spec. If so, cut off the shank.

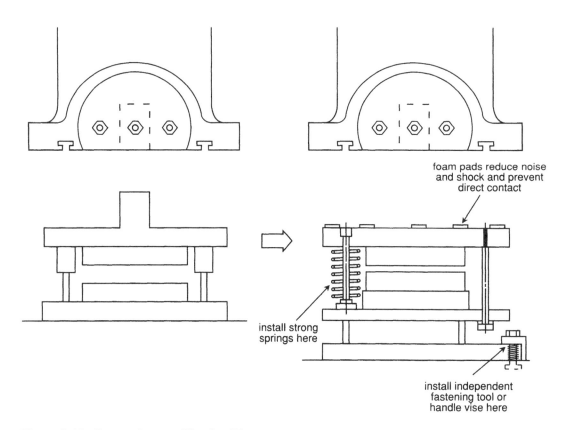

Figure 3-19. Converting to a Floating Die

Special considerations: If the die does not stay on specs, there is no point in having the shank. It is better to remove the shank and use a floating die. An independent fastening tool, such as the one shown in Figure 3-6, is recommended for easy fastening of the lower die. Or, you can use a handle-operated vise (see Figure 3-10).

If you are not sure about using such fastening tools on the upper die in a high-speed, high-precision press, try using an auto-clamp device on the upper die and using either an independent fastening tool or a handle-operated vise on the lower die (see Figure 3-20).

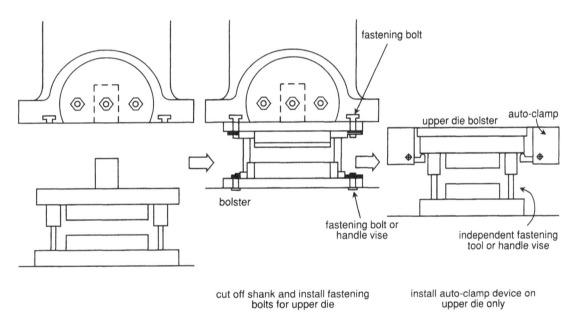

Figure 3-20. Converting to a Shankless Die with an Upper Die Auto-clamp

Point 8: Use Block Gauges for All Adjustments Done Visually with Scales

Block gauges generally come in three types:

• Loosening gauges
• Inserting gauges
• Tightening gauges

One of the more obvious cases for using block gauges is in setting the feed pitch on the end of a crankshaft. Setting the feed pitch often requires high precision; simply using a finely marked scale and your intuition is not good enough. Instead, you can devise block gauges. The ones shown in Figure 2-4 can be used for two different machine models. Readers are encouraged to combine gauges this way to eliminate the need to search for the right one.

Starting point: Find where all of the high-precision scale adjustments must be done.

Special considerations: Make block gauges for different standard settings. Remember, selecting a gauge is much less wasteful than making an adjustment. This is also true for point 7 of the formula.

Waste-elimination ideas:

1. Eliminate adjustment for setting the feed pitch
2. Eliminate adjustment of material feed devices (height, speed, etc.)
3. Eliminate adjustment for positioning in secondary processing equipment
4. Eliminate visual measuring work that uses scales, micrometers, calipers, dial gauges, etc.
5. Having to make a second test run is waste.

Figure 3-21 shows three improvement ideas for a product-length standard setting that are done using a handle. There are seven different product models whose lengths must be set.

As the figure shows, Plan A calls for making seven U-shaped block gauges, one for each product model. Plan B involves making two cross-shaped block gauges, each of which can be used for four product models. Plan C calls for making a roller-type block gauge that can be used for eight different product models. These block gauges are all good, and they all follow the principle of using stoppers for setting standard measurements.

In press shops that have a lot of workers, visual and intuitive setting of measurements and making of adjustments is a deeply ingrained habit. Veteran press operators are the most stubborn about making changes, since part of their professional pride lies in being the only ones who "understand" the press well enough to set it intuitively.

In such cases, it may be necessary to get the company president or other top managers involved in making the factory-floor improvements. They may be needed especially when it comes to integrating secondary processing equipment directly into the production line.

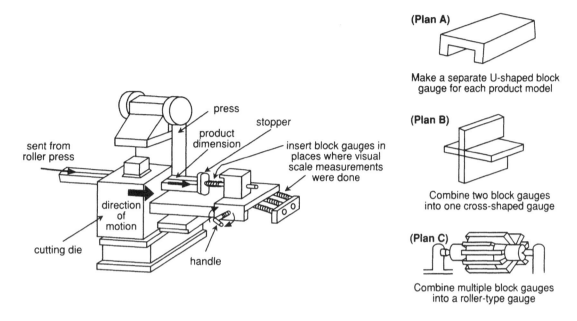

Figure 3-21. Use of Block Gauges for Product Length Cutting Device

Figure 3-22 shows four improvement plans for a positioning device in a secondary processing machine. Of these four improvements, the one shown as Plan A is the most commonly used, followed by the counter method shown as Plan B. The limit switch method, Plan C, is a more advanced type of improvement; it costs a lot more to implement and yet does not completely eliminate the need for fine-tuning adjustments. If the precision tolerance is ± 2/100 mm, as it is in most press shops, the block-gauge method shown as Plan D is fully adequate for the job. For high-precision products, such as aircraft parts, an index method must be used, but for presses the block-gauge method is fine.

Point 9: Find Ways to Carry Out Changeover Without Having to Stop the Press. Begin by Asking If the Changeover Operation Itself Can Be Eliminated.

This part of the formula should be used only by companies that have reached the most advanced level in achieving zero changeover. Readers who belong to medium-sized or small companies may think this level is beyond their abilities. Nevertheless, this section can help them, too.

Plan A: Manual positioning
The material feed pitch must be adjusted visually using
a scale, requiring several fine-tuning adjustments.

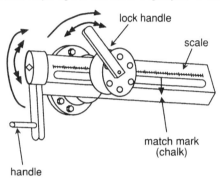

Plan B: Positioning using a counter

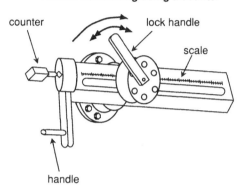

Plan C: Positioning using a limit switch

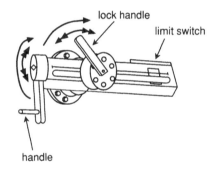

**Plan D: Positioning using a different block gauge
for each workpiece type**

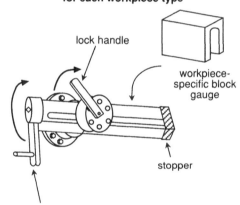

Figure 3-22. Block Gauges and Other Methods for Positioning Devices

Starting point: Find out if any of the changeover work can be mechanized using auto-feed or auto-stop devices.

Special considerations: The dies tend to get moved out of position at the moment of the upstroke, such as in rotary presses.

Waste-elimination ideas:

1. Integrate the press into the production line.
2. Use a rotary press.
3. Mechanize the die replacement process (auto-feed and/or auto-stop devices).

Figure 3-23 shows a transition for a one-operator-per-press line to a two-operator, multi-press line and finally a two-operator, U-shaped cell. The main drawback of forming a *line* of presses, each with its own operator, is that the presses must be lined up according to the processing sequence and there must be as many dies as there are presses. In other words, it becomes a line devoted to just one product model.

When this line is improved so that two operators each handle three presses, the presses' capacity utilization rate drops by two-thirds. Other drawbacks include the greater amount of time needed for model changes. However, if you were to install a rotary die changer, the changeover could be done without stopping the presses, and the use of auto-feed and auto-stop devices would

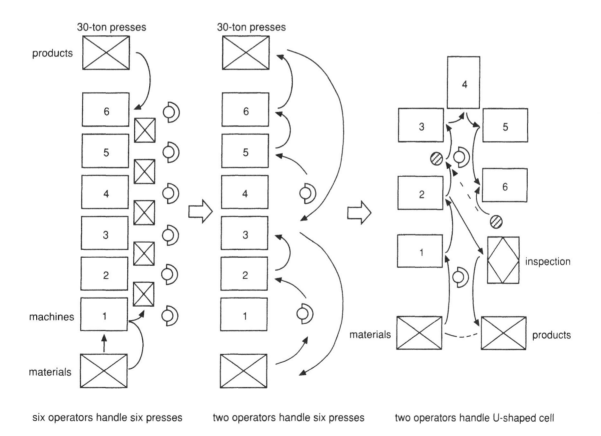

six operators handle six presses   two operators handle six presses   two operators handle U-shaped cell

Figure 3-23. Integrating Presses into a Line and a U-shaped Cell

eliminate the need for the safety devices used for manual operations. This would also allow you to decrease the number of presses, producing the following effects:

- The line would take up much less space in the factory
- Time loss due to walking waste could be reduced
- Operators can do their work outside of the press hazard zone, and the semi-automation of the line would both shorten the cycle time and increase safety
- Investment costs could be cut by about half
- Processing costs could be cut by about ¥135,000 ($1,100) a month

A slide-in cassette method for press die replacement enables the press to continue operating while handling two different product models (see Figure 3-24). When there are three or more product models, you must have external changeover of dies that are transported to the press when needed, as shown in Figure 1-4. This method is often used in sewing factories.

It may seem paradoxical, considering all the improvement work that you may be putting into changeover operations, but you must remind yourself

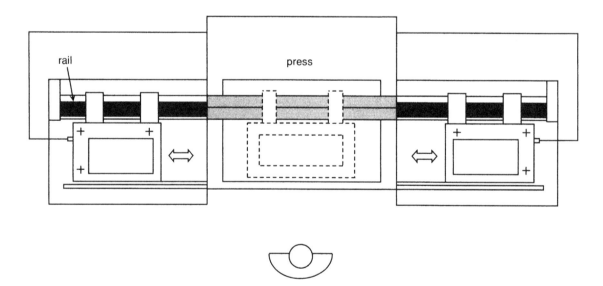

Figure 3-24. Slide-in Cassette Method for Die Replacement

that changeover itself is pure waste. It is best if you can do without change-over altogether.

Once you are sure that at least some changeover is unavoidable, ask yourself the following about the three main parts of changeover operations:

1. Since setup work is wasteful, is there a way to do without setup and external changeover?
2. Since replacement work is wasteful, is there a way to do the changeover with only minimal replacement work?
3. Since adjustment work is especially wasteful, are there better ways to set up standard measurements that will eliminate the need for adjustments?

With these three types of changeover waste in mind, take another close look at the current conditions in the factory to find where this waste exists. Without a deep commitment to eliminating waste, you cannot truly understand the 9-point formula, nor will you be likely to have much success in your changeover improvement efforts.

TEST YOUR SKILLS

Company D uses the kind of die shown in Figure 3-25. Workers fasten the dies into the presses using bolts. Naturally, there is a lot of setup and replacement work involved in using bolts and wrenches to do the changeover.

How would you apply the 9-point formula for achieving zero changeover in press operations in this case? Consider the following two guidelines:

Plan A: Find a method that does not incur much expense (¥100,000/$800 or less).

Plan B: Find a method that will enable zero changeover (3 minutes or less).

Solution

Plan A: Use the slide-pin method shown in Figure 3-26 or adapt one of the methods shown in Figures 3-6, 3-7, and 3-8.

Plan B: Remodel the die using the floating-die approach shown in Figure 3-14.

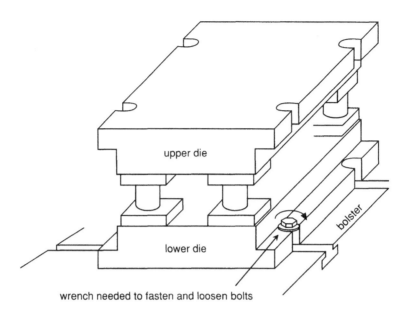

wrench needed to fasten and loosen bolts

Figure 3-25. Currently Used Die

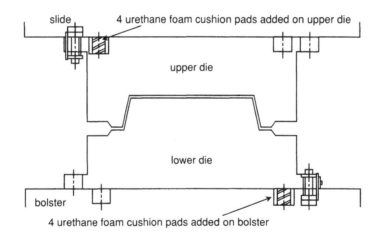

Figure 3-26. An Inexpensive Improvement

Part II
Processing Line
Changeover Improvement
Approaches

This part of the book describes steps and case studies of changeover improvements made in processing lines that consist of linked, stand-alone machines. Since some factories have not yet linked their machines into lines, we will begin this section with a brief description of process line linkage methods.

4
Changeover on Processing Lines

WHAT IS A PROCESSING LINE?

Figure 4-1 shows a production line made up of six large presses. This line has six processes:

- General pressing
- Drilling process
- Deep drawing
- Cutting out
- Bending
- Molding

There are two basic methods used for changeover in processing lines:

- Complete changeover
- Sequential changeover

Complete changeover follows the sequence of processes in shutting down the machines, and all changeover tasks are done while the entire line has been stopped. Likewise, the machines are started again according to the sequence of processes. Sequential changeover, on the other hand, leaves machines at other processes operating while shutting down only the process where changeover is being done. Here we will study sequential changeover rather than complete changeover, because the latter method incurs more time loss and is not conducive to achieving zero changeover.

If we assume that changeover at each process takes 3 minutes, sequential changeover on the 6-process press line shown in Figure 4-1 would take

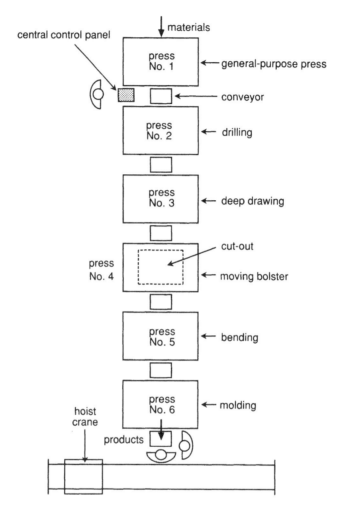

Figure 4-1. Large Press Line

(3 minutes × 6 processes =) 18 minutes. If such changeover is required 10 times per day, our changeover time loss would total (18 minutes × 10 times =) 180 minutes. If you take the total number of minutes in an 8-hour shift (8 hours × 60 minutes =) 480 minutes, you can figure the percentage of changeover loss as (180 ÷ 480 × 100 =) 48 percent of the shift.

Under these conditions, more than one-third of each 8-hour shift is spent performing changeover. In today's small-lot era, such conditions would not enable a factory to be profitable.

The point of changeover on processing lines is to carry out sequential changeover as zero changeover that is completed within the cycle time. To do this, you must, for example, begin performing changeover at process No. 2 while the die is being replaced at process No. 1. Figure 4-2 shows how 3 changeover workers can carry out sequential changeover on a 6-press processing line. Table 4-1 shows a waste elimination chart for the same large-scale press line.

When changeover includes operations that must be done from opposite sides of a machine (right and left or front and back), you should establish a 2-person procedure. This concept was discussed in the Chapter 3 description of point 3 of the 9-point formula.

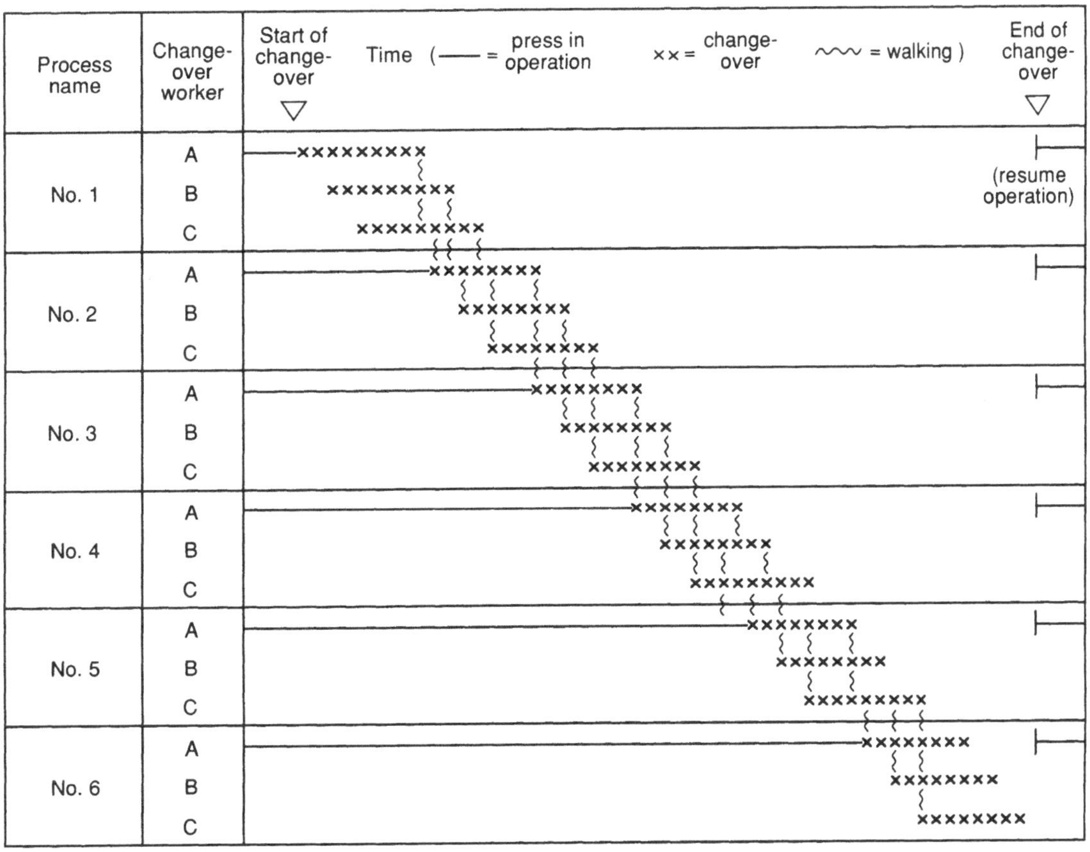

Figure 4-2. Standard Combination Chart for Three-Person Sequential Changeover

Table 4-1. Changeover Waste Elimination Chart

Waste Category	Types of Waste	Waste Reduction Plans	
		A (small improvements)	B (medium improvements)
Setup waste	1. Conveyance waste when die storage site is on first floor and press line is on second floor; setup and organization of tools	1. Move die storage site upstairs and organize dies and tools into addressed storage bins 2. Use changeover kanban (electronic kanban)	1. Specialized changeover carts 2. Improvement of process layout
	2. Storage for various items is too far from the press line	3. Use standardized locations and labels: keep die cushions and/or loading devices on the inside of the safety guards	
	3. Conveyor transfer waste (two-worker team)	4. Lay rails for wheels of conveyor carts (one-person operation)	
	4. Waste in opening and shutting scrap hopper	5. Simple operation: higher side walls, top lid, simplified opening and closing	
	5. Waste in cleaning up scraps that fall outside of the hopper	6. Raise the side walls on the scrap hopper	
Changeover waste (removing and attaching)	1. Variation in die dimensions	1. Attach risers to dies with low die heights	1. Standardization of dies (see Table 3-5) 2. Uniformity of cushion strokes; all cushion pins of same length
	2. Remove or attach chain	2. Attach chains to bolsters	
	3. Waste in adjusting angle of conveyor chute	3. Make chute angles easily adjustable	3. Uniformity in the angle of conveyor
	4. Waste in moving chutes (product chute, die scrap chute, etc.)		4. Shorten the chute and make it collapsible so it can fit through the press's side opening
	5. Waste in long material replacement times		5. Use double material feed device and double crane; install auto coil changeover mechanism
	6. Waste in difficult washer replacements and nut tightening; devise method that does not require wrenches	4. Permanently connect nuts and washers; raise nut heights so wrenches can be used from an above angle; switch to single-turn bolts	
	7. Waste in die transport time	5. Use a hook to lift out dies; attach dies by handles; and attach an anti-rebound brake for the rotary stoppers that position the dies	6. Build a slanted electric-powered die cart that can be operated by pushing with both hands
	9. Waste in air hose connections	6. Waste in changing air hose connections; color code air hoses, and bundle into pairs.	
	10. Waste of using robot for replacement	7. Replace only the hose ends.	
	11. Waste in connecting internal power sources in dies		8. Automatic connection in center of moving bolster
Waste in adjustment	1. Waste in press slide adjustments	1. Enable bolster to be moved to lower balance point	
	2. Waste in side guide adjustments	2. Pins should slide along side guide until they reach their designated holes	
	3. Waste in conveyor height adjustments	3. Simplify height control to avoid having to adjust	1. Use electrical devices (e.g., limit switch)
	4. Waste in robot hand adjustments		2. Simplify vertical movement of robot hand and lateral motion of bolt tightening
	5. Waste in die cushion sets		3. Install a height setting gauge to measure cushion pressure
	6. Waste in machine feet operations		4. Install a nearby switch or enable feed activation from front control panel.

ELIMINATING CHANGEOVER WASTE FROM PROCESSING LINES

Let us examine case studies of small and medium improvements cited in Table 4-1.

Die Addresses

In this case, the press line is on the first floor of the factory and the dies and tools are stored on the second floor. This results in a large amount of conveyance waste.

The improvement plan called for Group A dies and tools to be placed next to the press line and assigned specific addresses. This improvement is called standardized placement and identification of dies and parts.

Addresses should be assigned in categories that go from the most general to the most specific. For example, a die address of 123-A-35 might mean that the die belongs at storage site 123, storage shelf A, level 3, slot 5. Figure 3-2 shows an example of address-based die storage. It is also a good idea to use color coding for easier identification of addresses.

Changeover Kanban

There are two approaches for using kanban in the setup and start of changeover:

1. Use in-process inventory kanban (showing the processing sequence) as the changeover kanban. The person responsible for changeover setup must load all required charts, processing standards materials, dies, fastening tools, and inspection tools on an empty cart.
2. Use a bar-code reader as part of the changeover kanban, such as shown in Figure 4-3. This computerized system uses signal lamps to clearly indicate which items in the storage area are needed for a specific changeover.

Since small-lot production requires more frequent changeover, it is vital to improve the efficiency of changeover setup. Using electronic kanban is one good way to reduce changeover setup time. It is particularly effective in reducing searching waste and errors in selecting changeover tools or materials.

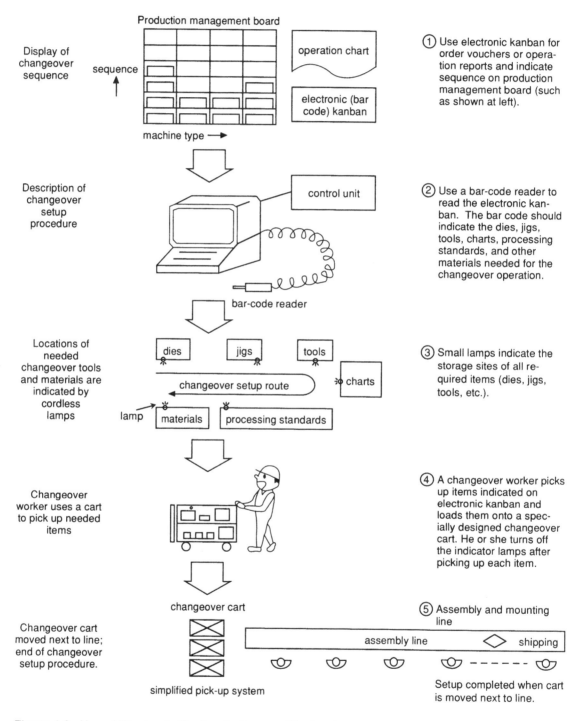

Figure 4-3. Use of Electronic Kanban to Prevent Missing Items

Scrap Hopper Improvement

As Figure 4-4 shows, before the improvement, the scrap hopper lid contained three sections. Each lid section had to be opened and closed manually. Furthermore, there was a gap between the scrap chute and the hopper. After the improvement, the hopper's walls are higher and there is only one lid to open and close.

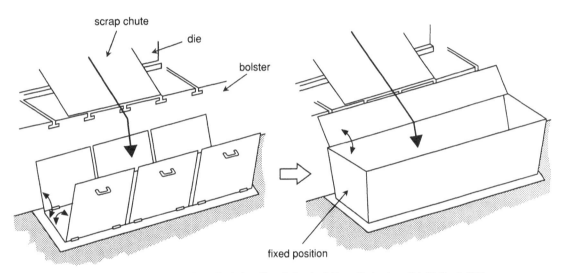

Source: Kanju Sato and Seiichi Maruhashi, "Case Study from Toyo Industries," *Press Technology*, Vol. 19, No. 3, 1981.

Figure 4-4. Simplification of Scrap Hopper Operation

Variation in Die Dimensions

Think back to point 5 of the 9-point formula from Chapter 3: Do not allow any deviation from die and jig standards. Setup for replacing dies can be summarized in the following four categories:

- Die centering standards
- Die height standards
- Die fastening standards
- Matching upper and lower die standards

Beginning with the height at which the dies are fastened, standardize the fastening height, the die height, and the die size (dimensions). The following is a hypothetical example of this standardization.

1. Organize the target dies into groups. Study frequency of the die use by conducting an ABC analysis. First standardize the fastening height, die height, and die centering for Group A.
2. List common structural components.
3. Make a second study of structural components that are not common among the target dies.
4. Decide on a standardized die structure.

Improvement of Conveyor Chute Angle

The short product chutes that are attached to the side of the conveyor are designed for specific product models and must be changed whenever production shifts to a different model. To eliminate this changeover waste, an improved chute was developed that can be easily set at different angles for different product models, as shown in Figure 4-6.

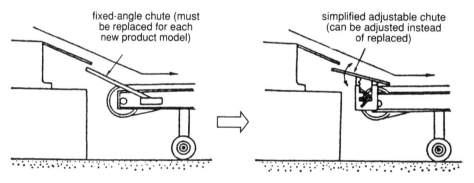

Source: Kanju Sato and Seiichi Maruhashi, "Case Study from Toyo Industries," *Press Technology*, Vol. 19, No. 3, 1981.

Figure 4-5. Improved Conveyor Chute with Adjustable Angles

Elimination of Chute Motion Waste

The fastening sections were shortened in two kinds of chutes: the product chute shown in Figure 4-6 and the scrap chute shown in Figure 4-7. These were also made to fold up so that more space could be given at the press's side opening.

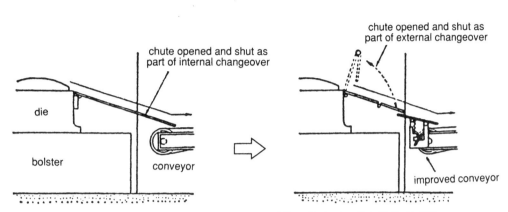

Source: Kanju Sato and Seiichi Maruhashi, "Case Study from Toyo Industries," *Press Technology*, Vol. 19, No. 3, 1981.

Figure 4-6. Improvement from Internal to External Changeover for Product Chute

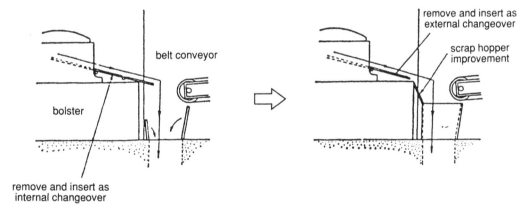

Source: Kanju Sato and Seiichi Maruhashi, "Case Study from Toyo Industries," *Press Technology*, Vol. 19, No. 3, 1981.

Figure 4-7. Improvement from Internal to External Changeover for Die Scrap Chute

Reduction in Material Replacement Time

The kanban-monitored material in this example are coils and the material supply device is an uncoiler. The improvement was to change the material replacement procedure from internal changeover to external changeover by using a two-headed uncoiler (see Figure 4-8). When one coil is depleted, the worker quickly switches to the other coil, which is ready and waiting.

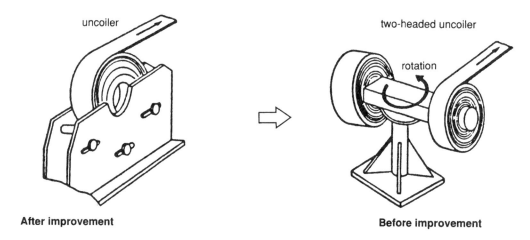

uncoiler

two-headed uncoiler

rotation

After improvement

Before improvement

Figure 4-8. Improvement of Uncoiler

Wrench-free Die Attachment

This example shows a closeup of the solution from the Test Your Skills problem at the end of Chapter 3. A bolt that can be removed simply and without requiring a wrench is used to attach the die, as shown in Figure 4-9 (see also Figures 3-25 and 3-26 in Chapter 3).

Installation of Coil Material Jointer

Figure 4-10 shows a jointer (an argon arc welder) that was installed between a cradle and a press to reduce the coil changeover time and to enable the coil material to be used all the way up to the coil end.

Simplification of Air-Hose Connection

In this example, an air hose is attached to a hose outlet near the operation panel for dies that are set into the press. As an improvement, a new hose outlet was installed in the bolster and a coupler-type connector was added for simple hose connection, as shown in Figure 4-11. In addition, a color-coded set of paired hoses were used to eliminate the waste involved in bringing in single hoses.

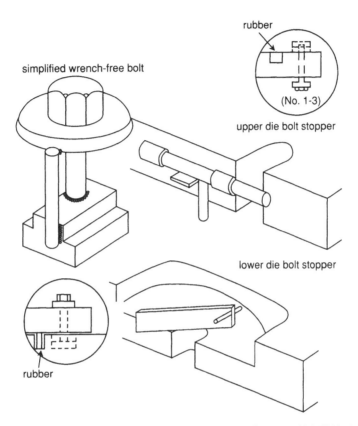

Source: Tsuyoshi Sokura, "Case Study from Daihatsu Industries," *Press Technology*, Vol. 25, No. 3, March 1987.

Figure 4-9. Wrench-free Die Attachment

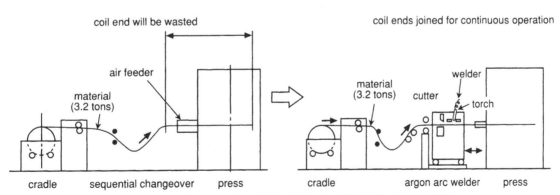

Source: Kosaburo Yamauchi, "Case Study from Isuzu Motors," *Press Technology*, Vol. 25, No. 3, March 1987.

Figure 4-10. Using a Welding Jointer to Reduce Time and Scrap

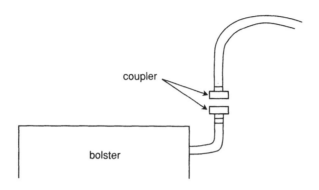

Figure 4-11. Simplified Air Hose Connection

Elimination of Slide Waste

Usually, the press die is lifted until it reaches the upper stopping point. Figure 4-12 shows how the lower stopping point can also be used.

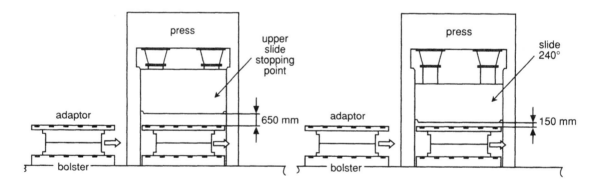

Source: Kanju Sato and Seiichi Maruhashi, "Case Study from Toyo Industries," *Press Technology,* Vol. 19, No. 3, 1981.

Figure 4-12. Improvement Enabling Bolster Movement with Press Slide Distance of 150 mm

Reduction of Die Removal Time

The task of removing dies from presses and onto carts is not only dangerous because of the weight of the dies; it is also just plain unpleasant. Electric cranes must be used to remove and insert the heavier dies. At one factory, employees developed an eye that they welded onto the dies (see Figure 4-13); this made it easier to attach wires or ropes to the dies and thus reduced labor.

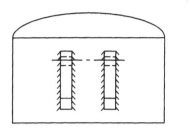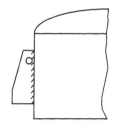

Figure 4-13. Die Removal Eye

There are other examples of improvements to remove waste from operations that insert, remove, or convey dies. Figure 4-14 shows how notch handles were made in the dies to facilitate simultaneous die removal and insertion. Figure 4-15 shows an improvement in which a hand-operated stopper was replaced by a foot-operated stopper to enable two-handed use of the die-conveyor cart. Figure 4-16 shows an improvement in which a wedge-shaped brake was added to a die conveyor cart to prevent dies from rocking or falling. Figure 4-17 shows a time-saving and fatigue-preventing improvement in which carts for heavy dies are motorized for easier transport. Figure 4-18 shows a stopper improvement that makes dies easier to insert and remove.

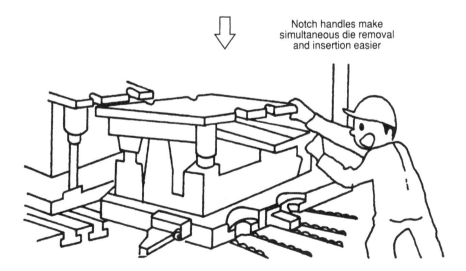

Source: Tsuyoshi Sokura, "Case Study from Daihatsu Industries," *Press Technology*, Vol. 25, No. 3, March 1987.

Figure 4-14. Simultaneous Die Removal and Insertion

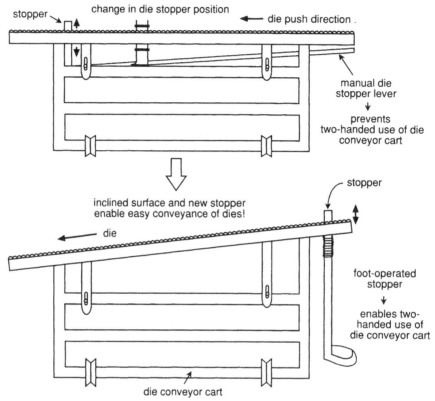

stopper

change in die stopper position   ← die push direction .

manual die
stopper lever
↓
prevents
two-handed use of die
conveyor cart

inclined surface and new stopper
enable easy conveyance of dies!

die

stopper

foot-operated
stopper
↓
enables two-
handed use of
die conveyor cart

die conveyor cart

Source: Tsuyoshi Sokura, "Case Study from Daihatsu Industries," *Press Technology,* Vol. 25, No. 3, March 1987.

Figure 4-15. Two-Handed Use of Die Conveyance Table

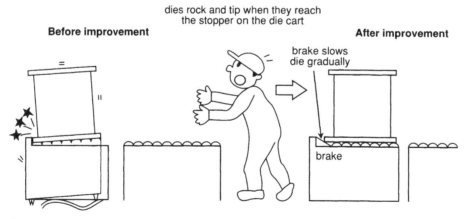

dies rock and tip when they reach
the stopper on the die cart

Before improvement

After improvement

brake slows
die gradually

brake

Source: Tsuyoshi Sokura, "Case Study from Daihatsu Industries," *Press Technology,* Vol. 25, No. 3, March 1987.

Figure 4-16. Installation of Brake on Die Conveyor Cart

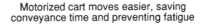

Motorized cart moves easier, saving
conveyance time and preventing fatigue

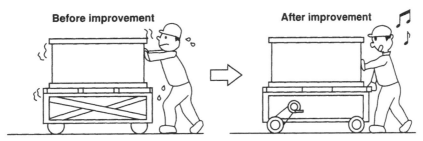

Source: Tsuyoshi Sokura, "Case Study from Daihatsu Industries," *Press Technology,* Vol. 25, No. 3, March 1987.

Figure 4-17. Motor-driven Die Conveyor Cart

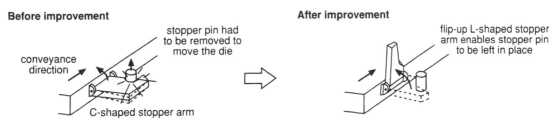

Source: Tsuyoshi Sokura, "Case Study from Daihatsu Industries," *Press Technology,* Vol. 25, No. 3, March 1987.

Figure 4-18. Improvement of Die Positioning Stopper

Improvement of Conveyor Height Adjustment

Figure 4-19 shows how a conveyor height-adjustment procedure was greatly simplified by installing an adjustable kickstand instead of using the height-adjustment crank.

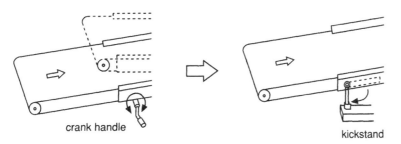

Source: Shoichi Terao and Masa Aizawa, "Case Study from Nissan Shatai," *Press Technology,* Vol. 25, No. 3, March 1987.

Figure 4-19. Improvement of Conveyor Height Adjustment

MULTI-PROCESS HORIZONTAL HANDLING OF EQUIPMENT

There are two ways to approach line organization of presses and other production equipment. One is called horizontal handling and the other vertical handling.

In large-lot production systems, horizontal handling is usually the better approach, since it creates much less changeover loss. In the example in Figure 4-20, roller conveyors are used to reduce changeover time between small presses in a line that uses the horizontal handling approach. This line features an automated system for moving and stopping press dies on the roller conveyors, and for automatically removing dies from the right side and inserting them from the left. This system reduced changeover time to 90 percent.

However, the biggest drawback in this horizontal handling system is its accumulation of inventory between processes. As mentioned earlier, having piles of work-in-process makes it much more difficult to trace the sources and causes of defects. A second drawback is the greater expense involved in establishing such an automated system and the fact that the system is not suited for medium or large presses.

An abrupt switch to a vertical handling approach, however, would create greater loss in the conveyance of dies and would disrupt the process flow until

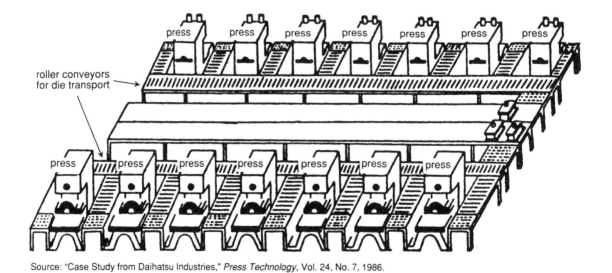

Source: "Case Study from Daihatsu Industries," *Press Technology*, Vol. 24, No. 7, 1986.

Figure 4-20. Reducing Changeover Time by Using Roller Conveyors Between Small Presses

all the bugs are worked out. Moreover, it is very difficult to keep changeover loss as low as in the horizontal handling approach; a much higher changeover loss would be likely (see Table 4-2).

To find out which approach is better for a particular production line, group processes into families and build the line on that basis. This family-based line organization method is described in Chapter 6. This chapter simply compares the relative advantages and disadvantages of these two approaches. Although either approach can produce good results, the vertical handling approach is generally preferable for wide-variety small-lot production lines.

Table 4-2. Comparison of Horizontal Handling and Vertical Handling

	Advantages	Disadvantages
Horizontal handling	1. Labor requirements can be reduced without substantially changing current conditions. 2. Very little need for retraining 3. Easy to reduce labor-hours 4. Easy to carry out changeover	1. Difficult to find the causes of defects and rework 2. Accumulation of work-in-process 3. Longer lead time
Vertical handling	1. Causes of defects and rework can be found quickly Full-lot inspection is easy to establish; defects can be addressed by preventive action at the source. 2. Reduction in work-in-process Market-oriented, just-in-time production: produce just what is needed, when it is needed, and in just the amount needed. 3. Shorter lead time 1/N connected processes. 4. Equipment factors Can be established simply (at low expense) using small general-purpose equipment that is relatively small and lightweight. Equipment can be moved around and modified easily. Automation devices can be easily added. 5. Cycle time production Production that uses fewer people, fewer machines, fewer materials. 6. Conducive to process razing for staffing reduction 7. Waste is made more visible and thus easier to eliminate	1. Changeover is more difficult 2. Requires training in multi-process handling; Some workers may not be able to get the hang of this 3. New workers must receive special training 4. Reduces capacity utilization rate for machines and devices

INEXPENSIVE U-SHAPED CELL DESIGN FOR PRESS PROCESSING

The diagram on the left side of Figure 4-21 shows the design of a press line before improvement. In this line, each press had its own operator. A die and some materials are brought to process No. 1, and after they are processed there, the work-in-process is conveyed to the in-process inventory storage area.

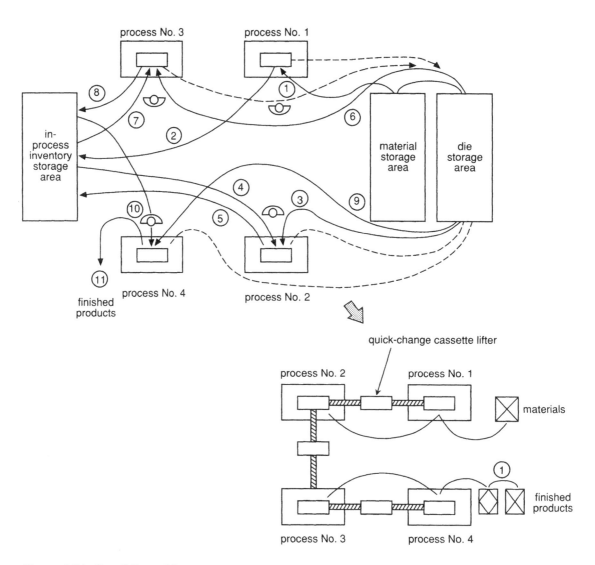

Figure 4-21. Small Press Line

From process No. 2 onward, Figure 4-21 shows the order of steps as circled numbers 3 to 9. Many of these steps involve repeatedly transporting dies and materials to and from the presses and the respective storage areas. The four most common types of waste in this line are:

1. In-process inventory waste (i.e., overproduction waste)
2. Defect production waste
3. Conveyance waste
4. Long-lead-time (slow-delivery) waste

Other types of waste can also be mentioned, but suffice it to say that this line is badly in need of process razing.

The diagram on the right side of Figure 4-21 shows how the line was re-designed as a U-shaped cell. Here, the processes have been linked and the die storage area moved to between the presses. If the budget allows, installing a quick-change cassette lifter will enable sequential changeover. If this is too expensive, the new dies should be prepared for changeover and set on the right or left of the presses where they will be needed.

The following are the basic steps for U-shaped cell design of press processing lines. Your first objective is to reduce the lead time. Unless a factory can guarantee quick deliveries, it is not very likely to receive orders to keep it running.

Figure 4-22 shows a line linking six processes, each handled by its own operator. Such a line is not conducive to quick delivery of product because it tends to accumulate in-process inventory.

To improve this line, the first step is to establish a trial straight line that is handled by just two operators, as shown in Figure 4-23. In this line, the operators walk from process to process and hand-carry the work-in-process.

Once production is going smoothly using this trial line, you are ready to take the next step, which is to establish a U-shaped cell handled by two operators, as shown in Figure 4-24. However, this U-shaped cell has three problems:

• Since each press uses its own die, the equipment's capacity utilization rate is low. In fact, the line includes more presses than it needs.
• Changeover becomes more difficult, and there is more conveyance loss.
• The cell is not conducive to sequential changeover.

As a further improvement, a rotating die table is installed at each press so that several dies can be moved around in just one press, lowering the cell's

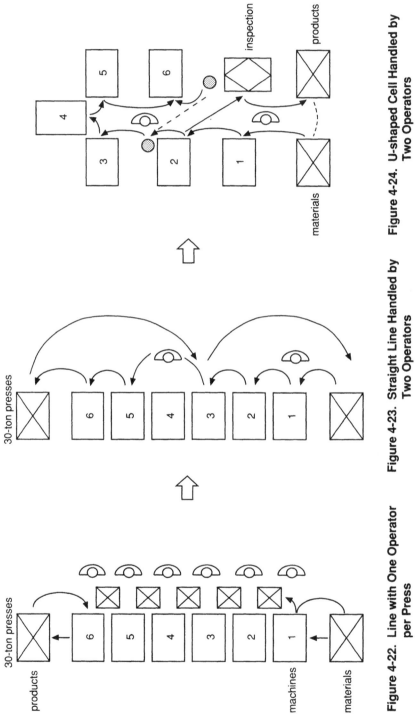

Figure 4-22. Line with One Operator per Press

Figure 4-23. Straight Line Handled by Two Operators

Figure 4-24. U-shaped Cell Handled by Two Operators

equipment cost dramatically (see Figure 4-25). With a cost per press of ¥2 million (about $15,000), the equipment cost reduction comes to ¥2 million X 7 = ¥14 million (about $100,000).

Look also at other improvement techniques that combine dies in fewer presses. Figure 4-26, for example, shows an improvement in which four dies are changed into a compound die that is handled at a single 300-ton press.

In small-lot production lines, changeover loss increases greatly when robots are used; you should think twice before choosing expensive FMS (flexible manufacturing system) options.

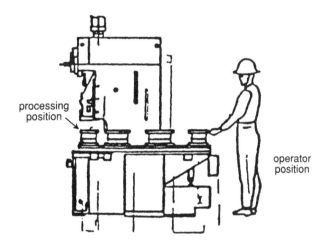

processing position

operator position

Figure 4-25. Rotating Die Table for Eight Dies

EXAMPLE OF A PROCESSING LINE CHANGEOVER IMPROVEMENT

This example was adapted from an article by Tsuyoshi Sokura, "Case Study from Daihatsu Industries," that appeared in *Press Technology* (Vol. 25, No. 3, March 1987). We have taken the liberty of including points from other companies' case studies and summarizing parts of the original article.

The first step in this changeover improvement was to organize an independent study group (actually, it is sometimes best to have top managers take the initiative in forming the first study group). The study group selected as their main objective the reduction of internal changeover time. They set a specific changeover time as their target.

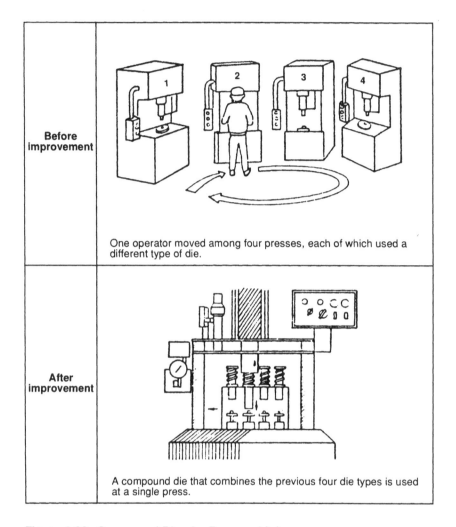

Figure 4-26. Compound Dies for Process Linkage

The study group took the following approach:

1. Studying Current Conditions

They began by trying to get a clear grasp of the changeover steps and work-hours required for changeover in the current line. The methods for studying changeover conditions were explained in Chapter 2. They used a walking route diagram (shown in Figure 4-27) and a standard operation combination chart (shown in Figure 4-28) to analyze and organize work-hour-related data.

They also made a videotape recording of the operators at work to facilitate motion study. Videotapes are a convenient way to study and reproduce actions repeatedly performed by line operators. Chapter 6 takes a closer look at how standard operation combination charts are drawn up.

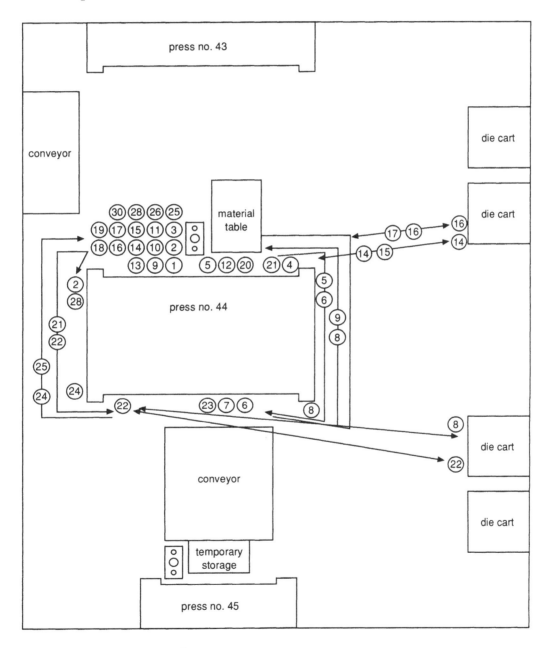

Figure 4-27. Walking Route Diagram

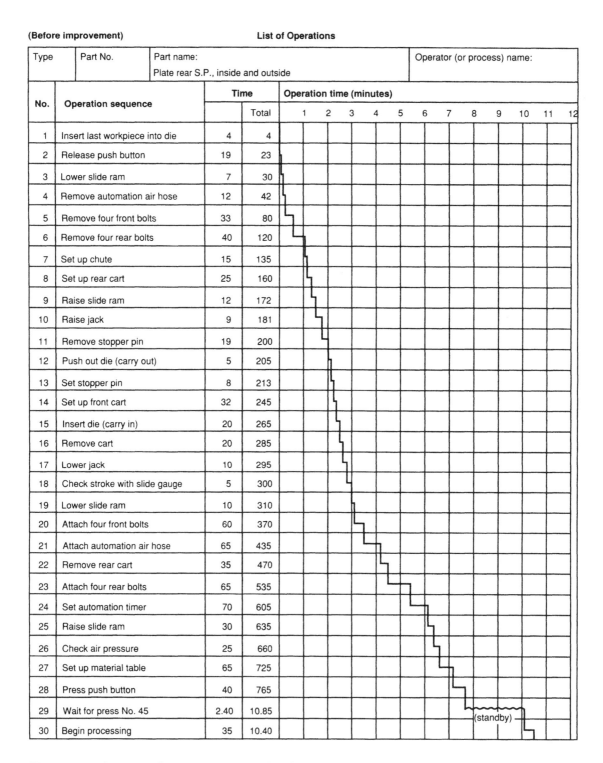

(Before improvement)   **List of Operations**

| Type | Part No. | Part name:
Plate rear S.P., inside and outside | | | | | Operator (or process) name: | | | | | | |

No.	Operation sequence	Time		Operation time (minutes)											
			Total	1	2	3	4	5	6	7	8	9	10	11	12
1	Insert last workpiece into die	4	4												
2	Release push button	19	23												
3	Lower slide ram	7	30												
4	Remove automation air hose	12	42												
5	Remove four front bolts	33	80												
6	Remove four rear bolts	40	120												
7	Set up chute	15	135												
8	Set up rear cart	25	160												
9	Raise slide ram	12	172												
10	Raise jack	9	181												
11	Remove stopper pin	19	200												
12	Push out die (carry out)	5	205												
13	Set stopper pin	8	213												
14	Set up front cart	32	245												
15	Insert die (carry in)	20	265												
16	Remove cart	20	285												
17	Lower jack	10	295												
18	Check stroke with slide gauge	5	300												
19	Lower slide ram	10	310												
20	Attach four front bolts	60	370												
21	Attach automation air hose	65	435												
22	Remove rear cart	35	470												
23	Attach four rear bolts	65	535												
24	Set automation timer	70	605												
25	Raise slide ram	30	635												
26	Check air pressure	25	660												
27	Set up material table	65	725												
28	Press push button	40	765												
29	Wait for press No. 45	2.40	10.85									(standby)			
30	Begin processing	35	10.40												

Figure 4-28. Standard Operation Combination Chart

2. Work-load Leveling

Internal changeover time is the changeover that follows the end of processing. It includes the changeover work starting when the previous process is finished and the product pallet has been loaded and ending when the next product pallet is ready to load.

In addition to changing dies, press changeover work includes moving and setting up conveyors and other peripheral equipment. You need to take into account these peripheral tasks as well when thinking of ways to level out the operators' work load.

3. Eliminating Deviation from Standards

You also must check whether the operators are following the standard operations instructions. If not, you need to find out why and see if it is because of some contradiction in the work sequence or process sequence. Videotape analysis can be especially helpful for studying such problems.

4. Eliminating Wasteful Operations

Any method, motion, or behavior that does not serve the process's objective should be seen as waste. Sometimes, videotapes can show wasteful motions or postures that are not easily perceived by the naked eye, especially if you speed up or slow down the tape playback. The changeover operators themselves should get together with their workshop leader to study videotapes of their work methods and to discuss and identify wasteful motions. This is a very good way to discover where improvements are needed.

5. Making Improvements so that Difficult Work Becomes Easier

Sometimes, a way of working that seems to be quite efficient and natural is found to include a lot of waste, unnecessary difficulty, or inconsistency when it is examined under the criterion of how well it serves the objective of the process. For example, tasks frequently become unnecessarily strenuous or difficult simply because the operator strays from standard operations. If a task is unavoidably strenuous, consider ways of mechanizing it to prevent operator fatigue.

In addition, it may be more efficient for a set of operations that is currently done sequentially to instead be done to some degree simultaneously. It may be possible to complete several different tasks at about the same time by changing the sequence of tasks. Shifting certain manual tasks to the feet, or devising ways of automating manual tasks with auto-feed or auto-stop mechanisms, can result in greater efficiency.

6. Making Process-specific Waste-Elimination Charts

General waste in changeover includes unnecessary difficulty, excess space or capacity, and inconsistency. As Table 4-1 showed, this general waste falls into the three categories of setup waste, replacement waste, and adjustment waste. After developing some improvement plans, sort them into small-scale, medium-scale, and large-scale improvement plans. Then you are ready to draw up a waste elimination chart.

The first step in implementing improvements is to start with the small-scale improvements that incur little or no expenses. Table 4-3 shows a change-over improvement waste-elimination chart. Table 4-4 shows a more detailed chart that lists specific problems and planned solutions. Whichever level of detail you choose, when you plan improvements remember that your primary goal is to reduce changeover time to enable single changeover, if not zero changeover.

7. Isolating External Changeover and Doing Changeover Setup

External changeover means changeover work that can be done without stopping the press. Changeover setup tasks include repairing dies, performing equipment maintenance checks, and other tasks preparatory to replacing dies. You must eliminate as much waste as possible from both external changeover work and changeover setup work.

It is also important to try to eliminate waste first from internal changeover work before trying to change internal changeover into external changeover. Simply changing internal changeover into external changeover does not make much of a net improvement, because it creates more work for people other than the changeover workers.

Table 4-3. Waste Elimination Chart for Changeover Improvement

Category	Type of waste	Waste elimination plan	
		A **(small-scale improvement)**	**B** **(medium-scale improvement)**
Setup waste	1. Jacking-up time is too long. 2. Front and rear scrap hoppers on press are hard to open and close. 3. Front and rear carts are too far away. 4. Front and rear scrap chutes are hard to set up. 5. Scraps are scattered on the bolster (behind the punch).	1. Change the size of the hydraulic pipe. 2. Combine the scrap chute with the workpiece chute.	1. Use an air cylinder to open and close the scrap hoppers. 2. Install automated transport system (with intermediate stop points) for die carts. 3. Install extendable or fold-up chutes.
Replacement waste	1. Connecting automation air hoses takes too long. 2. Upper bolts are hard to remove. 3. Waste occurs when extracted dies rebound out of position. 4. There is a wide variation in height settings for various dies. 5. Fastening and removing the front and rear bolts takes too long. 6. Time is wasted in carrying in the next die to be inserted; carrying and insertion are slowed down by the die's heaviness.	1. Color-code the hoses and pair them up. 2. Make the material feed chutes vertically adjustable. 3. Install die rebound stoppers. 4. Use bolts that can be loosened quickly; use bolt stoppers; attach urethane foam pads to the tops of the dies and to the beds. 5. Attach handles to the front and back of the dies; attach die stoppers, attach rotary die positioning stoppers, remove the die size stoppers from one side of the cart for die positioning.	1. Standardize die heights. 2. Use a die cart with an inclined surface.

8. Compilation of Improvement Points

Table 4-5 shows a compilation of changeover improvement points. Success in changeover improvement is built from the accumulation of small improvements such as these, each of which includes the identification of a problem and

Table 4-4. Line Changeover Problems and Responses

Problems and Responses

Item	Equipment	Problem	Response	Dept.	Period	Evaluation	Waste Type
1	#44	No safety barrier on materials table	Mount auxiliary plugs	Line	7/27		Setup
②		Automation air hoses hard to connect	Color-code hoses and pair them up	†	†	○	Replacement
3		Defective operation of rear gauge for die clamping	Conduct maintenance checks	Improvement	†		Adjustment
4		No adjustment screw on pusher speed controller	Install adjustment screw	Line	7/26		"
5		Front and rear carts too far away	Change crane operator's work sequence to enable external changeover	Study group	7/27	○	Setup
6		Stopper pin on workpiece chute hard to attach	Use metal bands to simplify stopper	Improvement	†	○	Replacement
7		Must walk too far to release push button	Move push button closer in	Line	†	○	Setup
8		Push button cord is too short	Attach longer push button cord	Production engineers	Undecided		"
9		Not enough rollers on bolster roller conveyor (hard to transport)	Install additional rollers	†	†		Replacement
10	Dies	When attaching dies, side stoppers catch on guide pins	Remove side stoppers from one side	Improvement	7/27	○	"
11	#44, 45, 46	Difficult to load heavy dies onto die carts	Use die carts with inclined tops	Line	8/7	◎	"
12	†	Bolt tightening takes too long	Install one-turn bolts on upper and lower dies	†	†	◎	"
13	†	†	Attach stoppers on upper and lower dies	†	†	◎	"
14	†	†	Attach urethane foam pads on bolsters	†	†	◎	"
15	Dies	†	Attach urethane foam pads upper dies	Die maintenance and line	†	◎	"

Waste Type	No.
Setup	11
Replacement	20
Adjustment	3
Total	33

No.	Ref.	Problem	Countermeasure	Responsible	Date		Waste Type
16	#45	Scraps scattered on bolster (behind punch)	Eliminate gap at scrap chute connection point	Improvement	8/3	O	Setup
17	↑	Upper bolts are hard to remove	Make the material feed chutes vertically adjustable	Line	7/27	O	Replacement
18	↑	Dies hard to transport (catch between bolster and cart)	Replace rollers on bolster conveyor	↑	↑	O	"
19	↑	Automation air hoses take too long to connect	Color-code hoses and pair them up	↑	↑	O	"
20	↑	Dents in dies' outer sleeves	Replace die sleeves	Die maintenance	7/30		"
21	↑	Rear scrap chute hard to connect	Develop simplified scrap and workpiece chute	Improvement	↑	◎	"
22	↑	Safety barrier in the way when moving conveyors	Train operators to avoid problem	Line	7/27		"
23	↑	Wide variation in die height settings during die replacement	Eliminate upper die shank	↑	8/7	O	"
24	↑	Lack of space hampers automation timer setting	Review operation sequence	Study group	7/27		Adjustment
25	#45, 46	Heavy conveyors difficult to move between lines	Develop automated transport system	Production engineers	Un-decided		Setup
26	#46	Upper die bolts hard to loosen/remove	Develop fold-up workpiece removal chutes	Improvement	8/3	◎	Replacement
27	↑	Automation air hoses hard to disconnect	Color-code hoses and pair them up	Line	7/27	O	"
28	↑	Workpiece removal conveyor too heavy	Improve rotation method and work sequence	Improvement, line	↑		Setup
29	↑	Jacking up takes too long	Install hydraulic jack	Production engineers	Un-decided		"
30	↑	Dies too heavy to remove easily	Install additional rollers on conveyor	↑	↑		Replacement
31	↑	Rear die carts too far away	Review work sequence	Study group	8/3	O	Setup
32	↑	Dents in sleeves used in setup	Replace sleeves	Die maintenance	7/30		"
33	↑	Scraps scattered on bolster (behind punch)	Eliminate gap at scrap chute connection point	Improvement	8/3	O	"
34	↑	Too much die rebound on conveyor carts	Develop unmanned transport system	Production engineers	Un-decided		Replacement

the implementation of a corresponding improvement plan. Slowly but steadily, you can whittle the overall changeover time until you reach the target, after which you are ready to set a new, even more ambitious target.

Table 4-5. Compilation of Improvement Data

Improvement Data Table							
Category	Item	Identification of problem		Implemented		Not implemented	
		Cases	Time (minutes)	Cases	Time (minutes)	Cases	Time (minutes)
Motion	Arrangement	2	20	2	20	0	0
	Operation ease	4	30	3	27	1	3
Route	Arrangement	6	42	4	37	2	5
	Distance	4	70	2	60	2	10
Switch to external changeover	Operation ease	2	15	1	8	1	7
	Storage areas	7	52	5	37	2	15
Equipment	Zero adjustments	5	52	3	38	2	14
	Fewer adjustments	2	30	2	30	0	0
Other	Operation standards	1	3	1	3	0	0
	Confirmation displays	1	6	0	0	1	6
Total	Net reduction in changeover (hours)	34 cases	320 seconds	23 cases	260 seconds	11 cases	60 seconds

Before improvement: 11'50" ⟹ After improvement: 7'30" ⟹ New target: 6'30"

9. Improvement Teams and Horizontal Deployment

One good way to carry out effective changeover improvement is to establish a model line on which to concentrate all your improvement efforts. Later, the same improvements can be deployed horizontally to similar processes in other lines, with the model line's improvement team providing guidance to the target line's team as they discover where waste exists and devise ways of eliminating it.

10. Using Standard Operation Combination Charts for Before-and-After Comparisons of Improvement Results

Table 4-6 shows a standard operation combination chart used to compare the line's conditions before and after improvement. This chart not only helps to show clearly how the line was improved, but also makes a useful reference material for horizontal deployment to other lines. When you demonstrate an improved changeover procedure to people from other lines, such a chart will help them understand how the improvement was made and what results it achieved. As such, it can be a valuable training tool.

Table 4-6. Standard Operation Chart: Before and After Improvement

Before Improvement

Type	Part No.	Part name: Plate rear S.P., inside and outside		Operator (or process) name: outside punch

No.	Operation sequence	Time		Operation time (decimal minutes)
			Elapsed	1 2 3 4 5 6 7 8 9 10 11 12
1	Release push button	—	.15	
2	Insert last workpiece into die	.05	.20	
3	Raise temporary storage stand	.08	.28	
4	Remove safety barrier from previous process	.07	.35	
5	Set up hopper	.02	.37	
6	Remove stopper from conveyor between lines	.03	.40	
7	Remove conveyor	.40	.80	*Workpiece extraction chute got in the way and caused bolts-tightening defects*
8	Lower slide ram	.15	.95	
9	Remove four front bolts	.85	1.80	
10	Remove automation air hose	.20	2.00	
11	Set up rear hopper	.10	2.10	
12	Remove 2 rear upper bolts	.40	2.50	
13	Set up chute	.05	2.55	
14	Remove 2 rear lower bolts	.35	2.90	
15	Set up rear cart	.20	3.10	
16	Raise slide ram	.20	3.30	
17	Raise jack	.05	3.35	*Dies got caught due to damaged rollers in conveyor bed*
18	Remove stopper pin	—	3.35	
19	Push out die (carry out)	1.25	4.60	
20	Set stopper pin	.10	4.70	
21	Set up front cart	.40	5.10	
22	Insert die (carry in)	.25	5.35	
23	Remove front cart	.15	5.50	
24	Lower jack	.10	5.60	
25	Check stroke with slide gauge	.40	6.10	
26	Lower slide ram	.10	6.20	
27	Lower slide adjuster	.20	6.40	
28	Attach four front bolts	.30	6.70	
29	Attach automation air hose	.25	6.95	*Scraps from punch scattered onto bed and required cleaning*
30	Remove rear cart	.30	7.25	
31	Attach four rear bolts	.65	7.90	
32	Set automation timer	—	—	
33	Raise slide ram	.35	8.25	
34	Set up conveyors between lines	.35	8.60	
35	Set up chute from previous process	.30	8.90	
36	Set up temporary storage for conveyor between processes	.30	9.20	
37	Set up safety barrier after previous process (right)	.10	9.30	
38	Set up safety barrier after previous process (left)	.35	9.65	
39	Set up safety barrier after temporary storage	.35	9.90	
40	Press push button	.25	10.15	
41	Begin processing	.38	10.35	
				Die replacement time: 10.35

After Improvement

Type	Part No.	Part name: Plate rear S.P., inside and outside		Operator (or process) name: outside punch

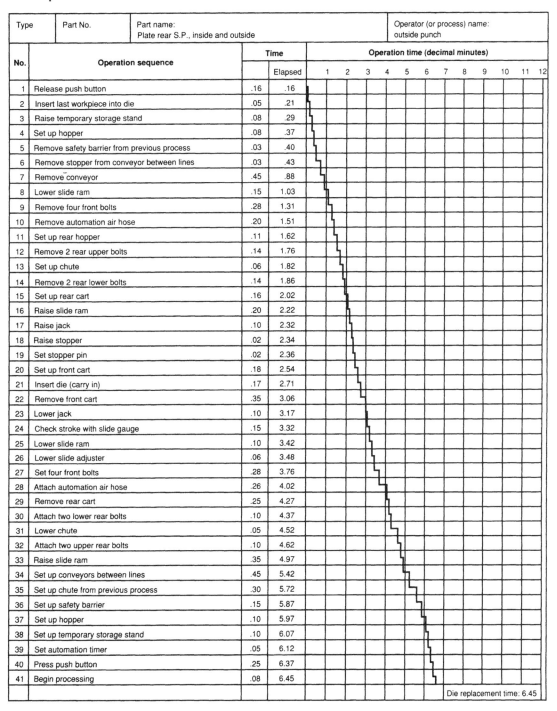

No.	Operation sequence	Time		Operation time (decimal minutes)
			Elapsed	1　2　3　4　5　6　7　8　9　10　11　12
1	Release push button	.16	.16	
2	Insert last workpiece into die	.05	.21	
3	Raise temporary storage stand	.08	.29	
4	Set up hopper	.08	.37	
5	Remove safety barrier from previous process	.03	.40	
6	Remove stopper from conveyor between lines	.03	.43	
7	Remove conveyor	.45	.88	
8	Lower slide ram	.15	1.03	
9	Remove four front bolts	.28	1.31	
10	Remove automation air hose	.20	1.51	
11	Set up rear hopper	.11	1.62	
12	Remove 2 rear upper bolts	.14	1.76	
13	Set up chute	.06	1.82	
14	Remove 2 rear lower bolts	.14	1.86	
15	Set up rear cart	.16	2.02	
16	Raise slide ram	.20	2.22	
17	Raise jack	.10	2.32	
18	Raise stopper	.02	2.34	
19	Set stopper pin	.02	2.36	
20	Set up front cart	.18	2.54	
21	Insert die (carry in)	.17	2.71	
22	Remove front cart	.35	3.06	
23	Lower jack	.10	3.17	
24	Check stroke with slide gauge	.15	3.32	
25	Lower slide ram	.10	3.42	
26	Lower slide adjuster	.06	3.48	
27	Set four front bolts	.28	3.76	
28	Attach automation air hose	.26	4.02	
29	Remove rear cart	.25	4.27	
30	Attach two lower rear bolts	.10	4.37	
31	Lower chute	.05	4.52	
32	Attach two upper rear bolts	.10	4.62	
33	Raise slide ram	.35	4.97	
34	Set up conveyors between lines	.45	5.42	
35	Set up chute from previous process	.30	5.72	
36	Set up safety barrier	.15	5.87	
37	Set up hopper	.10	5.97	
38	Set up temporary storage stand	.10	6.07	
39	Set automation timer	.05	6.12	
40	Press push button	.25	6.37	
41	Begin processing	.08	6.45	
				Die replacement time: 6.45

5

Making Inexpensive Improvements
to Reduce Staffing Needs

WHICH COMES FIRST: CHANGEOVER IMPROVEMENT OR NEW LINE LAYOUT? (A STUDY IN IMPROVING PROCESSING LINES THAT INCLUDE CHANGEOVER)

The trend toward wide-variety small-lot production has produced a conspicuous rise in work-hours lost to changeover operations. At automotive parts supplier factories, changeover occurs about ten times per shift on the average.

If the shift runs for 7.5 hours (450 minutes), that means changeover occurs, on the average, once every 45 minutes. If the changeover time is 9 minutes, only 36 minutes of each 45-minute block is actual processing time.

Of course, we have neglected to consider preparatory tasks other than changeover: tasks such as repairing molds, arranging, checking, and conveying parts, and changing machine programs. If these pre-changeover tasks take 30 minutes per changeover, we could say that the total changeover time (pre-changeover plus changeover) is 39 minutes.

That leaves us with a processing time/total changeover time ratio of 36 : 39. Obviously, this is not a well-balanced ratio. We define the production cycle as the processing time plus the changeover time plus the pre-changeover time, which in this case means:

36 minutes + 9 minutes + 30 minutes = 75 minutes

To have a well-balanced line, you must be able to complete the total changeover in less time than the processing time. To do this, it is important to make time-saving improvements in changeover, but it is even more important to integrate the pre-changeover tasks into the line to prevent the occurrence of missing items and standby time at the production line downstream.

Since so few press factories or machining factories in the automotive-parts industry or other industries have integrated pre-changeover into their lines, the purpose of this chapter is to describe steps for achieving this integration. People studying this subject often ask which comes first, changeover improvement or line-layout improvement? The answer: You must undertake both types of improvement at the same time.

Figure 5-1 shows a line-layout diagram that indicates various pre-changeover operations. The production management board shows the changeover sequence. Following the specifications given on the changeover kanban, the operator goes to the pre-changeover line shown on the left of the figure and picks up the specified dies, jigs, and frames. He or she then places these items, along with the program for the numerically controlled (NC) machine, processing standard specifications, and workpiece, on a specialized changeover cart.

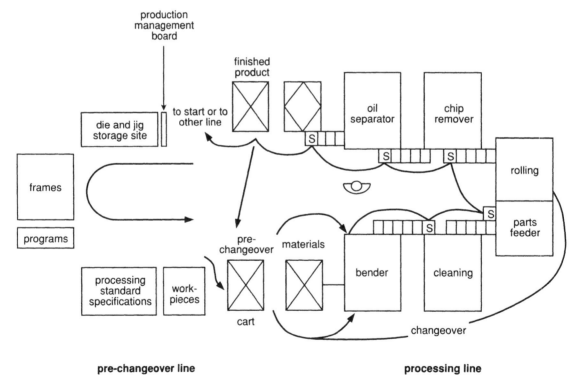

Figure 5-1. Processing Line with Pre-changeover Section

This completes the pre-changeover operation. Without a well-organized pre-changeover line such as this one, the changeover operator must do a lot of searching for items, which is wasteful. Most wide-variety small-lot production systems require that this pre-changeover step be completed within 3 minutes. Figure 4-3 showed electronic kanban as a method for preventing searching waste and assisting pre-changeover.

PRESS AUTOMATION

Figure 5-2 shows a dedicated press line that features single changeover (changeover within 9 minutes). Dedicated lines such as this one tend to require specialized dies and suffer from poor efficiency.

Figure 5-3 shows a robot-equipped press line that features sequentially fed dies. This type of automated line works best in large-lot high-yield production. In addition to industrial robots, press lines that are part of a flexible manufacturing system (FMS) also require automated transport devices and various transfer lines.

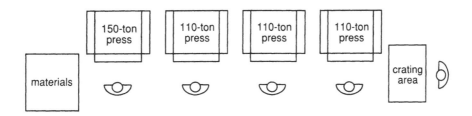

Figure 5-2. Simple Press Line

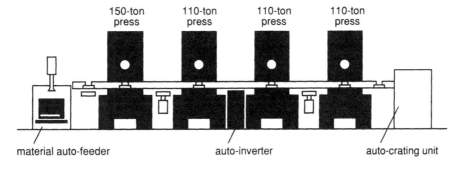

Figure 5-3. Robot-equipped Press Line

One of the drawbacks of the FMS approach is that it is very expensive. Perhaps the larger manufacturing companies can afford them, but small subcontractor companies generally cannot. A second drawback is that many aspects of an automated system are rendered useless when there is a major change in product models. While major manufacturers are basically able to estimate how long their product models will last, subcontractors must always be ready to adapt to their customers' model changes and cannot make such estimations. A third drawback is that changeover operations for automated lines generally consume more than half a day, which is not at all conducive to small-lot production by subcontractors.

In short, FMS is rarely a good idea for smaller manufacturers and for parts suppliers. They would be much wiser to find ways of building improved production lines without investing a lot of money.

BUILDING BETTER PROCESSING LINES AT LITTLE COST

Factories that perform only primary processing are generally not profitable. They must also include secondary processing equipment. If possible, it is best to invest in a line that includes both types of equipment.

The road to survival for smaller companies lies in inexpensively building processing lines that include primary and secondary processing. The first step in building a processing line is to set up a straight line of presses and other processing equipment, arranged according to the flow of processing operations. Figure 5-4 shows this type of line.

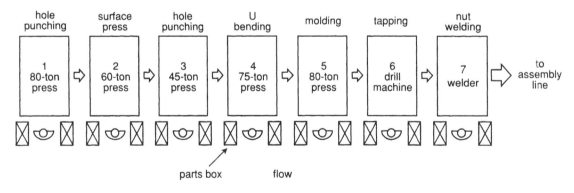

Figure 5-4. Press Line (No. 1)

To the casual observer, straight lines such as these appear to be the most neatly organized. The production methods used are also more obvious on straight lines. Such lines tend to use the traditional system of assigning one operator per machine. Of course, you can recognize right away that lines such as these are full of what the Toyota production system (TPS) approach defines as the seven types of waste (overproduction waste, standby waste, conveyance waste, processing waste, inventory waste, motion waste, and defect production waste).

To improve conventional lines such as these, you must raze some processes. Figure 5-5 shows how the line from Figure 5-4 would look after process-razing improvement. For a more detailed description of process-razing techniques, see Kenichi Sekine, *One-Piece Flow* (Portland, Ore.: Productivity Press, 1992). This chapter will touch on the general points of process razing.

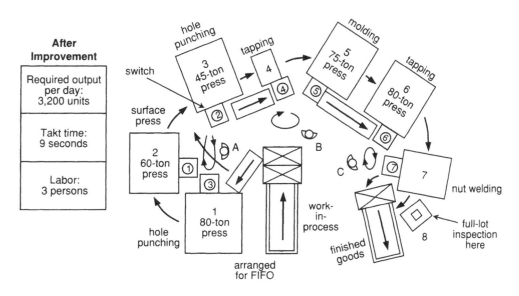

Figure 5-5. Press Line After Initial Process-razing Improvement

As the figure shows, the first round of process razing reduced the in-process inventory from 1,800 units to just 7 units. In addition, the switch to multi-process handling enabled a reduction in staffing from seven operators to just three. These results are remarkable, but they still fall short of the TPS objective, particularly since the defect rate is still above zero.

One reason why this line has not yet achieved the zero-defect goal is that it has different operators handling the entry and exit processes. A second reason is because the full-lot inspection process occurs only at the end of the line; it has not been incorporated into each operation in the line.

Figure 5-6 shows how the line looked after a second process-razing improvement. This improvement enabled a further staffing reduction, from three operators to just two.

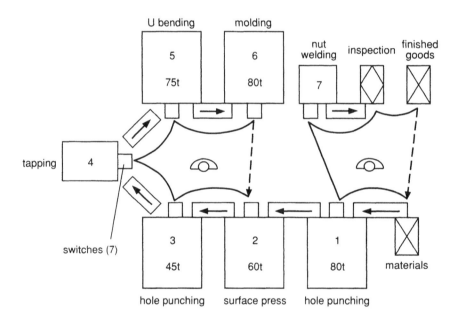

Figure 5-6. Press Line After Second Process-razing Improvement

PARALLEL MACHINING LINES

Figure 5-7 shows a parallel line arrangement. The top line (line A) is for product A and the bottom line (line B) is for product B.

The drawbacks of this layout include the difference in cycle times for the two lines, which interferes with multi-process handling. You can also see that

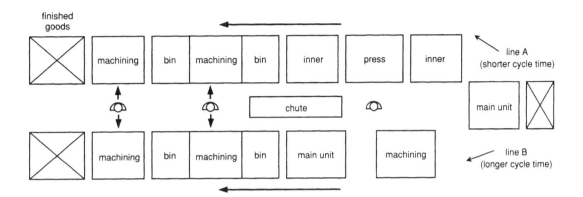

Figure 5-7. Parallel Machining Line

the chute in the center is isolated from both lines, and is therefore less efficient than a line-integrated chute.

Figure 5-8 shows an improvement that turns lines A and B into U-shaped cells and allows staffing to be reduced from three to just two operators. Since the third operator is no longer needed in this line, he or she can be trained as a changeover specialist or can be temporarily assigned as an improvement team member. As an additional improvement, a pre-changeover line should be built close to this line.

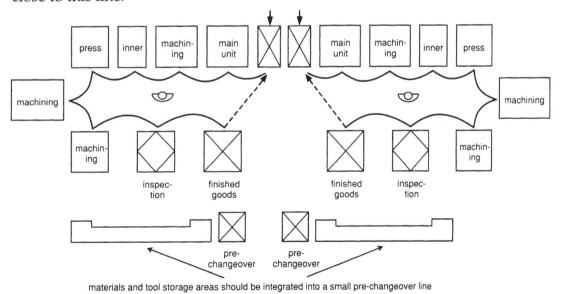

Figure 5-8. Opposite U-shaped Cells

EXAMPLE OF LABOR REDUCTION ON AN AUTOMATED PRESS/ROBOT LINE

A participant once presented a very interesting problem at a factory problem-solving seminar. This chapter offers a response to this problem.

Summary of Company A

Company A is a manufacturing company that uses high-speed, high-precision presses to make electronic components. The factory employs 50 people. Its factory equipment includes 30 automated presses that work on coil materials, 14 industrial robots, and 30 other types of presses. The equipment is laid out in rows, much like desks in a schoolroom. The factory also includes barrels and levelers. Figure 5-9 shows its factory layout prior to improvement.

Company A's Problem

In a nutshell, Company A's problem is that its factory is laid out for large-lot production but its customers send orders for both large lots and small lots. Having to deal with small lots causes the following specific problems:

1. Many extra work-hours spent on changeover
2. Increased production of defects following changeovers
3. Workpieces flow according to the needs of the robots
4. Large amounts of in-process inventory waste
5. Large amounts of standby waste (e.g., idle observation of robots)
6. Large cleaning equipment (all cleaning is done by one machine; operators must staff its entry and exit points)
7. Factory cannot meet short delivery deadlines, creating waste due to slow deliveries

The managers of Company A rank their problems in the above order of priority. The problem of changeover work-hours has top priority because of the loss in value added per employee that this problem creates. However, even the lowest-ranked problem of slow deliveries is serious, as it affects the customers' trust in Company A's ability to meet its obligations. Late deliveries ultimately result in loss of sales and loss of status among managers. This problem is actually the most serious one of the group. We will address these problems in their proper order of priority.

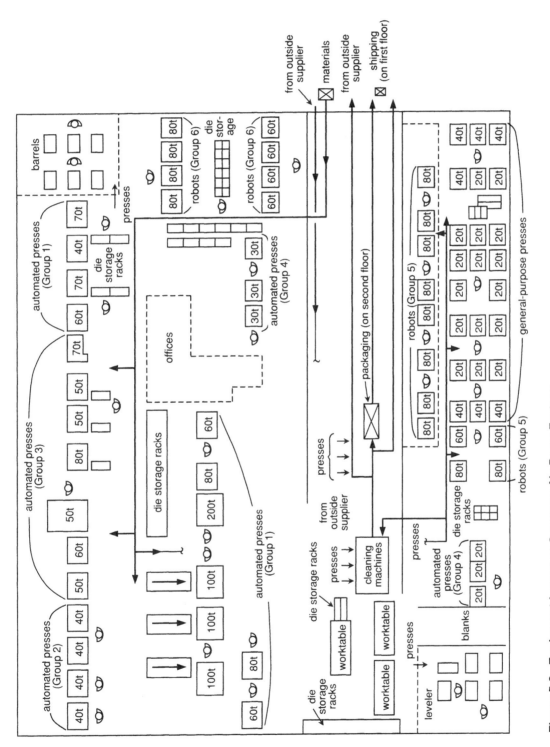

Figure 5-9. Equipment Layout at Company A's Press Factory

Problem No. 1: Waste caused by late deliveries

The cause behind this problem is the factory's volume-oriented management approach. The managers' main concern is the number of tons of product A or square feet of product B turned out each day.

The managerial priority, in other words, is large-lot production. Small-lot orders are treated as relatively unimportant and therefore little gets done to ensure their timely delivery. Only when the customer complains do the factory managers truly get concerned about the smaller lots. By then, it is usually too late to prevent a late delivery.

The waste-elimination approaches to this problem are:

Plan A: Establish zero changeover on the automated press and robot line.
Plan B: Build a new line layout oriented toward small-lot production.

Problem No. 2: Changeover waste (due to lack of zero-changeover operations)

Company A carries out four punch-die changeovers per day on its 20-ton and 40-ton punch presses, which means about 800 changeovers per month. Changeover takes about 90 minutes on the robot-equipped presses, 60 minutes on the automated presses, and 15 minutes on the general-purpose presses. Our first step would be to draw up a table listing the changeover times on each type of machine.

The cause for all this changeover waste is the factory managers' stubborn adherence to the philosophy of large-lot production. Like it or not, they can no longer afford to subscribe to that philosophy today, when the market demands small-lot production.

The waste-elimination plan for this problem would begin with a statistical report to the factory managers on the negative effect of large-lot production due to heavy changeover costs. It must then be impressed on them that the only way to turn the red ink into black is to build a small-lot production line.

Problem No. 3: Defect production waste (higher defect rate following changeovers)

Company A's managers had the mistaken notion that changeover is the same thing as die replacement. The fact is that changeover encompasses everything that needs to be done to prepare the equipment for a new set of processing standards. Unfortunately, people rarely enforce the standards strictly, and so a lot of time is wasted in making post-changeover adjustments to fix sloppy changeover that produces defective products.

The waste elimination plan for this problem would include forming a study group to learn the basic principles of changeover improvement. Since Company A has been receiving 5 to 15 complaints per month about late deliveries, this improvement study group obviously needs to get to work as soon as possible.

Problem No. 4: Workpieces flow according to the needs of the robots

After process No. 1 (punching out the outer-diameter blanks), the workpieces must be lined up for the robot at process No. 2. This arrangement of workpieces is a kind of motion waste, since it is done manually. Three improvement plans follow:

Plan A: Invent a jig that automatically arranges the workpieces for the robot.

Plan B: Use a single operator to operate auto-feed mechanisms for the robots.

Plan C: Attach a workpiece-sorting mechanism to the die at process No. 1. If this cannot be done in-house, contact an engineering company that can do the job.

Problem No. 5: In-process inventory waste

The main cause for this is the horizontal-handling type of layout in which the machines are separated into various clusters. When machines are separated this way, the inevitable result is the accumulation of in-process inventory due to retention in the flow of goods between processes. This retention is a fundamental cause of waste, since it lengthens the delivery chain, increases the amount of temporary storage, vertical conveyance, dust build-up, dents and other product damage, and adds to the production lead time. The work-in-process also hides defects, which creates even more waste. That's the thinking behind the belief that in-process inventory is dead inventory.

The improvement plan for this problem links the processes and groups the equipment into families to improve the flow of goods and to reduce in-process inventory drastically.

Problem No. 6: Large cleaning equipment

Here we run smack into the problem of adhering to the large-lot approach. The solution to this problem must therefore begin with education for factory managers and production engineers who have fallen behind the times in factory management know-how. Next, a test line consisting of dispersed small cleaning machines should be built and experimented with.

Without even going into the question of other types of waste, it is clear that the key improvement in this case is to prove to Company A's managers that only the small-lot production approach will meet today's needs.

Steps Toward Achieving Quick Delivery

Step 1: Group production equipment into families

Table 5-1 shows a process route analysis chart of the Company A production line (shown in Figure 5-9) that was used to make a family grouping. The key point here is to be able to group upstream presses and downstream robot-equipped machines into families.

In the table:

$$F_1 = \text{Press PB (large robot)}$$
$$F_2 = \text{Press PB (small robot)}$$
$$F_3 = \text{Press PG (large robot)}$$
$$F_4: \text{ Press PG (small robot)}$$

Among these groups, let's assume that the largest family of these four is F_2.

Step 2: Build a test line

A test line should be a single integrated line with a smooth flow of goods. The test line built for this case uses the largest family, F_2 (see Figure 5-10).

The workpiece-arrangement process that follows the 60-ton automated press should be an automated (or jig-operated) process; for now, we will leave it as a manual process.

Once the processes have been arranged in this sort of test line, it becomes easier to see where waste exists. Try to eliminate this waste, such as by developing automation devices.

Whenever the factory orders X amount of parts from an outside supplier, it should receive only that amount. To keep control of this, it is best to use kanban and set up a daily order system with deliveries due the following day (a 1-1-1 system).

Once this line is running smoothly, integrate the packaging process into the line as well. This will enable the factory to achieve a two-day production lead time for quick delivery.

Step 3: Launch a changeover study group

The initial objective of the changeover study group should be to cut the changeover time in half. After that, they should get it down to 15 minutes, then 9 minutes (single changeover) and, finally, down to within 3 minutes (zero changeover). Zero changeover can be done even when robots are involved if we find ways to minimize changeover by limiting it to the robot's extremities.

TEST YOUR SKILLS

The managers of Factory B have decided to raise their value-added rate by including more secondary processing in their production system. Among other things, their plans call for the introduction of automatic spot welders and in-line integration of presses.

Figure 5-11 shows Factory B's layout before improvement. As the figure shows, the layout is based on equipment type. One advantage of this type of layout is that it offers flexibility in responding to customer preferences. However, it tends to result in long lead times, making it difficult for the factory to meet customer needs for quick delivery.

To make their factory better suited to all customer needs, the managers decide to build a vertical-handling line using certain presses for secondary processing.

Step 1: Create a process-analysis flowchart

Figure 5-12 shows the flowchart created for product B (the major product).

Table 5-1. Process Route Analysis Chart for Company A

No.	Part name	Press	Press	Barrel	Arrange-ment (in-house)	Leveler	Large robot	Small robot	Press (outside supplier)	Cleaning machine	Tapping (outside supplier)	Chroming (outside supplier)	Heat treatment (outside supplier)	Crating (in-house)	Packaging	Lot size	Notes
		PB	PG	MB		ML	BP	BP	BP	CO	MT	T	N				
1	TUN	①								③	②				④	5,000	
2	INC	①			②	③		④		⑤	⑥				⑦	3,000	
3	GMN	①				②	③		④	⑤	⑤			⑥		15,000	
4	UC		①									②				5,000	
5	CTM		①		②	③				③	②				④	20,000	Ⓐ
6	GGM	①			②	③		④		⑤					⑥	5,000	
7	ATC		①							②					③	5,000	
8	GBN		①		②					③	②				④	5,000	
9	TUO	①			②	③				⑤			④		⑥	2,000	
10	DA		①	② ④									③		⑤	8,000	
11	BD		①	②							③	④				8,000	
12	TOH		①							②					③	10,000	
13	ZPL		①	②								④	③		⑤	5,000	

№	Code	Circled sequence values	Amount	(A)
14	ZPL	① ② ③ ④ ⑤	15,000	Ⓐ
15	CSU	① ② ③ ④	2,000	
16	NNN	① ② ③	10,000	
17	NCA	① ② ③ ④ ⑤	900	
18	BQJ	① ② ③ ④ ⑤	2,000	
19	IE	① ② ③ ④ ⑤ ⑥	500	
20	EM	① ② ③ ④	500	
21	CSL	① ② ③	5,000	
22	QHT	① ② ③ ④	5,000	
23	INJ	① ② ③ ④ ⑤	5,000	
24	ISED	① ② ③ ④	10,000	Ⓐ
25	CT	① ② ③ ④ ⑤ ⑥	30,000	Ⓐ
26	GBH	① ② ③ ④ ⑤ ⑥	20,000	Ⓐ
27	BHM	① ② ③	15,000	Ⓐ
28	DITJ	① ② ③ ④ ⑤ ⑥	15,000	Ⓐ
29	CLUN	① ② ③	20,000	Ⓐ
30	MCP	① ②	2,000	Ⓐ

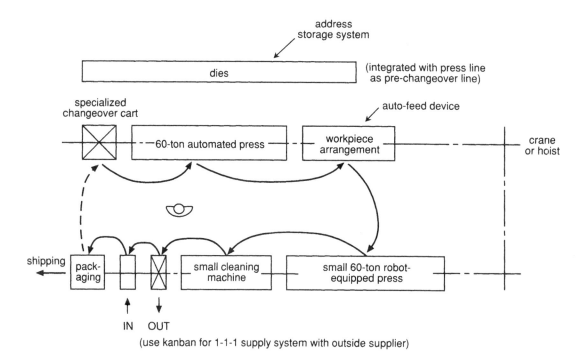

Figure 5-10. Test Line

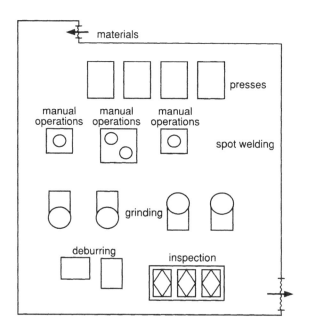

Figure 5-11. Layout of Factory B (Before Improvement)

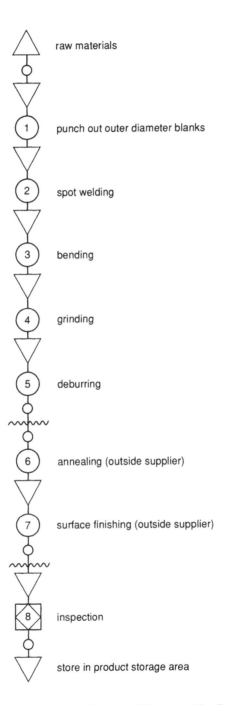

raw materials

1 punch out outer diameter blanks

2 spot welding

3 bending

4 grinding

5 deburring

6 annealing (outside supplier)

7 surface finishing (outside supplier)

8 inspection

store in product storage area

Figure 5-12. Process Analysis Flowchart for Product B

Step 2: Carry out waste elimination

All press factories share the problems of transport waste, retention waste, and standby waste.

Step 3: Carry out the first round of process razing to build a new line layout

The new line layout is shown in Figure 5-13. Suppose that you ran the automated spot welder without human assistance for 24 hours a day to make up for its heavy investment cost, but that this created the problem of overproduction and in-process inventory waste. Meanwhile, the rest of the line is operated only eight hours (one shift) per day.

In view of the above conditions, what would you suggest for the second round of process razing?

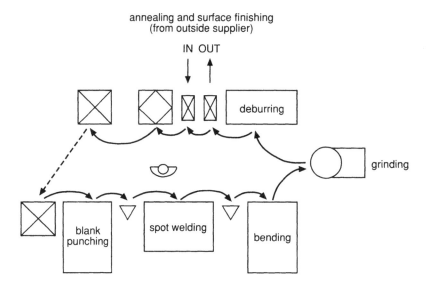

Figure 5-13. Factory B Line Layout After First Round of Process Razing

Proposed Solution

A two-shift system should be established. During the first shift, the automated spot welder should be operated within the line and in pace with the line's cycle time.

During the second (night) shift, the automatic spot welder should be left to run by itself, but not to handle any of the orders that go through the line. Instead, it should handle only spot welding orders that come in from other lines (possibly at other companies). To make this work, of course, you must achieve zero changeover.

Figure 5-14 illustrates this proposed second-round improvement.

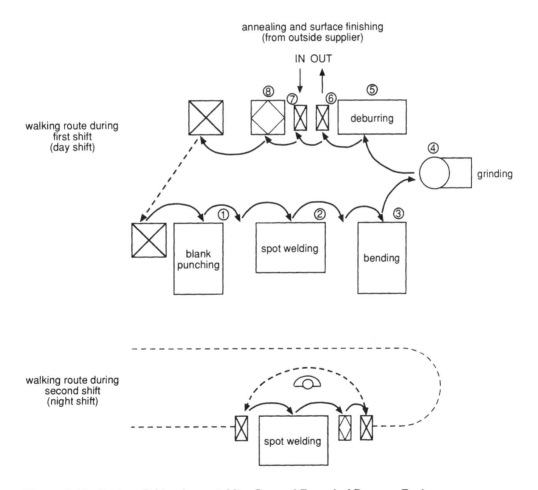

Figure 5-14. Factory B Line Layout After Second Round of Process Razing

6

Steps for Improving New Processing Lines

The previous chapter covered the main points about building improved production lines. This chapter will examine two methods for line improvement: the orthodox Toyota production system (TPS) method and the simplified (S) method.

THE TPS METHOD OF LINE IMPROVEMENT

The TPS method of line improvement follows this sequence:

Step 1: Form a labor-reduction (U-shaped cell) study group
Step 2: Study current conditions (P-Q analysis, etc.)
Step 3: Observe the factory
Step 4: Use process-route analysis to group products into families
Step 5: Draw up a part-specific capacity worktable for conditions before improvement*
Step 6: Draw up a standard operation combination chart for conditions before improvement*
Step 7: Draw up a standard operation chart (walking-route diagram) for conditions before improvement*
Step 8: Draw up a process-specific waste-elimination chart
Step 9: Draw up a part-specific capacity worktable for conditions after improvement

---

* The part-specific capacity worktable, the standard operation combination chart, and the standard operation chart (walking route diagram) are sometimes referred to as the three essential tools of the TPS approach.

Step 10: Draw up a standard operation combination chart for conditions after improvement

Step 11: Draw up a standard operation chart (walking-route diagram) for conditions after improvement

Step 12: Implement (factory supervisor)

Step 13: Write operation instructions

Step 14: Manage by SPH (strokes per hour)

This chapter presents a case study of how Company C followed the above steps. In particular, we will study the use of P-Q analysis, family grouping of processes based on a process-route diagram, part-specific capacity worktables, standard operation combination charts, standard operation charts, and process-specific waste-elimination charts created and used in this process of improvement.

STUDY CURRENT CONDITIONS (P-Q ANALYSIS, ETC.)

The best way to begin an effort to build improved U-shaped cells for wide-variety small-lot production is to study the wide-variety small-lot production conditions that already exist at the factory (see Figure 6-1).

The following are some objectives and advantages of P-Q analysis:

1. It enables you to estimate more easily how many processing-line families will be needed.

2. It gives a clear picture of which items are produced in-house and which are supplied by subcontractors.

   • It provides an easy-to-read list of the items handled in the production line.

   • It shows immediately how big a share is held by the most important items (Group A).

   • It enables you to estimate the number of changeovers and the changeover loss time, as calculated based on the average number of items per lot.

   • It helps give ideas for the design of wide-variety small-lot processing lines. For example, it might show that you need three processing lines for small workpieces and one line each for medium-size and large workpieces.

• If you compare the changeover times for the different lines, you can get a basic understanding of the amount of warehouse and in-process inventory and the production lead time.

What Is P-Q Analysis?

The "P" in P-Q analysis stands for product models (or items). The "Q" stands for quantity. The full name for a P-Q analysis chart is a customer-specific, part-specific product-quantity chart (see Figure 6-1). This looks similar to an ABC chart or a Pareto chart, but those are actually slightly different in that they evaluate products in terms of monetary value rather than quantity.

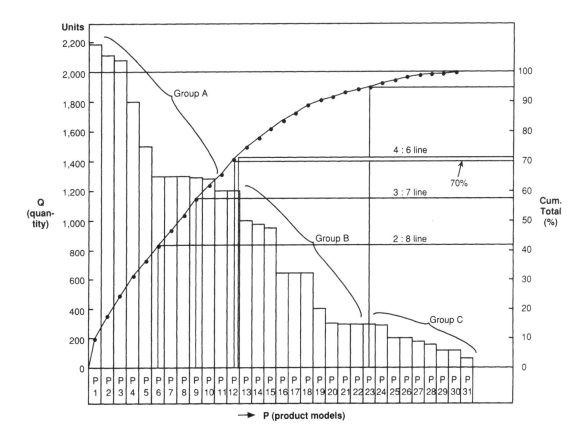

Figure 6-1. P-Q Analysis Chart

Table 6-1 shows a product-specific quantity table. By filling in the lot sizes, we can determine the average lot size. This also enables us to estimate the number of changeovers. The data can be taken from a period ranging from the past three months to the past year.

Although Table 6-1 shows only a product-model analysis, we could make a similar table showing customers as the first analysis category, product models as the second category, and marketing seasons as the third category. Thus, this type of table can be used for various purposes.

Implementation of P-Q Analysis

The P-Q analysis chart (Figure 6-1) is a graphic representation of the data listed in the product-specific quantity table (Table 6-1). It shows that:

- Group A occupies up to 70 percent of the total product volume.
- Groups A and B together occupy from 71 to 95 percent of the total product volume.
- Groups A, B, and C together occupy 96 to 100 percent of the total product volume.

It is not particularly difficult to create P-Q analysis tables and charts such as these, but to save time there are computer programs that can do it in about 10 minutes.

Study Current Wide-variety Small-lot Production Conditions

First, we need to determine whether the production line is currently a wide-variety small-lot production line, based on the ratio lines shown in Figure 6-1.

The 2:8 ratio line means that the first 20 percent of the product models should account for 80 percent of the total product quantity. If there are 31 product models, this means that 20 percent of those (about 6 products) should account for 80 percent of the total product quantity. Looking at the percent scale on the right side of the table, we see that the first 6 products account for only about 42 percent of the total product quantity; thus the 2:8 ratio does not apply in this case.

Table 6-1. Product-specific Quantity Table

No.	Product model	Quantity	Cum. Total (units)	Cum. Total (%)
1	P1	2,180	2,180	8.3
2	P2	2,100	4,280	16.2
3	P3	2,060	6,340	24.1
4	P4	1,780	8,120	30.8
5	P5	1,460	9,580	36.3
6	P6	1,320	10,900	41.4
7	P7	1,310	12,210	46.3
8	P8	1,300	13,510	51.3
9	P9	1,290	14,800	56.1
10	P10	1,280	16,080	61.0
11	P11	1,200	17,280	65.6
12	P12	1,200	18,480	70.1
13	P13	1,030	19,510	74.0
14	P14	1,000	20,510	77.8
15	P15	970	21,480	81.5
16	P16	690	22,170	84.1
17	P17	680	22,850	86.7
18	P18	680	23,530	89.3
19	P19	410	23,940	90.8
20	P20	310	24,250	92.0
21	P21	300	24,550	93.1
22	P22	300	24,850	94.3
23	P23	300	25,150	95.4
24	P24	280	25,430	96.5
25	P25	200	25,630	97.2
26	P26	200	25,830	98.0
27	P27	150	25,980	98.6
28	P28	130	26,110	99.1
29	P29	100	26,210	99.4
30	P30	100	26,310	99.8
31	P31	50	26,360	100.0

Next, we find out if this case falls under the 3:7 ratio category. To do that, the first 9 products must account for 70 percent of the total quantity. This time, it falls short again, at 58, although not so sharply. To meet the 4:6 ratio, the first 12 products must account for around 60 percent of the total product quantity. In this case, they reach about 72 percent.

Ultimately, we determine that the ratio in this case is closest to 4:6, and so that is the ratio to work with. Production lines that fall into the 4:6 ratio category can be called wide-variety small-lot production lines. The typical Japanese factory falls into this category, but many are having problems succeeding at this kind of production.

USE PROCESS-ROUTE ANALYSIS TO GROUP PRODUCTS INTO FAMILIES

Since Company C did not do a process-route analysis, we will instead use a typical example from another company (Company O), shown in Figure 6-2. Like Company C, Company O uses a machining line to process its products, and thus their process-route analysis chart will serve as a suitable example.

A P-Q analysis shows that Company O is also a wide-variety small-lot production company. It should be made clear, however, that this P-Q analysis deals with processes as the "P" instead of products, and processes (or rather, process routes) are grouped into families to reduce their number. Most factories have no more than five such process families.

In gathering the data via a process-route analysis, do not consider differences in product size, shape, or material as different varieties of parts. Figure 6-2 studies 13 product types that were selected from a total of 32. Try to work out the families on your own. Make no more than three families, with the restrictions that there are only two NC lathes, LB 15 and LB 20, and there is only one upright MC and one NC for making screw holes. No new equipment may be added.

THE TPS METHOD FOR DRAFTING OPERATION INSTRUCTIONS

Company C has three production lines: a rotor assembly line, stator-core processing line, and a motor assembly line. Figure 6-3 shows an assembly process flow analysis chart of the rotor assembly line before improvement.

No.	Part name	NC lathe		Horizontal mill	Upright mill	Compact mill	Upright MC	NC for screw holes	Marker	Drilling machine	Manual operations	Honing	Grinder	Quantity	Family
		LB15	LB20	M	VM	BM	6VA	TNC	MRK	B	MAN	H	G		
1	Slider (A)						①			②	③	④	⑤	1	
2	Slider (B)				①		②			③	④	⑤	⑥	1	
3	Press brace					①			②	③	④			1	
4	Bracket				①			②		③	④			1	
5	Table			①				②		③	③		④	1	
6	Damper	①			②			②		③	④			2	
7	Bracket	①							③	④	⑤			1	
8	Support				①			②		③				2	
9	Housing		①					②		③				1	
10	Flange		①							②				1	
11	Shaft			①						②	③		④	1	
12	Base			①	③		②				④		⑤	1	
13	Spacer				①③		②				④		⑤	1	

Figure 6-2. Process-Route Analysis Chart

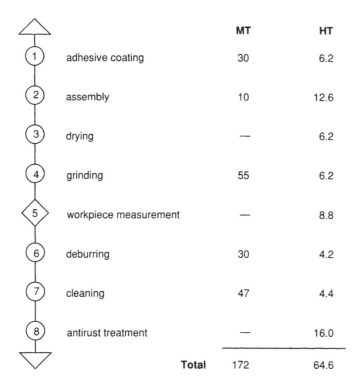

		MT	HT
1	adhesive coating	30	6.2
2	assembly	10	12.6
3	drying	—	6.2
4	grinding	55	6.2
5	workpiece measurement	—	8.8
6	deburring	30	4.2
7	cleaning	47	4.4
8	antirust treatment	—	16.0
	Total	172	64.6

Figure 6-3. Assembly Process Analysis of Rotor Assembly Line

For several years, these lines had been maintaining standard daily output of 400 units. Their strokes per hour (SPH) was 50 units. Due to pressures brought by appreciation of the yen, Company C's clients demanded price reductions, or else the clients would turn to cheaper imports from newly industrialized countries. Company C figured that to break even at the requested lower prices, they would have to achieve an SPH of 60 units.

The following line improvement can be worked out using the simplified method, but if time allows, you should use the TPS method instead. Here are the steps Company C took, using the TPS method.

Time Study

First, a time study was done by observing the operators at work and timing their operations. Table 6-2 shows the time measurements made on Company C's rotor assembly line. Improvement team members made five rounds of time measurements and then calculated the average values (X-bar), minimum values

(Min), and range of variation (*R*). They also determined the standard time (ST) by adding the minimum values (Min).

Part-specific Capacity Worktable for Conditions Before Improvement

For each machine (i.e., process), the team drew up a part-specific capacity worktable to find the current processing capacity for each type of part. In addition to the data shown in Table 6-2, they gathered time measurement data for auto-feed (MT) devices and for blade replacements and other changeover operations. Then they drew up the part-specific capacity worktable shown in Figure 6-4.

The process capacity was calculated using the following formula.

$$\text{Process capacity} = \frac{\text{Operation time}}{\text{Completion time/unit} + \text{blade replacement time/unit}}$$

For Process No. 4 (grinding):

$$\text{Process capacity} = \frac{8 \text{ hrs./shift} \times 3{,}600 \text{ sec./hr.}}{61 \text{ sec.} + \dfrac{6{,}000 \text{ sec.}}{1{,}500 \text{ units}}} = 443 \text{ units (rounded)}$$

Table 6-2. Time Measurement Chart for Rotor Assembly Line

No.	Work element	Measurement No.					$\bar{X}$	Min	R
		1	2	3	4	5			
1	From adhesive coating application to cup placement	5	6	7	7	6	6.2	5	2
2	Assembly	13	13	12	13	12	12.6	12	1
3	From adhesive reinforcement to drying and insertion	6	6	7	6	6	6.2	6	1
4	Conveyance to grinding	6	6	7	6	6	6.2	6	1
5	Workpiece measurement (micrometer)	11	7	10	7	9	8.8	7	4
6	Deburring	4	4	5	4	4	4.2	4	1
7	Cleaning	4	4	3	3	4	4.4	3	1
8	From antirust treatment to packaging	15	15	16	17	17	16.0	15	2
	Total	64	61	67	63	64	64.6	58	
	Average								1.6

Section mgr.	Plant mgr.	Part-specific Capacity Worktable (Before Improvement)	Part No.	Model	Dept.	Name
			Part name: Rotor processing	Quantity		

Process No.	Process name	Machine No.	Basic time measurements			Cutting tools		Process capacity	Comments
			Manual operation time (HT)	Auto-feed time (MT)	Completion time	No. replaced	Replacement time		(Diagram lines:)
			min. sec.	min. sec.	min. sec.				Manual operation = ——— Auto-feed = – – –
1	Adhesive coating		5	30	35			822	5" ⊢ 30" – – – – ⊣
2	Assembly		12	10	22			1,309	12" ⊢ 10" – – ⊣
3	Drying		6		6			4,800	6" ⊢
4	Grinding		6	55	61	1,500	6,000"	443	6" ⊢ 55" – – – – ⊣
5	Workpiece measurement		7		7			4,114	7" ⊢
6	Deburring		4	30	34			847	4" ⊢ 30" – – – ⊣
7	Cleaning		3	47	50			576	3" ⊢ 47" – – – – ⊣
8	Antirust treatment		15		15			1,920	15" ⊢
	Place on bracket insertion tool		1		1				
	Total		59						

Figure 6-4. Part-specific Capacity Worktable (Before Improvement)

Standard Operation Combination Chart for Conditions Before Improvement

In making a standard operation combination chart oriented toward keeping pace with the cycle time (CT), our objective is to determine the combination of operations that produces the least waste. One part of this objective is to prevent standby waste among operators.

The time measurements for operators, work-in-process, and machines consist of manual operation time (HT), mechanical auto-feed time (MT), and walking time. The part-specific capacity worktable shows the HT and MT.

Operator standby tends to occur most frequently during MT, as operators idly observe auto-feed devices at work. TPS stresses the need to eliminate this type of standby waste.

The following steps were taken in drawing up the standard operation combination chart shown in Figure 6-5.

1. Process sequence
2. Operation description: Insert the operation and equipment names from the part-specific capacity worktable.
3. Time: Insert the manual operation time (HT) and auto-feed time (MT) from Figure 6-4.
4. Operation times: Use different lines to indicate the various times.
   Solid line: manual operations
   Broken line: auto-feed
   Wavy line: walking

In this case, the walking time is two seconds.

5. Cycle time (CT): The cycle time is the amount of time required to produce one product.

At Company C, the target SPH is 60 units and the target SPD is 480 units. However, actual results show an SPH of 60 units and an SPD of 400 units. Line stoppages occur every day. In February, Company C experienced an average of 1.5 line stoppages per 45-minute time block. Based on these figures, we can calculate Company C's cycle time using the following formula:

$$CT = \frac{\text{Operation time}}{\text{Required output/day}} = \frac{\left(8 \text{ hrs.} - 1.5 \text{ times} \times \frac{45 \text{ hrs.}}{60 \text{ units}}\right) \times 3{,}600 \text{ sec.}}{480 \text{ units}} = 51 \text{ sec. (rounded)}$$

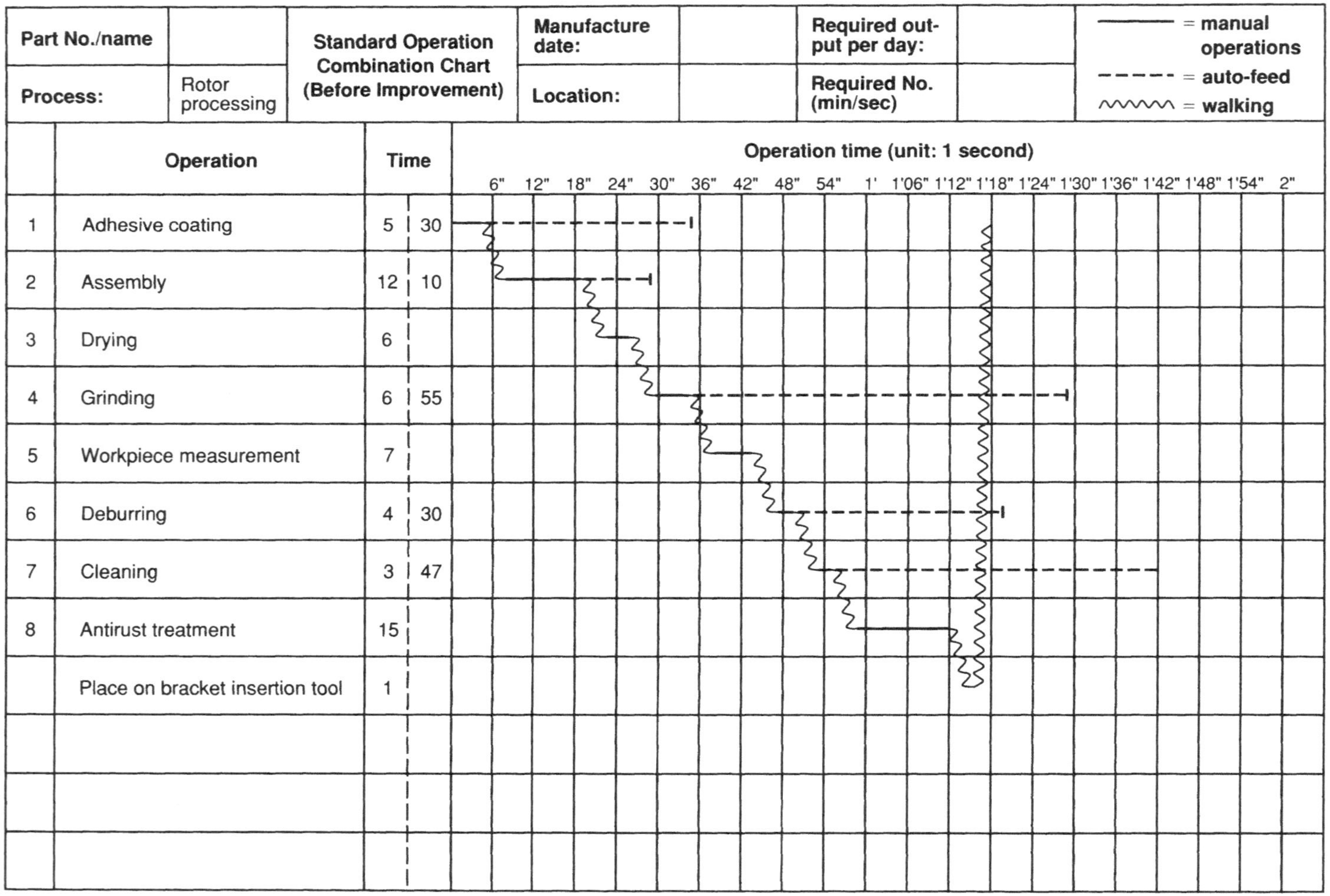
Part No./name
Process:
Rotor processing
Standard Operation Combination Chart (Before Improvement)
Manufacture date:
Location:
Required output per day:
Required No. (min/sec)
= manual operations
= auto-feed
= walking
Operation
Time
Operation time (unit: 1 second)
6" 12" 18" 24" 30" 36" 42" 48" 54" 1' 1'06" 1'12" 1'18" 1'24" 1'30" 1'36" 1'42" 1'48" 1'54" 2"
1 Adhesive coating 5 30
2 Assembly 12 10
3 Drying 6
4 Grinding 6 55
5 Workpiece measurement 7
6 Deburring 4 30
7 Cleaning 3 47
8 Antirust treatment 15
Place on bracket insertion tool 1

Figure 6-5. Standard Operation Combination Chart (Before Improvement)

Figure 6-5 shows that it takes 1 minute and 42 seconds to complete one rotor. Unless this time can be reduced to one-third this amount, it will not fit into the standard operation combination. Consider the following points when attempting to shorten this time.

- Shorten the MT time for grinding
- Shorten the MT time for cleaning
- Shorten all the HT times
- Pay special attention to the assembly and antirust processes.

Standard Operation Chart (Walking-Route Diagram) for Conditions Before Improvement

The purpose of standard operation charts is to explain to operators the standards that will enable them to work as part of an effective combination of people, material, and machines to produce high-quality products safely and at low cost. This type of standard is unique in that it emphasizes the correct sequence of operations over the method of operations. Figure 6-6 shows how operations on the rotor assembly line are written as standard operations.

1. The equipment layout diagram includes numbers corresponding to the operation sequence indicated in the standard operation combination chart; it uses a solid line to link them according to the walking route. A broken line shows the walking-route link where the operator returns from the last operation to the starting one.
2. A diamond symbol marks the machines that require quality checks.
3. A cross symbol marks processes that warrant extra caution for safety.
4. The standard stock on hand is the minimum necessary in-process inventory (stock on hand) at various processes. Black dots mark the machines that have standard stock on hand; the quantity of standard stock on hand should also be indicated.
5. The cycle time should also be entered.
6. The net operating time should be entered, too.

Process-specific Waste Elimination

After carefully observing each process, we start devising ways to eliminate the various types of waste we have found. Waste is defined as any motion,

Standard Operation Chart (Before Improvement)

Description of operation:	From: adhesive coating application	Date:
	To: antirust treatment	

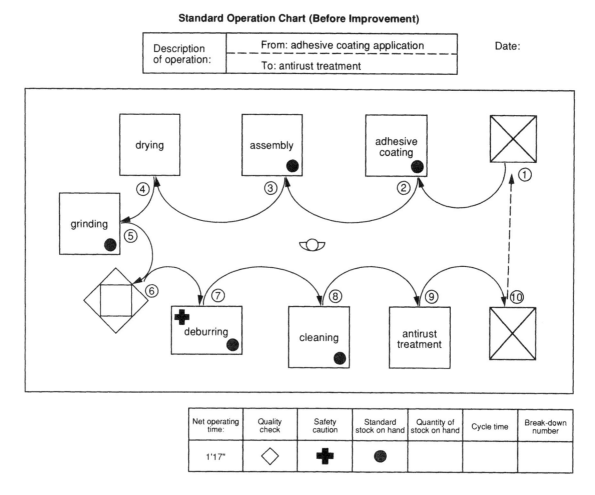

Net operating time:	Quality check	Safety caution	Standard stock on hand	Quantity of stock on hand	Cycle time	Break-down number
1'17"	◇	✚	●			

Figure 6-6. Standard Operation Chart (Before Improvement)

method, or behavior that does not serve the purpose of the process. Generally, this means that the waste is an operation method, action, or step that does not add value to the product. Table 6-3 shows a waste-elimination chart.

The key points in eliminating waste include:

1. *Shortening the MT time for the grinding process:* They tested various brands of grinding stones and established optimal processing conditions, based on speed, time, and other factors. As a result, they were able to reduce the MT time to 40 seconds and cut the HT time to just 4 seconds.

Table 6-3. Process-specific Waste-Elimination Chart (Company C)

(1) Rotor processing line

Waste	Cause	Waste-elimination plan
1. Inserted and removed vertically for assembly	No notch	Establish horizontal insertion and removal
2. Manual antirust treatment	Use of flange requires manual handling	Use revolving sprayer instead
3. Workpiece measurement	Overdivision of labor	Combine workpiece measurement with deburring
4. Waste in production of defective shafts	Defectives produced by outside supplier	Link shaft processing with rotor assembly and main assembly line (see Figure 6-10)

(2) Stator core process line

Waste	Cause	Waste-elimination plan
1. Waste in wiping off oil (cleaning waste)	Done during adhesive coating (prior process)	Develop method for spraying oil only onto tip of cutting tools before cutting
2. Overflow of CM card adhesive	Card is dropped into adhesive solution	Insert card slowly, then remove and let stand
3. Walking waste	Line is too long	Establish specialized lines instead of joint lines
4. Switch is pressed from above	Wrong type of switch	Install a switch that can be activated by a horizontal touch

(3) Motor assembly line

Waste	Cause	Waste-elimination plan
1. Screw pick-up	Screws are fed in random positions	Make a box that will align screws (with heads up)
2. Screw-fastening check		Devise an analog device for foolproofing the torque check procedure
3. Attaching and removing connectors	Separate operation	Combine with other operation and use changeover switch
4. Recording of data on checksheet	First and last items must be recorded (not suitable for small-lot production)	Record checksheet data only for lots larger than ten units
5. Method for storing items		Devise more obvious indicators, such as by outlining, addressing, and colorcoding

2. *Shortening the MT time for the cleaning process:* They switched from using cleaning fluid to using a high-frequency cleaner. This shortened the MT time to 40 seconds.
3. *Shortening the HT times:* Look at Figure 6-5. By eliminating waste in the assembly process, they shortened the assembly time from 12 seconds to just 4 seconds. By automating the antirust treatment process, they were also able to shorten the HT time there from 15 seconds to 3. Combining the workpiece measurement process with the deburring process brought a further decrease, from 11 seconds to 3.

Part-specific Capacity Worktable (After Improvement)

After carrying out process-specific waste elimination, they drew up a new part-specific capacity worktable to show conditions after improvement, as shown in Figure 6-7.

Standard Operation Combination Chart (After Improvement)

Figure 6-8 shows the improvement team's standard operation combination chart with conditions after improvement. This chart was drawn up in almost exactly the same way as the before-improvement chart (Figure 6-5), but in this case the processing is completed within the cycle time.

1. Sequence of operations
2. Description of operations
3. Times
4. Operation times
5. Cycle time line is entered in red ink

Taking the post-improvement HT time and walking time from the part-specific capacity worktable shown in Figures 6-6 and 6-7, we can check whether they fit within the cycle time.

total HT	= 33 sec.
walking time = 2 seconds × 9	= 18 sec.
total	= 51 sec.

Revision date:

Section mgr.	Plant mgr.	Part-specific Capacity Worktable (After Improvement)	Part No.		Model		Name
			Part name: Rotor processing		Quantity 480 units/day	Dept.	

Process No.	Process name	Machine No.	Basic time measurements			Cutting tools		Process capacity	Comments (Diagram lines:) Manual operation = ——— Auto-feed = - - - - -
			Manual operation time (HT)	Auto-feed time (MT)	Completion time	No. replaced	Replacement time		
1	Adhesive coating		5 min. sec.	30 min. sec.	35 min. sec.			822	5" 30"
2	Assembly		4	10	14			2,057	4" 10"
3	Drying		6		6			4,800	6"
4	Grinding		4	40	44	1,500	6,000"	600	4" 40"
5	Workpiece measurement		3		3			9,600	3"
6	Deburring		4	30	34			847	4" 30"
7	Cleaning		3	40	43			669	3" 40"
8	Antirust treatment		3	20	23			1,252	3" 20"
	Place on bracket insertion tool		1						
	Total		33						

Figure 6-7. Part-specific Capacity Worktable (After Improvement)

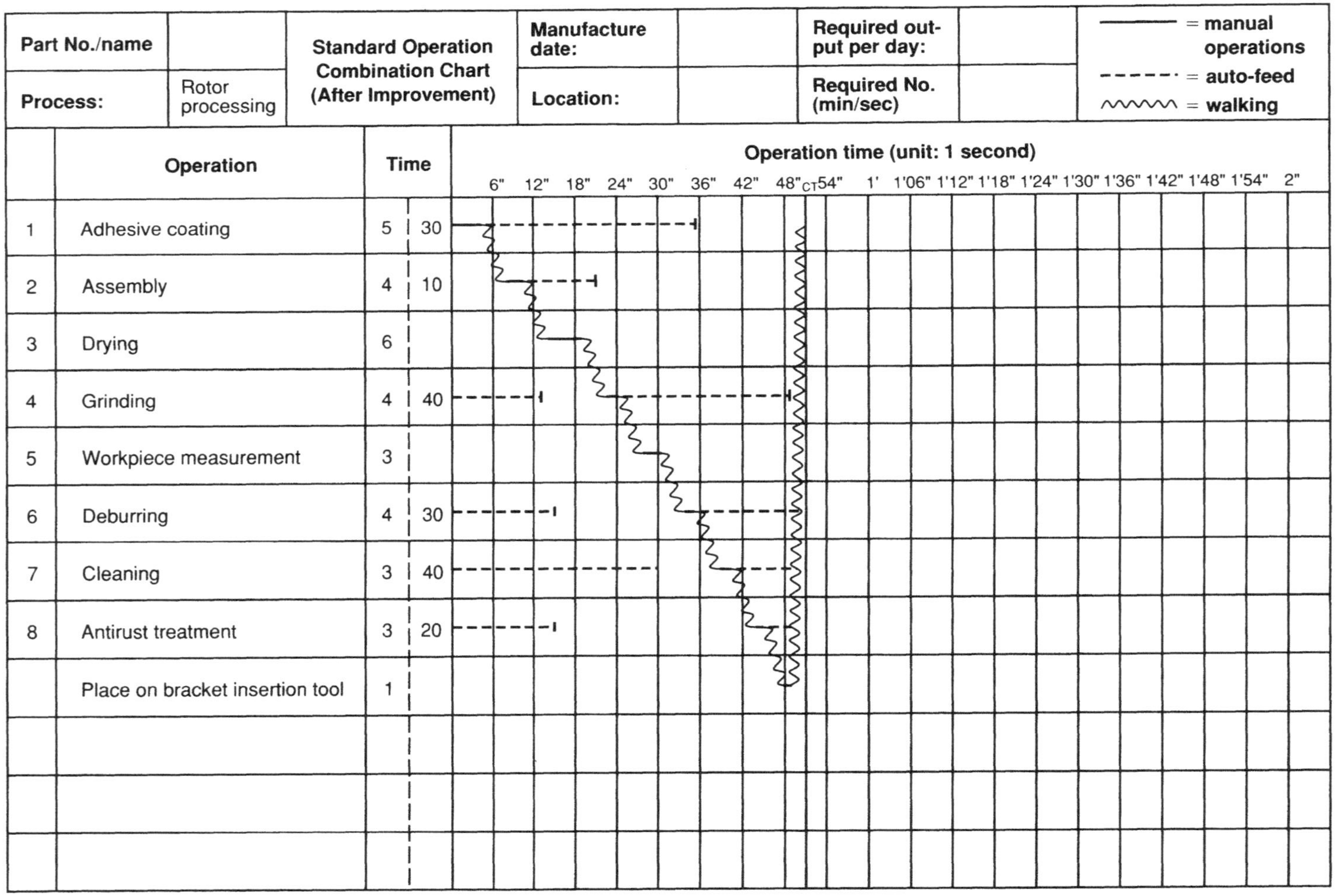
Part No./name
Process:
Rotor processing
Standard Operation Combination Chart (After Improvement)
Manufacture date:
Location:
Required out-put per day:
Required No. (min/sec)
= manual operations
= auto-feed
= walking
Operation
Time
Operation time (unit: 1 second)
6" 12" 18" 24" 30" 36" 42" 48" CT 54" 1' 1'06" 1'12" 1'18" 1'24" 1'30" 1'36" 1'42" 1'48" 1'54" 2"
1 Adhesive coating 5 30
2 Assembly 4 10
3 Drying 6
4 Grinding 4 40
5 Workpiece measurement 3
6 Deburring 4 30
7 Cleaning 3 40
8 Antirust treatment 3 20
Place on bracket insertion tool 1

Figure 6-8. Standard Operation Combination Chart (After Improvement)

6. Check combination of operations

If the auto-feed time is longer than the cycle time, we can subtract the difference from the starting point. If the manual operation times do not work out together, however, the operation combination is no good. In such cases, we must consider other combinations.

Since the MT at the grinding process (process No. 4), for example, exceeds the red CT line, we should subtract the difference from the starting point. However, if this subtracted time interferes with the HT and causes standby waste, we should try to improve the process and study other possible operation sequences. In Figure 6-8, process No. 4 is 7 seconds short of the CT line, so it is OK.

7. Check the quantity of work

At process No. 9, the operator sets the workpiece on the bracket press table and returns to process No. 1. The point of return to process No. 1 meets the red CT line, which means the combination is OK for cycle-time production.

If this point of return was considerably short of the red CT line, it would indicate that another operation could be added while remaining within the range of cycle-time production. When the point of return goes past the red CT line, it means that cycle-time production is not possible until further time-saving improvements are made. It also means the line will not be able to meet its SPH target.

Standard Operation Chart (Walking-Route Diagram) for Conditions After Improvement

The improvements described so far have focused on the rotor processing line. Next, we will see the part-specific capacity worktable and standard operation combination chart that Company C drew up to indicate the results of improvements on the stator core processing line and the motor assembly line.

In the rotor processing line, the improvement team dealt with the problem of defective shafts, which were manufactured by an outside supplier (see Table 6-3). They solved this problem by establishing the shaft processing as in-house work. The abbreviated names for the newly designed three lines are line S (shaft processing), line R (for rotor processing), and line A (for motor assembly). The standard operation chart for this new line layout is shown in Figure 6-9.

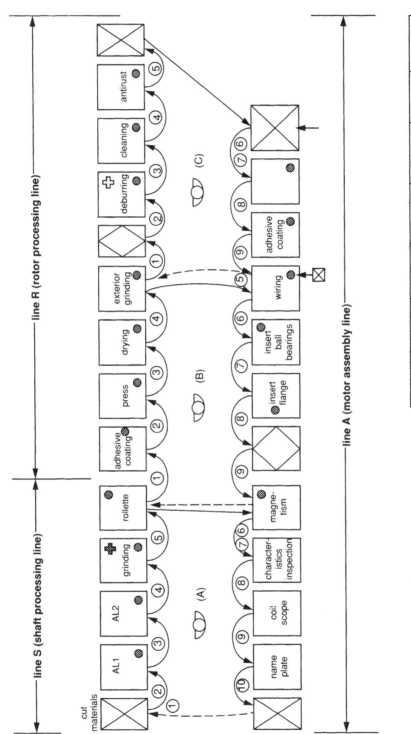

Figure 6-9. Standard Operation Chart (After Improvement)

Net operating time:	Quality check	Safety caution	Standard stock on hand	Quantity of stock on hand	Cycle time
1'17"	◇	✚	●	17'	51"

The next step is to have the factory supervisor try out the test line to see whether it is actually capable of operating according to the standard operation chart. If it cannot be operated as the chart specifies, further improvements must be made. Once we have it working right, we can write specific operation instructions and begin training the operators.

After the regular operators begin running the line, the managers must keep track of the SPH and must be on hand to respond immediately to any abnormalities that occur at any of the processes.

SIMPLIFIED METHOD (THE S METHOD)

Company C could use the following simplified method to make its process-razing improvements.

- Step 1: *Study current conditions (P-Q analysis) (see Figure 6-2).* Select the target equipment (or product). In this case, the target is the rotor processing line.
- Step 2: *Observe factory operations.*
- Step 3: *Do a process analysis or assembly process analysis.* On the chart, record separate HT and MT times. Figure 6-10 shows an assembly process chart for the rotor processing line.
- Step 4: *Use the process-route analysis to make family groupings.*
- Step 5: *Draw a flow diagram of current conditions.* Figure 6-11 shows a flow diagram of the rotor processing line.
- Step 6: *Calculate the CT (cycle time), then use the CT to calculate the minimum number of workers.* Use the cycle time formula given earlier:

$$CT = \frac{\left(8 \text{ hrs.} - 1.5 \text{ times} \times \dfrac{45 \text{ hrs.}}{60 \text{ units}}\right) \times 3{,}600 \text{ sec.}}{480 \text{ units}} = 51 \text{ sec. (rounded)}$$

Use the following formula for calculating the minimum number of workers:

$$n = \frac{HT}{CT} = \frac{58 \text{ sec.}}{51 \text{ sec.}} = 1.1 = 1 \text{ person}$$

- Step 7: *Implement process-specific waste elimination.* Draw up a process-specific waste-elimination chart (see Table 6-3).

		MT	HT
1	adhesive coating	30	5
2	assembly	10	12
3	drying	—	6
4	grinding	55	6
5	workpiece measurement	—	7
6	deburring	30	4
7	cleaning	47	3
8	antirust treatment	—	15
	Total	172	58

The HT times are taken as the minimum values from the measurement data.

Figure 6-10. Assembly Process Chart

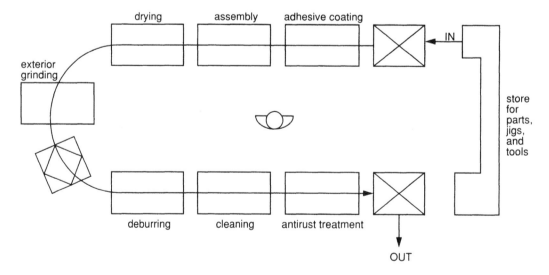

Figure 6-11. Flow Diagram of Current Conditions on Rotor Processing Line

- Step 8: *Determine a starting point for waste elimination*. The improvement team in this case selected standby waste. Their improvements to eliminate standby waste consisted of shortening manual operation time by turning HT into MT (i.e., automation) and eliminating shaft defects by shifting shaft processing in-house and by linking lines S, R, and A.
- Step 9: *Implement process razing*. Figure 6-12 shows a basic diagram of the new line layout.
- Step 10: *Build a test line and try it out*.
- Step 11: *Compare before and after results*. Table 6-4 lists the before and after figures.
- Step 12: *Draw up a new part-specific capacity worktable, standard operation combination chart, and standard operation chart*. Use the conventional TPS methods for drawing them up.
- Step 13: *Prepare for another round of process razing*.

TEST YOUR SKILLS

A certain factory includes a line that processes pinion components. Figure 6-13 shows the current sequence of processes in this line. There are five machines arranged in a U-shaped cell, all equipped with auto-feed and auto-stop mechanisms. The target SPD (standard production output per day) for this line is 1,252 units. The operation time is 16 hours, or two 8-hour shifts. For simplicity's sake, assume that there are no breaks during these shifts and that the walking time between any two processes is always 2 seconds.

Problem 1: Calculate the cycle time.
Problem 2: Calculate the process capacity.
Problem 3: Draw up a standard operation combination chart.

Proposed Solutions

Problem 1:

$$CT = \frac{\text{Total operation time per day}}{\text{SPD}} = \frac{8 \text{ hrs.} \times 2 \text{ shifts} \times 3{,}600 \text{ sec./hr.}}{1{,}252} = 46 \text{ sec.}$$

Problem 2: See the process-capacity column in Figure 6-13.
Problem 3: See Figure 6-14.

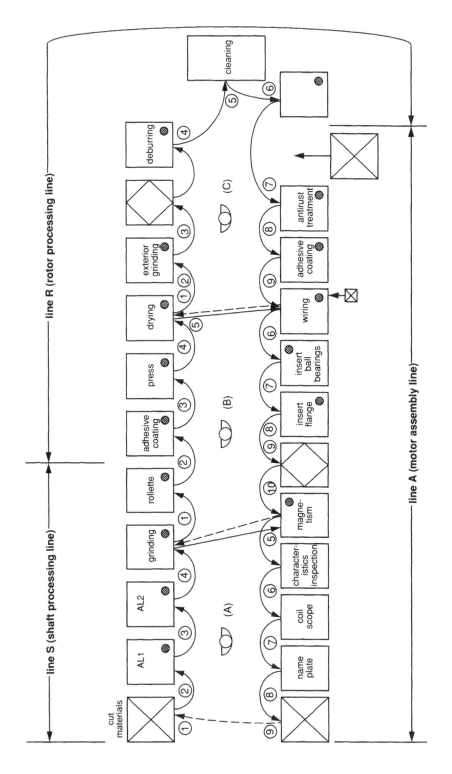

Figure 6-12. New Line Layout (After Process Razing)

Table 6-4. Comparison: Before and After Improvement

	Before improvement	After improvement
Operators	1 person	1 person
Cycle time	1 minute, 17 seconds	51 seconds
SPH	50 units	60 units
Missing items	Shafts	None
Outside processing	Shaft processing	None

Revision date: ___

Section mgr.	Plant mgr.	Part-specific Capacity Worktable	Part No.	41211-20092	Model	RY	Dept.	Name
			Part name:	8-inch pinion	Quantity	1	432	Nagadanigawa
							442	Nakamura

Process No.	Process name	Machine No.	Basic time measurements			Cutting tools		Process capacity (1,294)	Comments (Diagram lines:) Manual operation = ——— Auto-feed = – – –
			Manual operation time (HT) min. | sec.	Auto-feed time (MT) min. | sec.	Completion time min. | sec.	No. replaced	Replacement time		
	(Pick up materials)	—	1	—	1			(—)	
1	Coarse grinding of gear teeth	GC614	5	38	43	300	2'30"	1,324	5" 38"
2	Chamfering of gear cutting edges	CH228	6	7	13	2,000	1'00"	4,330	6" 7"
3	Surface finish grinding of gear's forward edges	GC1444	6	38	44	300	2'30"	1,294	6" 38"
4	Surface finish grinding of gear's backward edges	GC1445	6	30	36	300	2'30"	1,578	6" 30"
5	Pin diameter measurement	TS1100	7	3	10			5,760	7" 3"
	(Put down finished product)		1		1			(—)	
	Total		32						

Figure 6-13. Part-specific Capacity Worktable

Part No./name	41211-20092	Standard Operation Combination Chart	Manufacture date:		Required output per day:	1,252 units	——— = manual operations
Process:	Rotor processing		Location:		Required No.	1 every 46 seconds	- - - - = auto-feed ∿∿∿ = walking

	Operation	Time	
	(Pick up materials)	1	
1	Coarse grinding of gear teeth	5	38
2	Chamfering of gear cutting edges	6	7
3	Surface finish grinding of gear's forward edges	6	38
4	Surface finish grinding of gear's backward edges	6	30
5	Pin diameter measurement	7	3
	(Put down finished product)	1	

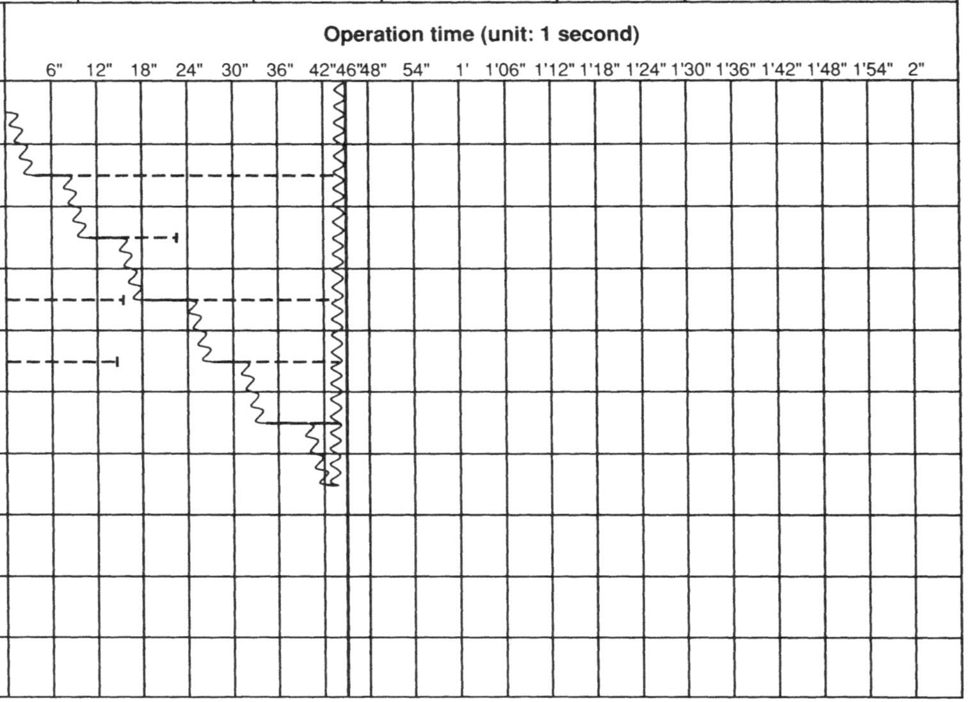

Figure 6-14. Standard Operation Combination Chart

Part III
Improvement Case Studies

- Zero Changeover Campaign in Press Line Processing
- Single Changeover in the Steel Forging Industry
- Zero Changeover for Transfer Machines
- Changeover Improvement Steps for the Process Industry
- Zero Changeover for PCB Auto-Inserters
- Zero Changeover for a Sheet Metal Factory
- Zero Changeover for Plastic-Molding Equipment
- Zero Changeover for Die-Cast Machines
- Zero Changeover for Assembly Lines

7

Zero Changeover in Press Line Processing

This chapter describes the zero changeover campaign undertaken by Takamori Manufacturing (hereafter, Company T) on its press line as part of the company's business strategy that emphasizes wide-variety small-lot production with high turnover and small profit margins. The types of small improvements described in this chapter may serve as especially helpful examples to smaller manufacturing companies.

Company T is located in the town of Takamori in Nagano Prefecture, a region of Japan famous for its apple orchards. The company has monthly sales of about ¥100 million and employs 80 people, subcontracts much of its work, and makes almost all of its earnings from processing fees. Its products include pieces fabricated on its press line from rolled strips of material.

Company T does not attempt to develop its own products. Instead, it works to maintain and develop the latest in processing technology to keep costs down for its parent company. One of Company T's specialties is the processing of metal cores used in computer peripheral motors. The factory flow begins with die design as soon as the customer's order is received, after which comes fabrication, press processing, parts processing, and assembly, all in an integrated production system.

Amid ever more stringent market demands for high-tech product components that can be produced at low cost yet with short delivery deadlines and high quality, Company T is totally committed to wide-variety small-lot production. Its business strategy is to succeed by operating with a high turnover and small profit margins.

In particular:

- It strives to meet the challenges posed by orders for high-precision products.
- It specializes in prototype production and small-lot production.
- It also tries to specialize in low-cost production of prototype dies. Company T fabricates steel dies for prototype products and has the technology for switching over to full-scale production by hardening only the cavity section.
- It manufactures its own high-precision dies. Following the belief that quality dies make quality products, Company T has invested heavily in top-grade die fabrication equipment.

STEPS IN COMPANY T'S ZERO CHANGEOVER CAMPAIGN

To achieve zero changeover as part of its wide-variety small-lot production approach, Company T took the following steps:

Step 1: Analyze current changeover loss conditions

Table 7-1 shows various changeover-related data gathered to study current changeover conditions. Table 7-2 was used to assess the resulting losses. It shows that Company T's changeover loss amounted to over ¥500,000 ($4,000) per month.

Step 2: Form a changeover improvement team

Company T's next step was to form a changeover improvement team. They observed changeover demonstrations and analyzed them using time study techniques. If no one in the improvement group has a basic knowledge of time study, the group can still profit from observing current changeover operations even without analyzing the operations. The danger of performing analyses such as time study is that improvement groups tend to become concerned primarily with performing the analysis and forget their main objective of identifying and eliminating waste.

Table 7-1. Sample Changeover Time Data

Factory Dept. 1   March 3, 19--

Factory	Machine	Item	Die	Changeover frequency		Changeover cost			
				Output for past 3 months (units)	Changeovers in past 3 months	Time (min.)	Labor (person)	Total labor-hours (min.)	Labor/ equipment charge
Process No. 1	300-ton press (automatic)	W	trimming	406,100	102	48	1	4,896	¥50
Process No. 2	150-ton to 300-ton press (manual)	"	"	340,100	139	48	1	6,672	"
Machine	100-ton to 125-ton press	R	trimming, cutting	625,400	116	36	1	4,176	"

Table 7-2. Changeover Loss Table

Item \ Description	Processing time	Changeover time	Changeover as a percentage of processing time	Loss calculation
Category B	7343^H	339^H	5.4%	7,972 minutes/month × ¥50 = ¥398,600/month
Category R	775^H	114^H	11.7%	2,320 minutes/month × ¥50 = ¥116,000/month
Overall average	8318^H	513^H	6.2%	10,292 minutes per month × ¥50 = ¥514,600 per month

Step 3: Carry out changeover waste elimination

After gathering data from their observations, the improvement group drew up a changeover waste-elimination chart. Table 7-3 shows their list of changeover waste. While referring to this table, the group members devised various waste-elimination measures and noted them as small, medium, or large improvement plans.

Table 7-3. Changeover Waste-Elimination Table

Category	Per-centage	Type of waste	Small improvement
Setup	7%	• Waste in removing bands from materials • Waste in making two trips to carry dies • Waste in lining up tools • Waste in not having inspection tools already prepared • Waste in not having product loading boxes already prepared • Walking waste • Waste in not switching to external changeover	• Divide changeover into internal and external changeover
Replacement	26%	• Waste in having to fasten many screws • Waste in failure to use the most appropriate tools • Waste in adjusting die positions • Waste in walking around equipment • Waste in having too many fastening tools • Waste in having too many types of bolts • Waste in having to attach chutes • Waste in using hard shanks	• Switch spectacle-type ratchet • Use springs for pressure braces • Hook-on chutes • Unify type of hex bolt used
Adjustment	67%	• Waste in having to adjust the ram several times • Waste in having to adjust the feed length several times • Waste in having to do several test operations • Waste in having to do several inspections • Waste in having to reposition processing oil • Waste in checking cutting tools • Waste in turning screws to release devices • Waste in making adjustments during processing • Waste in performing manual feed • Waste in having to change cart height for removing and attaching dies • Waste in having to connect many wires	 • Adjust cart height during conveyance • Bundle connectors

At this step, the point is simply to develop improvement ideas with no concern of whether the ideas are feasible or make engineering sense.

Step 4: Draft a changeover improvement schedule

In the zero-changeover approach, another name used for this type of improvement scheduling is "flag deployment." At this stage, the changeover im-

Medium improvement	Large improvement
• Use a larger cart to enable all dies to be carried in one trip • Make specialized product loading boxes • Make material storage boxes, use clamps for materials (instead of bands)	
• Redesign the shank holder, as shown below 	• Create new die design standards • Unify the die height • Standardize die set • Standardize the clamping method • Unify the positioning method
• Make bumper blocks, as shown below • Make a feed length adjustment gauge, such as shown below 	

provement group begins to consider the feasibility of improvement plans proposed so far and works out a specific schedule of improvements on targeted ("flagged") processes. Figure 7-1 shows the improvement schedule worked out by Company T's changeover improvement group.

It is important to remember that not all improvement plans work; it will at times be necessary to produce alternative plans. The improvement schedule should not be treated as if it were carved in stone. It may be difficult for the

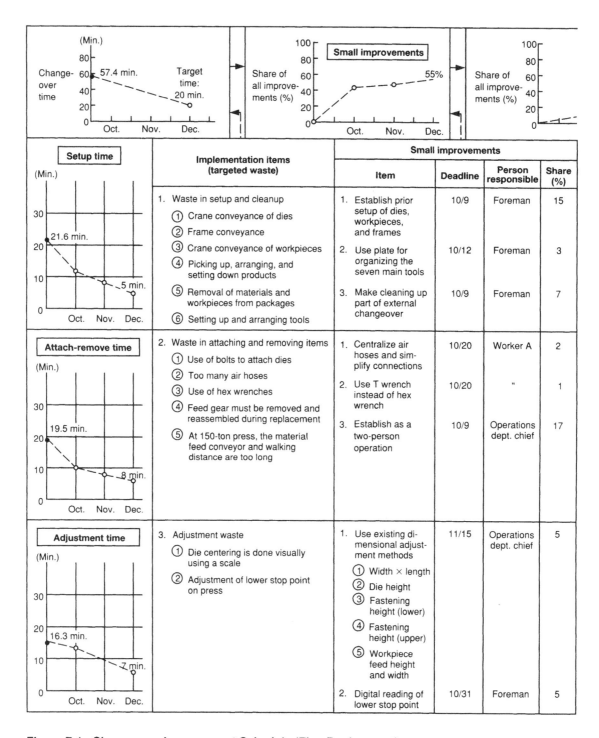

Figure 7-1. Changeover Improvement Schedule (Flag Deployment)

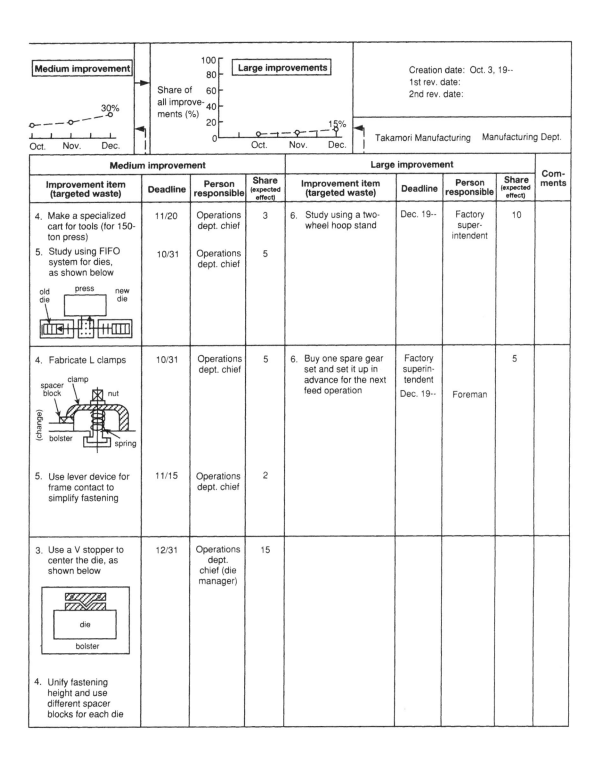

Medium improvement				Large improvement				Com-ments
Improvement item (targeted waste)	Deadline	Person responsible	Share (expected effect)	Improvement item (targeted waste)	Deadline	Person responsible	Share (expected effect)	
4. Make a specialized cart for tools (for 150-ton press)	11/20	Operations dept. chief	3	6. Study using a two-wheel hoop stand	Dec. 19--	Factory super-intendent	10	
5. Study using FIFO system for dies, as shown below	10/31	Operations dept. chief	5					
4. Fabricate L clamps	10/31	Operations dept. chief	5	6. Buy one spare gear set and set it up in advance for the next feed operation	Factory superin-tendent Dec. 19--	Foreman	5	
5. Use lever device for frame contact to simplify fastening	11/15	Operations dept. chief	2					
3. Use a V stopper to center the die, as shown below	12/31	Operations dept. chief (die manager)	15					
4. Unify fastening height and use different spacer blocks for each die								

creator of an improvement plan to see it fail and be discarded in favor of another person's plan, but such things must be accepted as part of the creative process and also part of teamwork. The important thing is to keep the improvement group on the right track toward the goal of zero changeover.

IMPROVEMENT EXAMPLES

Specialized Carts

There are seven main types of tools required for changeover, including dies, hand tools, diagrams, and inspection tools. Among the best ways to minimize waste in setting up for changeover is to keep all these tools together in an orderly manner on a cart custom-made for this purpose. This cart should be kept as close as possible to the press or other equipment where the changeover tools will be used.

One of the things to avoid during changeover operations is spillage of oil onto the floor, since spilled oil gets things dirty and creates a risk of slippage. The specialized changeover cart shown in Figure 7-2 is designed to prevent such oil spillage.

Die Clamp

Press dies vary in size and thus must be clamped at different heights. The clamp used at Company T has a strong spring instead of fastening bolts. It is

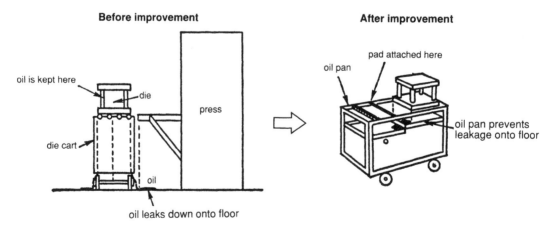

Figure 7-2. Specialized Changeover Cart Designed to Prevent Oil Spillage

affixed to an L-shaped support to prevent the clamp from falling over. This clamp makes die replacements much simpler. As a further improvement, the changeover group added a guide that uses the grooves in the press.

Subplate

When fastening positions vary from die to die, changeover time tends to take longer than expected. To shorten fastening time, a standardized subplate is used to make it possible to shift all sizes of dies in and out of position laterally.

Company T made groups of subplates in different sizes to make them work for die replacements on all sizes of presses. They made two subplate sets for each press, so that one set could be used for external changeover and the other for internal changeover. A number of holes are drilled into a subplate for use with cushion pins. The subplates are color coded to indicate which equipment models they go with.

Uniform Height for Fastener Sections

When the fastener sections are different heights, the changeover worker must make height adjustments during changeover, which is wasteful. In this case, the clamp with the L-shaped support does not help. The problem here is that the existing dies must be remodeled. This problem is best solved by making new dies, all having the same height.

Company T devised special clamps for dies that were above and below standard height. What makes these devices efficient is that the clamps adjust to the die height, so the dies do not have to be adjusted for the clamp height.

Horizontal Die Feed

Company T had used scales for measurements and markings for alignment to feed dies sequentially and horizontally. A pin method and block method were used to improve this horizontal die feed operation.

The pin method is used only when holes can be made in the press's bolster, but the block method can be used with any press.

The main operation in using the pin method is to set the pins in the correct position for the size of the die. The left and right pins are simultaneously set against blocks that have notched pieces welded to them.

The notched block does not look very useful for smaller dies, but it is an excellent device because it enables quick and easy operation.

Air Hoses

When problems not predicted by the designers occur during complicated sequential-feed operations, air hoses are sometimes needed to clean off products and blow away debris. When attaching air hoses, we must be careful about where the hoses go and how they are connected.

An improvement makes it possible to connect all air hoses at just one place (in front of the equipment). This keeps the hoses out of the way of the dies and eliminates hose adjustment waste.

Simplified Attachment of Product-removal Chute

Quite often, factory workers make their own product removal chutes; they sometimes unwittingly complicate the fastening method by using screws or wires to fasten the chutes. Company T's improvement over screws and wires involved chutes spot-welded into a frame so that they can be attached directly to the dies at one time. This simple improvement enables them to attach chutes in only two or three seconds (see Figure 7-3).

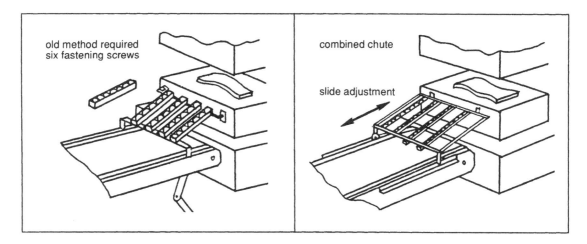

Figure 7-3. Combined Chute

Two-headed Uncoiler

Company T decided to buy a two-headed uncoiler, such as shown in Figure 4-9, to enable zero changeover for their coil changeover procedure. The uncoiler stocks a fresh coil of material that can be put in loading position with one quick turn.

SUMMARY OF RESULTS AND ISSUES FOR THE FUTURE

1. Company T achieved zero changeover on part of its press line.
2. As of this writing, Company T has not yet taken the initiative for horizontal deployment projects, which admittedly is not always easy for small companies with limited time and energy for such projects.
3. Estimating that process razing to put one worker in charge of two lines would cost too much, Company T decided instead to build only one test line and to implement the improvement when it builds a new line.
4. Managers at Company T began to take a keen interest in making improvements once they realized such improvements promised to ease their heavy daily workload.

8

Single Changeover in the Steel Forging Industry

Nagano Steel's single-changeover success story started when a visiting group from the Tashuken (Wide-variety Production Research Council) came for an inspection tour. The visitors told Nagano Steel's managers that its changeover methods were 20 years out of date. This realization spurred them to accept the challenge of single changeover. As a result, they undertook a slow-but-steady campaign to reduce the changeover times for the 1,600-ton press from the original 2 hours to the "single changeover" time of 9 minutes. It took them almost 2 years, but they did it. Since then, they have succeeded at an even more ambitious project: achieving zero changeover (under 3 minutes).

Founded in 1953, Nagano Steel was capitalized at the time at ¥30 million ($240,000) and employs 145 people. Its major products include engine valves, tappets, internal combustion engine parts, agricultural equipment parts, and high-precision forged products. Annual sales amount to about ¥3 billion ($24,000,000).

A FACTORY FROM 20 YEARS PAST

When Nagano Steel finally got around to pursuing the goal of establishing single changeover for its 1,600-ton press, Japan's large manufacturers had already whittled their press changeover times to a few minutes. Even the quickest changeover operator at Nagano Steel was unable to perform the 1,600-ton press changeover in less than 60 minutes.

In August 1982, members of the Tashuken visited Nagano Steel to help with the elimination of waste in the company's press operations. The result is the improvement schedule shown in Figure 8-1.

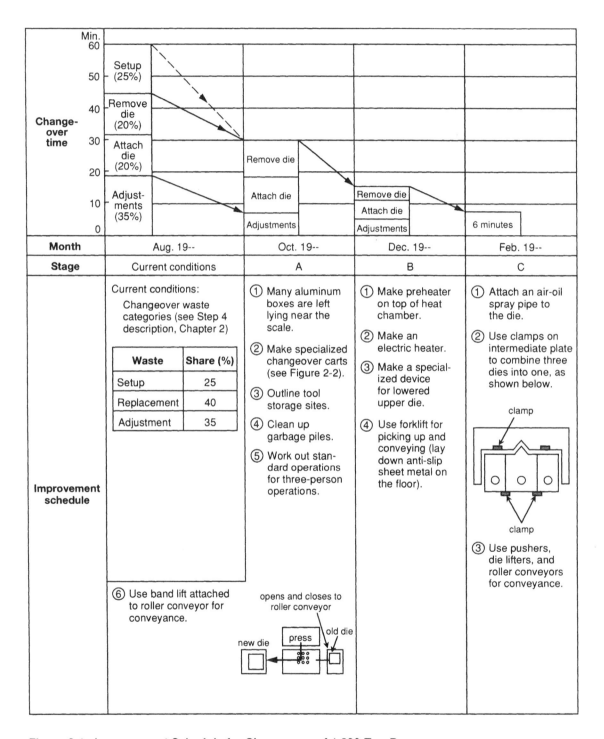

Figure 8-1. Improvement Schedule for Changeover of 1,600-Ton Press

At the initial visit, one of the Tashuken members noted that it was his first time in a steel forging plant. "Do all steel forging companies have such complex changeover operations?" he asked. Another group member replied: "Well, perhaps 20 years ago, but not today." The factory managers were shocked to hear this. They had been under the impression that only the large companies had taken on the challenge of single changeover.

Today, forging plants must be prepared to accept orders for lots as small as one unit. Obviously, when a press changeover takes up to 2 hours, the factory cannot afford to accept such a small order. The plant truly was 20 years behind the times.

After concluding a study session, the Tashuken members worked with Nagano Steel's forging staff and production engineering staff in planning improvements toward single changeover. Their main press was coming due for an overhaul, and they saw this as a good opportunity to introduce a new 1,600-ton press line as a model line for single changeover.

BEFORE IMPROVEMENT: CHANGEOVER IN 1 TO 2 HOURS

Before improvement, the changeover procedure began when four-piece sets of coarse finishing and fine finishing dies were brought close to the 1,600-ton press and two internal-changeover workers stood by waiting to start.

The time required for each changeover operation varied greatly, ranging from 1 to 2 hours. Figure 8-2 (a) shows the changeover steps that were followed before improvement.

Step 1: Remove

1. Remove the die-lubricating device.
2. Loosen bolts on upper and lower die clamps.
3. Insert die-changing tray and remove two pieces from upper die set.
4. Remove two pieces from lower die set.
5. Clean off lower die holder.

Step 2: Attach

Follow the removal procedure in reverse:

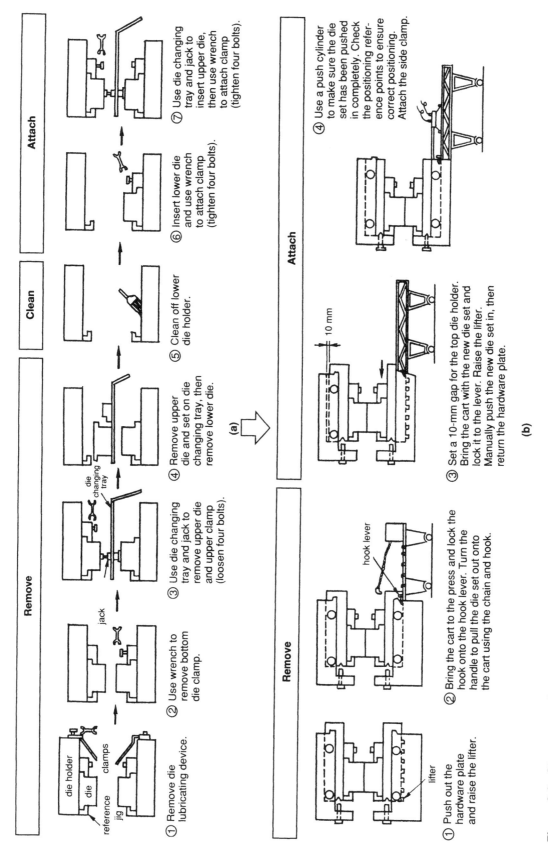

Remove

① Remove die lubricating device.

② Use wrench to remove bottom die clamp.

③ Use die changing tray and jack to remove upper die and upper clamp (loosen four bolts).

④ Remove upper die and set on die changing tray, then remove lower die.

Clean

⑤ Clean off lower die holder.

Attach

⑥ Insert lower die and use wrench to attach clamp (tighten four bolts).

⑦ Use die changing tray and jack to insert upper die, then use wrench to attach clamp (tighten four bolts).

(a)

Remove

① Push out the hardware plate and raise the lifter.

② Bring the cart to the press and lock the hook onto the hook lever. Turn the handle to pull the die set out onto the cart using the chain and hook.

Attach

③ Set a 10-mm gap for the top die holder. Bring the cart with the new die set and lock it to the lever. Raise the lifter. Manually push the new die set in, then return the hardware plate.

④ Use a push cylinder to make sure the die set has been pushed in completely. Check the positioning reference points to ensure correct positioning. Attach the side clamp.

(b)

Figure 8-2. Changeover Steps Before (a) and After (b) Improvement

1. Attach the two pieces of the lower die set.
2. Attach the two pieces of the upper die set.
3. Tighten the clamp holders.
4. Attach the die-lubricating device.
5. Make any needed adjustments.

THE FIRST MOVE TOWARD SINGLE CHANGEOVER

The managers adopted the following plan for reaching their goal of completing changeover within 10 minutes after shutdown.

1. *Standardize dies.* Standardizing the heights of different dies used for different products eliminates the need for die height adjustments (see point 5 in Chapter 3).
2. *Change internal changeover into external changeover whenever possible.* Use a specialized die-changeover cart (as described in Figure 2-2), simplify die replacement by using cassette-type die sets (hardware plate integrated with die), and make die preheating an external changeover operation.
3. *Reevaluate the selection of changeover tools.* Try to minimize the number of tools required by establishing more common use of tools or by improving the tools to make them more versatile. Also look for more efficient methods for storing tools.
4. *Change the die-lubricating method.* They decided to replace their graphite lubricant with one that is more conducive to faster changeover.
5. *Carry out process razing to minimize removal and attachment work.* They decided to minimize the use of bolts and to simplify replacement of spray nozzles and other parts.
6. *Standardize internal changeover procedures.* This enables shorter changeover time and minimum variation.

SUCCESS IN SINGLE CHANGEOVER

The conventional method for single changeover of large presses is to remove the old die set, then use a crane to separate the halves of the die or use a large die inverter.

Both of these external changeover methods require large and expensive equipment, to handle die sets that weigh as much as three tons. Small companies

such as Nagano Steel cannot easily afford such equipment. The following is
an alternative approach for smaller companies.

1. *Think of the die set as part of the press.* There is no need to change the
   whole die set. After all, part of the reason for having a die set is so that
   dies can have reference jigs for standardized positioning.
2. *Use die cassettes.* Recognizing that it is best to establish unvarying standards (see point 5 in Chapter 3), it makes sense to use die cassettes that
   consist of only the hardware plate and the die. This cassette is prepared
   as external changeover, as in Figure 8-2 (b).
   Before this improvement, the changeover team had to use a jack to raise
   the upper die before removing it. After the improvement, the lower die
   holder includes a built-in roller conveyor lifter, so that it is no longer
   necessary to jack up the die or use a die changing tray. As a result, the
   die changeover can be done by sliding the dies onto and from simple
   carts (see layout shown in Figure 8-3).

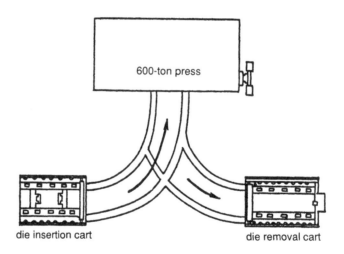

Figure 8-3. Path Used by Changeover Carts

3. *Use guide walls for quick positioning.* By attaching guide walls on the rear
   and right side of the cassette slot to standardize the sides of the cassette,
   there is no longer a need for the internal procedure of using blocks or
   guide pins to attach separate guide walls for each die set (see Figure 8-
   4). The use of die cassettes (integrated hardware plates and dies) allows
   die removal to be done as an external changeover procedure.

	Before improvement	After improvement	Improvement goal
Diagram	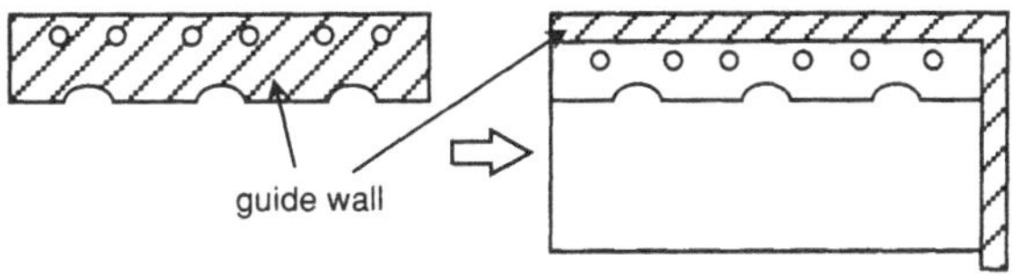 guide wall		
Improvement points	Each die had to be positioned against its own individually devised guide wall.	Die cassettes are made with built-in guide walls on the rear and right side.	Positioning along the guide wall, formerly an internal procedure, is now an external procedure, thanks to the use of die cassettes. This reduces the positioning time.
Effect of improvement	No need for die positioning.	1. Replacement of manual positioning with simple die switching operation eliminates variation between changeover workers. 2. Two-sided guide walls reduce positioning time. 3. The time was reduced from 1 minute and 30 seconds to just under 1 minute.	

Figure 8-4. Simplification to Reduce Changeover Time

4. *Use a locking clamp.* When the next preheated die cassette is fed into the press, the side clamp and plate clamp are hydraulically locked, thereby eliminating the previous bolt-tightening work.

EFFECTS OF SINGLE CHANGEOVER

Reduced Internal Changeover Time

This improvement greatly reduced the amount of time taken by internal changeover for the 60-ton press. Table 8-1 compares the changeover time scales before and after this improvement. Table 8-2 compares the internal changeover times before and after this improvement. It shows an annual time savings of 450 hours, which converts to over one month of operation time using two workers.

Table 8-1. Overall Changeover Time Before and After Improvement

Before improvement

| 10 | | 30 | | 60 | Min. 85 |

	Setup	Remove	Attach	Adjustment	Preheat die	Heater
Internal changeover	Remove lubricator	Clamp	Clamp	Check die centering	Upper and lower die pieces	Make adjustments
	Prepare tools	Die fastening bolts	Die fastening bolts	Adjust die height		Supply new materials
	Clean die set			Check knock-out amount		

Note: Before improvement, no distinction was made between internal and external changeover, so everything was done as internal changeover (two changeover workers took 85 minutes to complete it).

After improvement

| 10 | | 30 | | 60 | Min. 70 |

	Setup (attach-remove)			Preheat die	Heater			
External changeover	Clamps Die fastening bolts Cleaning			Upper and lower die pieces	Make adjustments, supply new materials, etc.			
Internal changeover	**Note:** After improvement, they clearly distinguish between internal and external changeover. One changeover worker performs the external changeover in 70 minutes. The other changeover worker performs the internal changeover in 10 minutes.				Remove	Clean	Attach	Other

Reduced Changeover Workload

The amount of changeover work has also been substantially reduced (see Figures 8-4, 8-5, 8-6, and 8-7).

Table 8-2. Internal Changeover Times Before and After Improvement

Internal changeover time	Before improvement	After improvement	Result (amount of reduction)
Average changeover time	85 min.	10 min.	75 min.
One month (30 times)	42.5 hours	5 hours	37.5 hours
One year	510 hours	60 hours	450 hours

	Before improvement	After improvement	Improvement goal
Diagram	lower rear guide wall swaging finishing coarse finishing clamp	swaging coarse finishing finishing	
Improvement points	1. Two clamp bolts were turned as part of internal changeover (2 workers)	1. Only one clamp bolt was turned, now as part of external changeover (1 worker)	3. Press downtime was shortened by shifting internal to external changeover; die replacement was speeded up
	2. Clamp length 200 mm	2. Clamp length shortened to 140 mm	Attachment time was speeded up and work load was lightened
Effects of improvement	Two people took 61 minutes to do the attachment work as internal changeover.	1. Two people take 6 minutes and 20 seconds to do the internal changeover part of the attachment work. 2. The acceleration of die replacement time and the lighter work load enabled a large reduction in the press downtime, which had impeded the processing flow.	

Figure 8-5. Acceleration of Attachment and Replacement During Changeover

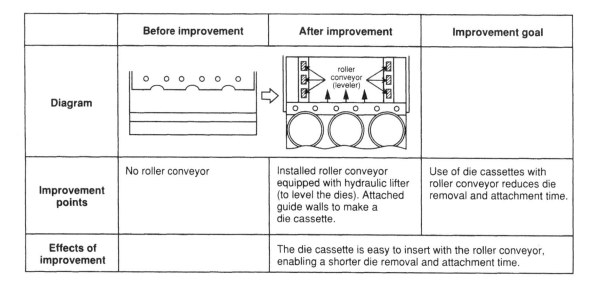

	Before improvement	After improvement	Improvement goal
Diagram			
Improvement points	No roller conveyor	Installed roller conveyor equipped with hydraulic lifter (to level the dies). Attached guide walls to make a die cassette.	Use of die cassettes with roller conveyor reduces die removal and attachment time.
Effects of improvement		The die cassette is easy to insert with the roller conveyor, enabling a shorter die removal and attachment time.	

Figure 8-6. Reduction of Changeover Time via Use of Die Cassettes and Roller Conveyor

	Before improvement	After improvement	Improvement goal
Diagram		clamps	
Improvement points	Two changeover workers tightened clamp bolts.	Clamp bolts replaced with hydraulic clamps.	Hydraulic clamps eliminate the need for clamp fastening bolts.
Effects of improvement		Use of hydraulic clamps eliminated the need for clamp fastening bolts, saving time.	

Figure 8-7. Boltless Method for Die Clamps

Reduced Cleaning Time

Changing the lubricant allowed a big reduction in time used for cleaning die holders and dies. Before improvement, this took two workers 15 minutes. After improvement one worker did it in 2 minutes.

Eliminated Searching

Creating an outlined board for the changeover tools instead of storing them in a box also eliminated waste in searching for tools.

Eliminated Die Preheating Time from Internal Changeover

By making die preheating into external changeover, the press can be test-operated as soon as the die cassette is inserted. This eliminates 20 minutes of die preheating time that used to be part of internal changeover.

EXPANDING SINGLE CHANGEOVER

Previously, the people at Nagano Steel had thought that single changeover was something that cost a lot of money to establish and could be done only by large companies with ultramodern, spacious factories or by factories that use only small presses.

They had also thought that establishing single changeover would be particularly difficult for hot forging plants such as theirs, which must spray lubricants to remove dirt from dies and must deal with scale that builds up on dies and die holders during forging.

Figure 8-8 is a time analysis of changeover time improvement for Nagano Steel's 60-ton press. The ups and downs in the line show that their attempted improvements did not always result in reduced changeover time.

By experimenting with various improvement plans and by integrating their dies and hardware plates as die cassettes, Nagano Steel built a successful model line for single changeover. As of this writing, Nagano Steel planned to extend this single changeover success to its other forging lines.

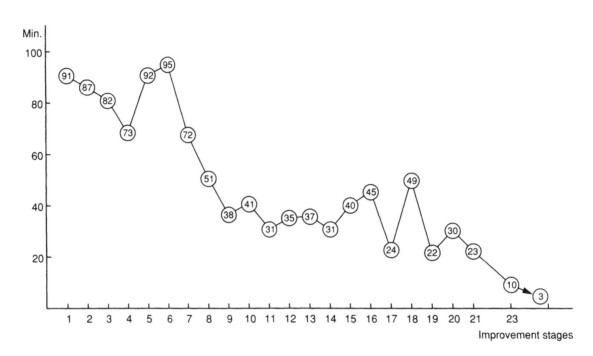

Figure 8-8. Changeover Time Improvement for 60-Ton Press

9
Zero Changeover for Transfer Machines

This chapter is adapted from a report by the Tashuken (Wide-variety Production Research Council).* The report describes the success of Fujikoshi Machines (Company F) in establishing zero changeover for its 40-meter-long transfer machine. It offers insights into the obstacles that must be cleared in studying changeover problems and implementing improvements to achieve zero changeover.

The secret of changeover improvement for machining lines lies in establishing strict adherence to processing standards. One of the primary methods for doing that is to create die sets for presses. You may find this chapter easier to understand if you refer again to the description of the fundamentals in Part I. This would help particularly during the discussion of die sets, and later during the discussion of correct development.

Company F was founded in 1952; it is capitalized at ¥60 million ($480,000) and employs 140 people. Its organization includes a hydraulic valve and pneumatic cylinder manufacturing division, a semiconductor processing equipment manufacturing division, and a precision processing division for electronic component materials such as ferrite, crystal, and ceramics.

The following case study comes from Company F's hydraulic valve and pneumatic cylinder manufacturing division; it concerns improvements to achieve zero changeover for transfer machines used in the production of solenoid valves in manufacturing department No. 1.

---

* The Tashuken report was originally published in the May 1984 issue of *Factory Management*.

175

PROBLEMS IN MANUFACTURING DEPARTMENT NO. 1

This division's growth, seen in terms of total sales, had been rather sluggish during the previous six or seven years, and the division still contributed only about 15 percent toward companywide total sales. Finally, the managing director in charge of that division (currently Company F's president) personally visited the division to inspect its operations and identify problems. He began with the most visible ones.

Dirty Floors and Machines

The division obviously had not yet adopted the principles of *seiri* (organization) and *seiton* (cleanly orderliness). The floors and machine surfaces were covered with lubricating oil and scattered swarf. Some of the machines were coated with a thick layer of oil that had built up since they were installed in 1972. The scattering of cutting oil made the floors slippery and gave the division's workers a reputation for having the dirtiest coveralls.

Customer Complaints, Defects, and Equipment Breakdowns

Even after receiving many customer complaints about product quality, the division's employees still saw on-time shipment as their top priority. Clearly their factory operations had some fundamental problems. Manufacturing department No. 1, which had a 37-station solenoid-valve-machining line connected by a transfer machine, was facing the most obvious problems.

Around 1981, the division experienced several occasions when entire lots of products were defective; the equipment problems took up to a week to fix, resulting in lengthy down time that delayed shipments. As a first attempt to eliminate waste, they addressed the problem of small line stops.

Their cause-and-effect study taught them that the apparent source of their problems was the lack of *seiri* and *seiton* and the frequent occurrence of small line stops (and equipment breakdowns). The underlying cause for all of these problems is lack of interest and enthusiasm among factory managers for the process of manufacturing products.

OVERHAUL STRATEGY

In October 1981, the division's managing director made a drastic decision. Fearing a total collapse of customer confidence, he ordered a full-fledged overhaul of the division's operations.

With the cooperation and consent of their customer, Nachi-Fujikoshi (Hydraulics Manufacturing), the division employees began using their off-hours overhauling their transfer machine and milling machines. To keep track of the changes wrought by this overhaul strategy, they began compiling data in 1982. These data showed that as the overhaul progressed, improvements became evident and defects declined conspicuously.

This overhaul strategy made everyone acutely aware of the need to overhaul not only the division's equipment but also its approach to production.

Machines Build Quality into Products

One of the most important things the overhaul strategy taught the division's employees was that quality is built into products by machines. Figure 9-1 shows the improvement in the defect rate this strategy produced: processing defects shrank from 50 percent to just 3 percent. This hugely successful improvement was the result of many small improvements that were planned and implemented during the overhaul, such as improvements in the replacement of O rings and other seals as well as bearings, in the centering of jigs and spindles, in the organization and maintenance of lubrication systems, and in bolt-tightening practices.

Material Defects Become Apparent

The factory employees had tended to believe that all equipment defects are the fault of the foundry products manufacturer, but as the processing defect rate rose, they began to pay more attention to materials defects. They worked with the foundry products manufacturer, comparing data and establishing improved processing standards and foundry product designs. The result was a 20 percent reduction in defects. This taught them that by giving up their notions

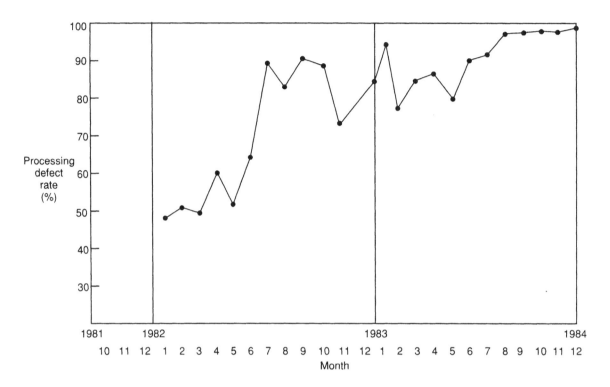

Figure 9-1. Processing Defect Rate (Oct. '81 to Dec. '84)

about what is possible and simply striving to make improvements, equipment defects can be substantially reduced. Figure 9-2 is a "weather chart" they devised as a humorous way of displaying data on core interval defects.

Reduction in Small Line Stops: An Improvement-oriented Factory Is Born

To launch these efforts toward eliminating customer complaints, the changeover team gathered data and made charts to identify the factory's worst problems. They then went to work devising covers to prevent oil from spattering, which helped keep the floors cleaner. Once they had cleaned and organized their workshops, they found that the frequency of small line stops dropped dramatically. They also noticed a big reduction in loss due to equipment problems.

They carried this momentum forward into other improvements in manufacturing department No. 1. Before long the entire factory was jumping on the improvement bandwagon. The installation of machine covers to prevent the

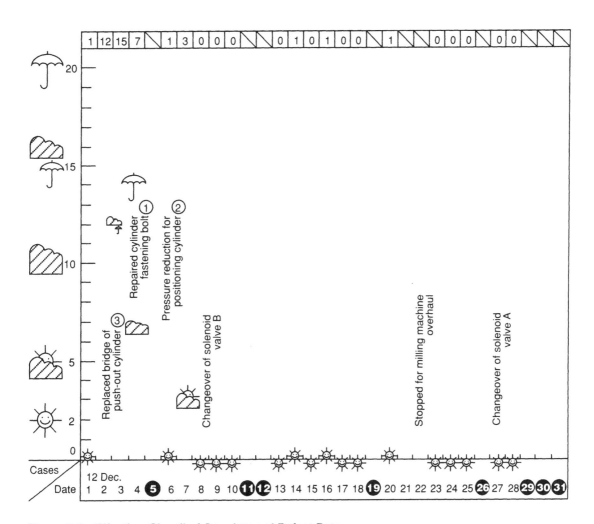

Figure 9-2. "Weather Chart" of Core Interval Defect Data

scattering of oil and swarf was just one part of a comprehensive program of implementing the principles of *seiri*, *seiton*, and *seiso* (cleaning). The result was a clean and well-organized factory. The compilation and display of data on abnormalities made everyone more aware of quality. These cleaning and organizing steps laid the groundwork for profound improvements to come.

Process-razing Efforts

When the Tashuken group arrived in 1983, the managers at Company F had been struggling to improve their factory without having studied the Toyota production system (TPS) or its U-shaped cell designs. Right away, the Tashuken consultants began teaching what the TPS approach had to offer, such as:

- Factorywide use of U-shaped cell designs
- Zero changeover for the transfer machine

Company F decided to introduce a new production system based on these themes.

ELIMINATION OF SETUP WASTE

Before the Tashuken group arrived, Company F had taken the traditional approach to changeover; this meant allowing the individual changeover operators to do the changeover work however they saw fit, based on their own experience and sensibilities. The managers assumed that the veteran changeover operators knew how to do the job right by virtue of their long experience. Therefore, they were reluctant at first to discuss improvements in changeover procedures.

The Tashuken group nevertheless proposed a changeover improvement theme and helped carry out a program (begun on April 12, 1983) to gradually reduce changeover time over the next year. Figure 9-3 shows the improvements planned under this program, which was implemented according to the following steps:

Step 1: Gather data for studying current conditions and eliminate setup waste (April 12 to August 31)

Step 2: Replace current changeover operation manual with new instructions to cut changeover time by half (October 20 to November 19)

Step 3: Break the review council into study groups who will carry out small improvements to reduce standby waste and thereby achieve the midterm goal of 55-minute changeover.

Compilation of Changeover Time

First, they studied current changeover conditions. They entered their changeover time measurements on the chart shown in Figure 9-4. They found the average changeover time was about 400 minutes and that about 30 percent of that time was spent in setting dimensions. These discoveries surprised them greatly and fired their enthusiasm toward making time-saving improvements.

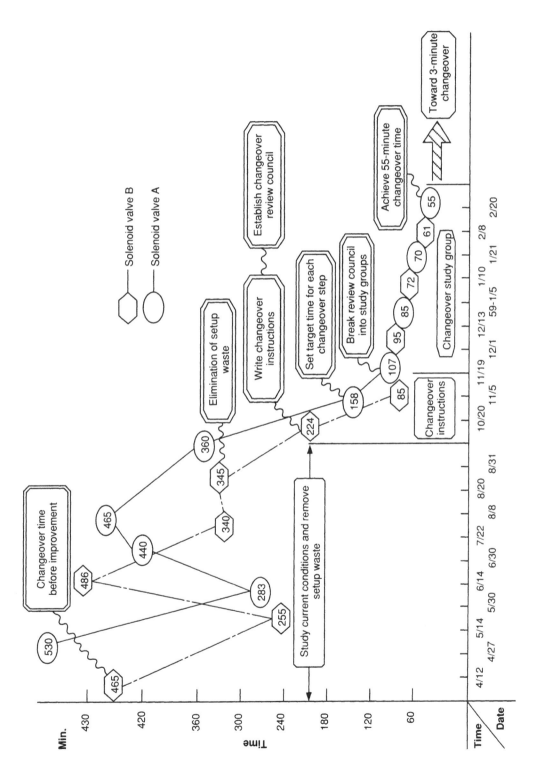

Figure 9-3. Trend Chart for Changeover Time Improvement

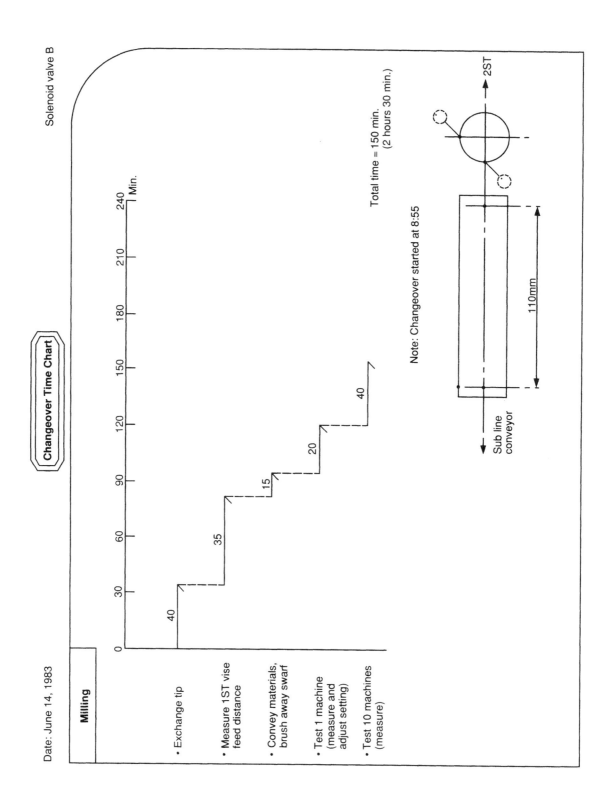

Date: June 14, 1983

Changeover Time Chart

Solenoid valve B

Milling

- Exchange tip
- Measure 1ST vise feed distance
- Convey materials, brush away swarf
- Test 1 machine (measure and adjust setting)
- Test 10 machines (measure)

40   35   15   20   40

Total time = 150 min.
(2 hours 30 min.)

Note: Changeover started at 8:55

Sub line conveyor

110mm

2ST

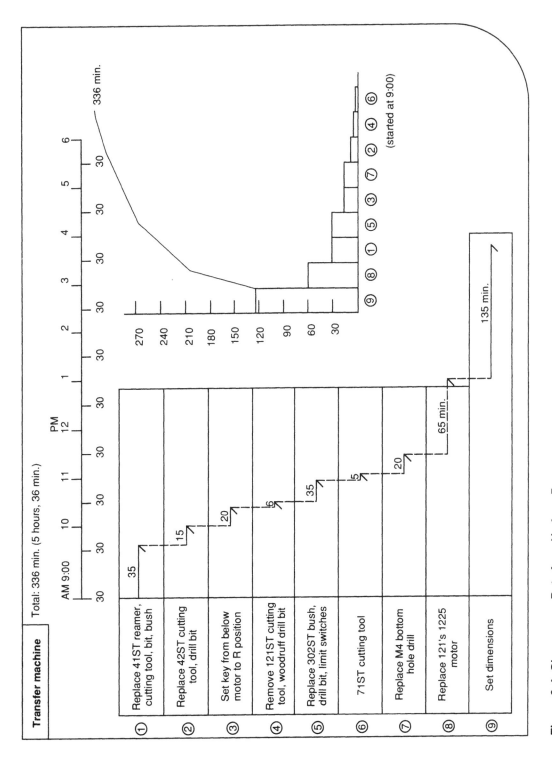

Figure 9-4. Changeover Data from Various Processes

Observation of Changeover Operations

In addition to the data compiled in August, they made other time measurements by observing changeover operations with a stopwatch.

1. *Dimension-setting time.* They found that the changeover operation often began with a lot of searching for tools, or retrieval of tools lent to other workshop teams. Sometimes changeover operators had to wait for the previous process to be completed. The study group learned that these wasteful activities had been included in the dimension-setting time.

2. *External changeover mixed with internal changeover.* They also discovered that external changeover tasks, such as cleaning out swarf, conveying materials, and replacing tool tips, had been included as part of internal changeover.

3. *Standby.* In one workshop, the three people who performed changeover tasks such as replacing blades, bushes, motors, and other parts cooperated well in their work, but only one of the three was skilled in adjusting dimensions; while he was doing that, the other two just stood idly by.

These observations led the factory managers to realize that it was not a good idea to leave things up to the changeover operators. It would not be easy to reach the changeover improvement targets. On August 20, they tried an experiment: they installed specialized changeover carts to hold the tools and measuring instruments needed for the solenoid valve A changeover operation. Figure 9-5 shows the process analysis they created based on their observations.

Changeover Operation Manual

Referring to their process analysis chart, on August 31 they began observing "changeover procedure memos" that described the steps taken by the three changeover workers (see Figure 9-6). They found a lot of standby waste remaining among the three changeover workers; standby time in fact totaled 81 minutes. This led one member of the changeover improvement group to suggest that they should create a single form for describing the steps and recording the time measurements.

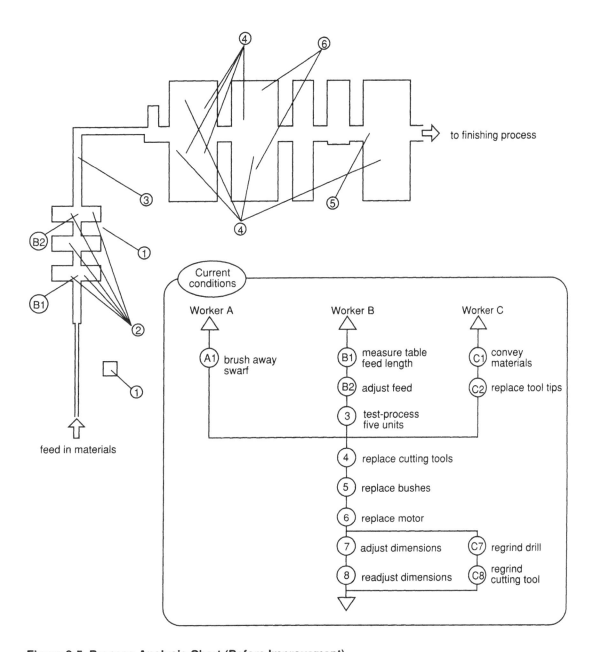

to finishing process

feed in materials

Figure 9-5. Process Analysis Chart (Before Improvement)

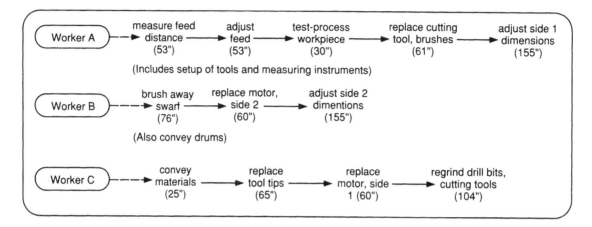

Figure 9-6. Changeover Procedure Memo

After completing their observations (Step 1), the improvement group began the Step 2 task of creating new changeover instructions. These instructions describe the division of tasks among the changeover workers. The improvement group's goal was to minimize the standby waste among the three workers.

EFFECTS OF NEW CHANGEOVER INSTRUCTIONS

On September 6, a Tashuken member gave a progress report on Company F's yearlong improvement project. At the same time, he helped Company F's managers revise their time chart of changeover steps into new changeover instructions that would help achieve the goal of reducing the total changeover time from the current 3 hours and 30 minutes to within 1 hour.

Creation of new instructions

At first the improvement group at Company F was uncertain as to how they would develop the new set of changeover instructions that the Tashuken had asked them to complete by October 20. They decided that the instructions should show each changeover worker's flow of operations, with times noted on the same form. They thought it should also have room for comments about the changeover operations.

Figure 9-7 shows the new changeover instruction form that they devised. As it shows, it reduces the total changeover time from the previous 400 minutes to 224 minutes, meeting the target set at Step 1. Everyone was amazed at the dramatic improvement these instructions proposed.

Appreciating the potential value of these new instructions, the improvement group decided to form a review council to help plan their effective implementation.

Review Council

The review council's first session was marked by high-spirited enthusiasm for changeover improvement. In just 30 minutes, some 50 problems in need of improvement were brought up before the council. Participants proposed ambitious goals, such as finding a way to get the 15-minute workpiece-positioning procedure for the milling process down to 5 minutes or less.

No one had any idea that the session would draw out such strong optimism and creative thinking. The Tashuken adviser proposed that they implement a series of small improvements to bring the total changeover time down to within an hour.

Meetings by Individual Improvement Groups

The implementation of the new changeover instructions started smoothly and had a powerful impact. However, one item overlooked during the review council's session was the monthly equipment model changeover. No one knew how long the previous model changeovers had taken.

To overcome this problem, the review council photocopied previous changeover instructions and asked each member to write down a proposed target time. Next, improvement groups met to hear progress reports on small improvements, and the members held a 10-minute meeting to decide on a target time for equipment model changeover.

Ready for Action

Finally, everyone was ready to implement the new changeover instructions. They held a countdown, yelled "Go!" and ran to their stations. Fueled with ambition, they managed to reduce the total changeover time using the new instructions. The changeover instructions were a big help, leading everyone toward the target changeover time.

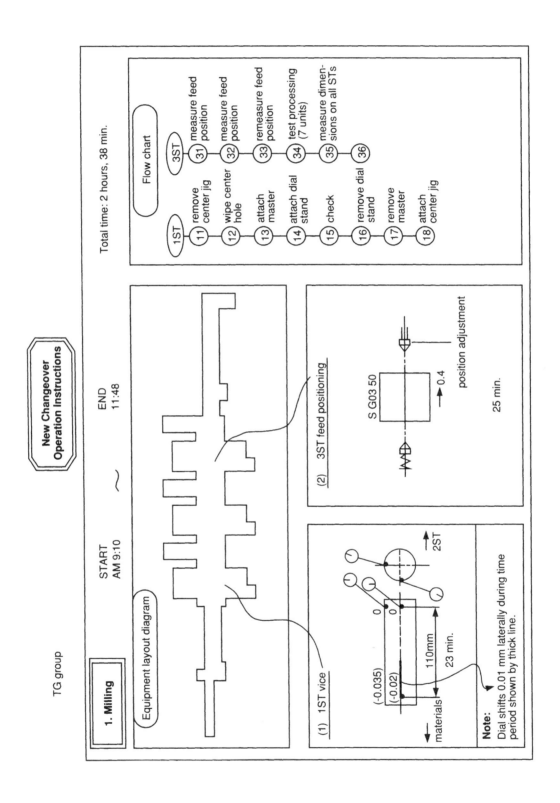

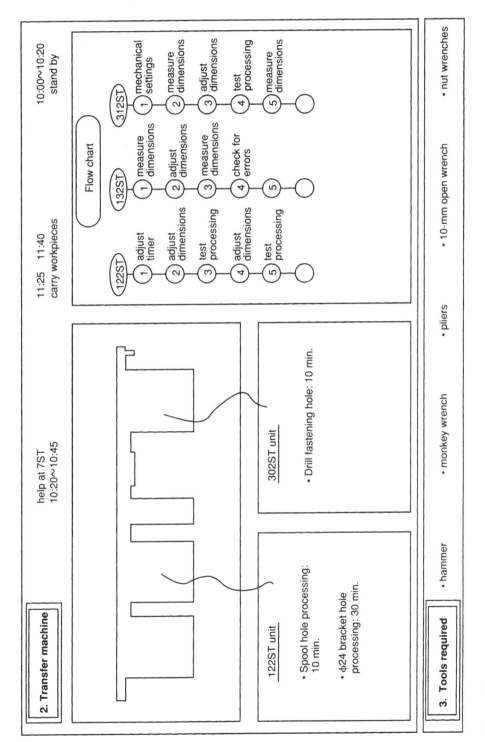

Figure 9-7. New Changeover Operation Instructions

ESTABLISHING IMPROVEMENT STUDY GROUPS AND SMALL IMPROVEMENT PROJECTS

Before describing Company F's Step 3 efforts, we will consider the sequence of changeover operations for the transfer machine.

Stage 1: The changeover improvement group held a meeting to briefly discuss recent improvements and operational points based on the new changeover instructions and the changeover analysis materials.

Stage 2: Individual group members set their own target times.

Stage 3: They implemented new changeover procedures based on the new changeover instructions.

Stage 4: They held improvement study group meetings at which target values were compared with measured values. They rooted out causes by repeatedly asking why problems occur, then planned small improvements.

After implementing the new changeover procedures, a second review council session was held; this time the discussion veered from problematic processes to problematic behavior by workers. This caused some anxiety and it was soon recognized that some improvement groups were much more enthusiastic than others about making improvements. Therefore, the council decided to form a number of improvement study groups that could meet independently.

The purpose of these study group meetings was to focus each group's discussion on the same improvement themes, as well as to encourage individual group members to use their own strengths and resources to solve problems. Their basic procedure was to select an improvement theme, devise an improvement plan and try it, meet to discuss problems encountered while trying the plan, and then implement a revised plan that addressed those problems.

By 1984, Company F's improvement groups had reduced the changeover time to within the range of 70 to 95 minutes. On February 20, they met to tally the results from a new changeover plan that promised to bring the total changeover time to within 1 hour. At long last, they felt they were about to reap the harvest of their many small improvements, proudly achieved over the past several months.

The tally revealed an average total changeover time of 46 minutes, a maximum of 55 minutes, and a minimum of 35 minutes. They did it! Their faces lit up with even greater enthusiasm for future improvements. One person said "I know we can get our changeover time below 50 minutes!" Everyone was confident in their choice of improvement themes and proud of their accomplishments.

Figure 9-8 shows a process analysis based on these results.

TOWARD SINGLE CHANGEOVER

Thanks to the diligence and ingenuity of individual group members, the department was able to achieve the target time of 60 minutes. Their next target was equally challenging: Shrink the total changeover time down to the "single changeover" time of 9 minutes or less. They pursued this new challenge according to the following four steps.

Step 1: The groups conducted motion studies using a video camera, then used the videotape to study group improvement themes related to the elimination of motion waste.

Step 2: They changed internal changeover operations into external operations, trimming away adjustment waste in the replacement of cutting tools.

Step 3: They universalized foundry product dimensions and achieved zero changeover for the milling process.

Step 4: They attached an inverter to help with motor replacement in the transfer machine process, thereby enabling zero changeover for that replacement operation.

They repeated the cycle of meet → try new changeover plan → study results → make improvements. These and other efforts earned them success in reaching the single changeover goal. They ultimately took on and won the challenge of establishing zero changeover — 3 minutes or less — for all of their changeover operations.

As part of their plan to carry this success over to other departments in the factory, they wrote out improvement case study sheets and sent them to everyone in the factory.

EXAMPLES OF IMPROVEMENTS LEADING TO ZERO CHANGEOVER

The following improvements mentioned in Company F's case study sheets regarding transfer machine changeover operations exemplify many of

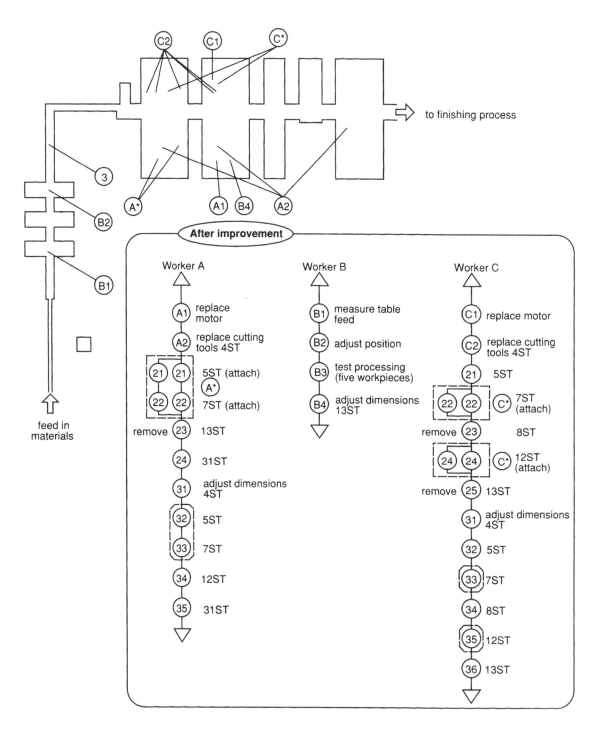

Figure 9-8. Process Analysis Chart (After Reaching Target Time)

the elements of the 9-point formula for achieving zero changeover in press changeover operations (see Chapter 3).

1. *Ensure that everything needed for setup is already organized and on hand.* "Until now, we had tried to keep all of our measuring tools neatly organized in one place in the factory. Now we have improved this situation by using specialized carts that hold the tools needed for changeover and that are kept right next to the process where the tools will be needed."

2. *It is OK to move the arms, but not the legs.* "By using three workers to do a changeover that had been previously done by only one worker, they can cue each other and work on both sides of the equipment at once, without having to walk around it."

3. *Do not remove bolts completely.* "Instead of having to remove the four fastening bolts, we made pear-shaped holes for them, so that the bolts can be loosened without being removed" (see Figure 2-3).

4. *Regard bolts as enemies; do whatever you can to get rid of them.* "We now use an inverter motor for changing the RPM during blade changeover, which makes it a one-touch operation with no bolts."

5. *Do not allow any deviation from standards.* "When milling solenoid valves 50 and 10, there was a 0.5 mm difference in these two valves' dimensions between their reference plane and their core. Therefore, we had to make an adjustment using a reference spacer during changeover. As an improvement, we unified the reference plane-to-core dimension in the 50 and 10 solenoid valves to eliminate the need for the spacer adjustment."

6. *Adjustment is waste. Do not move the base section. If you have to adjust anything, adjust the extremities.* "During the drill changeover, we used to remove the entire drill and spent a lot of time cleaning the spindle. Now we do a quick and simple dimension adjustment with a spacer instead."

7. *Use block gauges for all adjustments that are currently done visually with scales. This limits versatility, but it also reduces adjustment waste.* "At station 32 in the transfer machine, there is a processing depth difference of about 40 mm between solenoid valves 50 and 10, so we had to adjust the dogs. However, because the processing has to follow a line, some variation occurs in the dimensions and we have to make numerous dimension adjustments that take up a lot of time."

   "As part of our improvement, we installed a stopper block. When the dog hits the stopper block, it stops there, which stabilizes the processing dimensions and eliminates the need for the dimension adjustments."

8. *Install blocks and guides to help set standard dimensions.* "After setting up this machine, we used to do a trial operation, then use calipers to adjust the stepped reamer. Now, we install preset reamers that have been set up as part of external changeover, so we no longer have to do any adjustments."

9. *Universalize intermediary jigs.* "Before, this machine could only mill solenoid valves 10 and 50, but now we have universal intermediate jigs that enable the machine to mill other models too."

THE BUSINESS ADVANTAGES OF ZERO CHANGEOVER

Company F's President Ichikawa noted the following advantages zero changeover brought for his company:

- Higher productivity and a higher value-added ratio in production
- Better training of employees
- Shorter delivery lead times
- Zero defects arising from changeover
- Greater trust and confidence from customers

In particular, before these improvements Company F's factory had a poor performance record in its handling of rush orders, a bad sign for any wide-variety small-lot production factory. Once it achieved zero changeover, the factory could respond smoothly to rush orders while also improving productivity.

By achieving what seemed at first to be impossible goals, Company F's employees became better and more confident in their work. Moreover, each success has inspired them to achieve even more ambitious goals. What could be better staff education and training than this?

Noboru Furukai, one of the leading members of the changeover improvement movement, offered the following four points as "musts" for successful changeover improvement.

1. Top management policies must motivate the improvement group. The improvement drive must be initiated by top management.
2. Encourage close cooperation between the engineering staff and the changeover workers.
3. Always keep equipment maintained at its best.
4. As an improvement leader, show strong enthusiasm for achieving the improvement goals.

MACHINING CENTER CHANGEOVER IMPROVEMENT

We will briefly examine a case study of a machining center improvement made by one of Company F's improvement groups.

Machining centers are a type of processing equipment that can perform several different types of machining within the same processing cycle. Since each machining center includes several types of machines, when we discuss machining center changeover, we usually break down the changeover operations into machine-specific changeover times.

The use of machining centers has proven to be an effective method for substantially raising both machining precision and productivity. However, machining centers do have some drawbacks, one of which is the time it takes to do changeover on them.

Company F's machining center changeover improvement efforts included the following two steps:

Step 1: *Study current conditions.* Table 9-1 lists the results of an operation analysis of current conditions in a machining center. The changeover for this machining center had been taking about 200 minutes (3 hours and 20 minutes). The improvement group developed an intermediate jig that could be inserted to prevent deviation from standards. This cut down the changeover time to just 44 minutes, but that was still much too long.

Eventually, they were able to reduce the changeover time to the single changeover time of 9 minutes, and finally to the 3-minute zero-changeover range (see Figure 9-9).

Step 2: *Carry out a second round of improvements.*

To reach the changeover goal of single changeover, they decided they needed to spend no more than 3 minutes each, on each of the three changeover stages: setup, replacement, and adjustment. Table 9-2 shows the changeover waste-elimination table they made based on their observation data.

Their goal in eliminating setup waste was to reduce the setup time to 3 minutes. The improvements they made to achieve this goal included:

- Adding a hoist to the crane operation for conveying replacement parts
- Making a plate to hold the seven changeover tools

Table 9-1. Reductions in Changeover Time for Machining Center

Before Improvement (Four Machining Processes)				
Process	**Item**	**Time (min.)**	**Qty/Frequency**	**Total**
1	Set fixture	25	1	25
	Set individual jig	3	3	9
	Set hydraulic pipe	3	1	3
	Preset seal	2	6 units	12
	Set tape	1	1	1
	Input offset amount	0.33	6 pairs	1.98
	Margin = 1.18			
2	Remove process 1 individual jig	3	3	9
	Set process 2 individual jig	3	3	9
	Preset seal	2	7	14
	Set tape	1	1	1
	Input offset amount	0.33	7	2.31
	Remove fixture	20	1	20
	Margin = 1.18			(65.2)
3	Set process 3 individual jig	3	3	9
	Set hydraulic pipe	3	1	3
	Preset seal	2	2	4
	Set tape	1	1	1
	Input offset amount	0.33	2	0.66
	Remove individual jig	3	3	9
	Margin = 1.18			(31.5)
4	Set individual jig	3	4	12
	Set hydraulic pipe	3	1	3
	Preset seal	2	4	8
	Set tape	1	1	1
	Input offset amount	0.33	4	1.32
	Remove individual jig	3	4	12
	Margin = 1.18			(44.0)
			Total	201.7

After Improvement (One Machining Process)			
Item	Time (min.)	Qty/Frequency	Total
Set individual jig	3	3	9
Set hydraulic pipe	3	31	3
Preset seal	2	12	24
Set tape	1	1	1
Input offset amount	0.33	8(*1)	2.64
Margin = 1.10 (see Note 2.)			(43.6)
Notes 1: Offset dial can be set for up to 8 only. The remaining four cannot be offset. 2: Process shortening reduced the margin from 1.18 to 1.10. * When the target item is used continuously over two or more days, the individual jig removal is not required.			
		Total	43.6

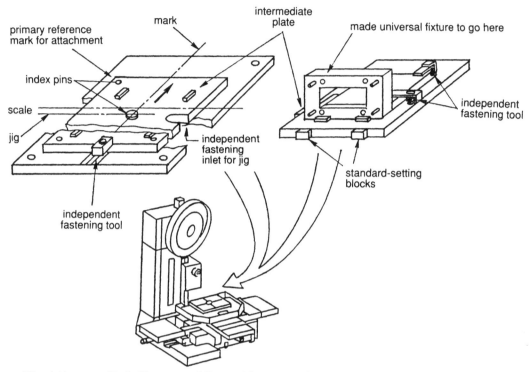

Source: "Special Issue on Single Changeover," *Factory Management*, Vol. 26, No. 6, 1980.

Figure 9-9. Universal Fixture for Intermediate Plate

- Doing a walking-route analysis and changing the layout of tools and materials to enable a U-shaped walking route
- Reducing the number of threads on the eye bolts

In addition, they made the following improvements to reduce replacement time to 3 minutes:

- Used the crane for removing old plates and the hoist for bringing in new plates
- Switched to independent fastening tools
- Used auto-clamps whenever financially possible

They also made the following improvements to bring adjustment changeover time down to 3 minutes:

- Emphasized greater accuracy and logical sequences
- Used index pins to mark standards

Table 9-2. Machining Center Changeover Waste Elimination Table

Category	Type of waste	Waste elimination plan	
		Small improvement	Medium improvement
Setup waste	• Air blown on leveling stand • Conveyance via crane • Cleaning • Setup of braces and caps	1. Install a table for external changeover. 2. Set up a plate to hold the 7 changeover tools. tools	1. Add one more hoist (500 kg/unit). 2. Reduce eye bolt threads from 15 to 5.
Replacement waste	• Remove bolt • Remove nut • Remove temporary leveling stand • Too many threads on eye bolt	1. Install an intermediate plate for external changeover. lathe 15 holes in workpiece M/C T groove moving bolster	match marks origin point spring
Adjustment waste	• Frog meter checks • Setting standard values (x, y, z) when empty • Sequence errors • Waste in calculating offset value • Waste due to lack of processing standards chart	1. Use a marker line to determine x-y coordinates for intermediate plate and for workpiece. Also use an index for making reference holes in the workpiece. 2. Make a chart to list the changeover sequence. 3. Set up input board on the work table (instead of doing tape offset). 4. Start processing standards from the x-y intersection. Design for clockwise operation (see diagram). 5. Set up standard settings for next job at the external changeover table.	

Source: "Special Issue on Single Changeover," *Factory Management*, Vol. 26, No. 6, 1980.

- Eliminated the need for tape offsetting by removing the cause for variation in standards
- Universalized and standardized tools and magazines

Finally, they used the following tools and methods as part of their machining center process-razing efforts:

- P-Q analysis
- Part-specific process route analyses (they did separate analyses for each type of machining material, station, and holder tool, and also changed some horizontal handling to vertical handling)
- New designs to reduce the number of stations.

Through these and other efforts, the improvement group at Company F was eventually able to achieve zero changeover for their machining center.

10

Changeover Improvement Steps for the Process Industry

In process industries, stand-alone machines are linked and run at high production speeds. From the perspective of changeover improvement engineering, these linked machine systems resemble other types of large-lot production systems. The only differences worth noting are:

1. Linked machining lines are more difficult to clean because different chemical substances must be used on different machines without being mixed.
2. It is more difficult to set optimum processing conditions (in terms of temperature, speed, pressure, etc.) when the machines are closely linked.
3. Standards must be set in a series, since upstream processes in a linked machining line have a big impact on adjacent downstream processes.
4. The longer the linked machining line is, the more time its changeover will require. A line with N machines will take N times longer than a single machine.

Because changeover takes a long time, process-industry factories tend to favor large-lot production which emphasizes maximum capacity utilization. However, large-lot production always carries heavy losses due to high inventory costs. Surprisingly, some large-lot factory managers are not even aware of this.

Among the many managers who recognize that inventory is the root of all evil, some still oppose inventory-reducing improvements. Some of these opponents feel that the Toyota production system is simply not adaptable to the process industry. The best way to counter such arguments is to prove them wrong. Perhaps the best place to start is by introducing the TPS approach to change-over improvement.

Many process-industry factories are obvious examples of the large-lot production approach in that their production systems handle combinations of many types of materials, from steel, glass, and petroleum to chemicals, paper, and foodstuffs. Process-industry factories that adhere strictly to continuous production do not need to be concerned much with changeover, but even they are finding themselves gradually swept up by the new wave of wide-variety small-lot production.

Overview of Company B

Company B is a large company, capitalized in the tens of billions of yen (hundreds of millions of dollars) and employing about 6,000 people. It is known as a specialist in the process industry field. It has four factories in Japan as well as joint-venture factories in Japan and overseas. It exports about 10 percent of its products made in Japan. Company B has branch offices all over Japan, and at least one of its products can be found in virtually any store in Japan that sells food.

Problems at Company B

Riding atop the rapid-growth wave that swept through Japan beginning around 1955, Company B built factory after factory — all designed for large-lot production, which means they were equipped with giant, expensive machines that can handle huge batches of product. When Japan's economic growth began slowing down around 1975, Company B found it was not immune to the new consumer trends toward diversity and individuality. Its product variety soon expanded to the point where it became necessary to begin developing a wide-variety small-lot production system.

For a while, Company B tried to apply its large-lot inventory management methods toward its new small-lot production methods. The managers found, however, that the steadily expanding product variety was adding to warehouse stocks and resulting in much higher warehousing and distribution costs, such as interest payments, management personnel, conveyance, and commercial warehouse leasing. Eventually, such costs reached 7.2 percent of total sales.

Figure 10-1 shows the layout of Company B's distribution system. In addition to the commercial warehouse costs, the company has invested nearly a billion yen ($8 million) in an automated warehousing system.

As Company B continues to follow the trend toward wide-variety small-lot production, it finds itself having to expand its automated warehousing system or lease new commercial warehouse space. It also finds its branch offices asking for more and larger regional distribution centers.

Naturally, the company's sales division would like each branch office to have its own warehouse and distribution center so that it could fill orders quickly to help ensure customer satisfaction. However, because so many of the company's products are seasonal goods, their distribution must be pooled in one way or another.

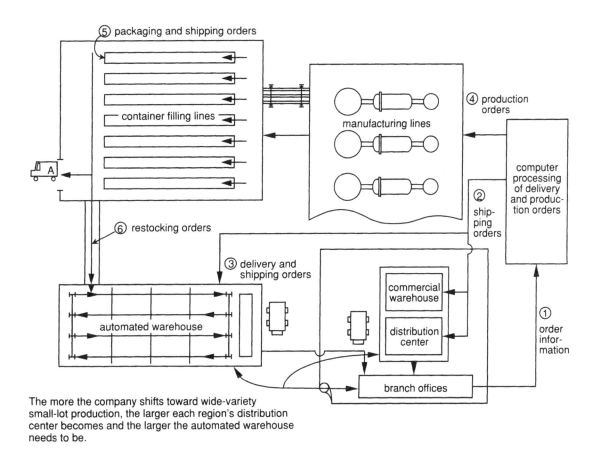

The more the company shifts toward wide-variety small-lot production, the larger each region's distribution center becomes and the larger the automated warehouse needs to be.

Figure 10-1. Distribution System Layout Diagram for Company B

Company B's managers debated the following two distribution strategies.

Plan A: Set up as many distribution centers as branch offices request and lease more commercial warehouse space in those areas to build a strong nationwide rapid-delivery system.

Plan B: Stop leasing any commercial warehouse space and instead ship all products directly from the factory's container filling lines to the sales outlets.

Their decision was to give Plan B a try.

SEVEN TYPES OF WASTE IN PROCESS-INDUSTRY FACTORIES

Process-industry factories have their own set of seven principal types of waste, many of which are similar to the TPS approach's seven types of waste. These wastes include:

1. Inventory waste
2. Standby waste (idly observing machines at work)
3. Minor stoppages waste
4. Changeover loss waste
5. Defect and rework waste
6. Yield loss waste
7. Handling operation waste

Inventory Waste

The chief culprit on this list is warehouse waste. Process-industry factories find large-lot production particularly convenient and small-lot production particularly inconvenient. The reason is that they have such long manufacturing lines.

The long changeover times for the process-industry factory's long manufacturing lines can turn small lots into big headaches. The factory can solve this problem in only one of two ways: return somehow to large-lot production scheduling or implement zero changeover improvements for small-lot production.

Figure 10-2 shows how the most apparent warehouse costs are like the tip of an iceberg. There is not only interest to pay on related capital loans, but also warehouse operation costs, management costs, transport personnel costs, costs for buying shelves, pallets, boxes, forklifts, and carts, antirust treatment, voucher and data processing costs, dead inventory disposal costs, and more. All these costs may run as high as 20 percent of the company's total sales value.

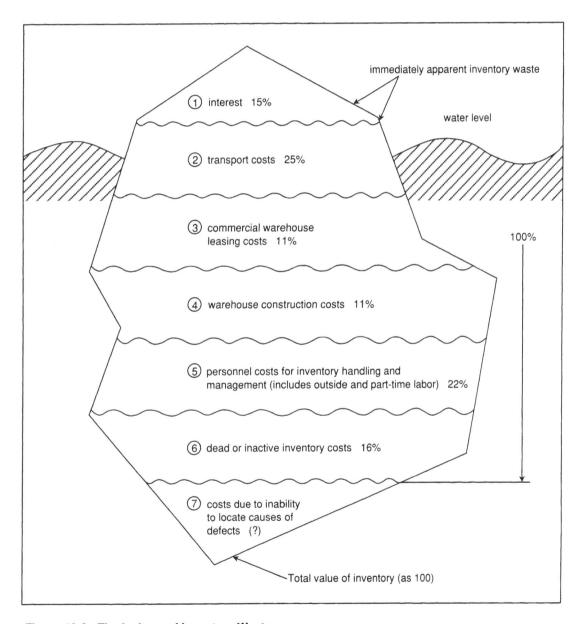

Figure 10-2. The Iceberg of Inventory Waste

As a rule of thumb, for every dollar saved in warehouse costs, you can save another 40 cents in other indirect costs. Consider also the intangible costs of keeping big warehouse inventories, such as:

1. Loss of urgency and diligence in production due to sense of security that arises from having a well-stocked warehouse.
2. Loss due to hidden problems; large piles of inventory hide equipment imbalances, overemployment, and other problems.
3. Slower responses to chronic small problems, such as equipment break-downs and defects.
4. Difficulties in enforcing first-in, first-out (FIFO) sequencing and priority-based sequencing of production.

These tangible and intangible losses are what led Toyota's improvement leaders to proclaim that inventory is the root of all evil. Inventory hides and protects waste. Having a large inventory can almost be called waste in itself, since it always means that the company has bought more materials and made more products than it can sell at the moment.

Standby Waste

Standby waste occurs when more people are assigned to the production line than are needed. Much of standby waste takes the form of operators doing nothing but monitoring control panels. Nowadays, factories use a wide variety of distribution boards, gauges, and other control panels, so it is not surprising that workers spend a lot of time watching them. In many cases, such standby waste is caused by the overspecialization of job assignments, which leaves workers with time where they having nothing to do but watch their machines work. Even in process-industry manufacturing lines, where the managers boast very high degrees of automation and centralized control, there are still an awful lot of workers idly monitoring decentralized devices and control panels.

Another cause of standby waste is the fact that so many changeover workers are needed to carry out the lengthy and troublesome changeover procedures for the factory's long manufacturing lines and its long finishing and packaging lines.

Minor Stoppages Waste

There are many types and quantities of machines in process-industry factories, and each type can include many different kinds of hoses, hose fittings, gauges, electrical components, and other parts. It is therefore difficult for the operators of these machines to gain even a basic grasp of all of their mechanisms, which makes it impossible to master their maintenance techniques. Therefore, such factories have a separate department for maintenance specialists. This gives rise to an attitude among operators: "I just run it; the maintenance staff fixes it." This attitude keeps operators from daily involvement in the maintenance needs of their machines.

An operator with this outlook is merely concerned with operating the machine and does not care how dirty the machine gets. Unless something breaks down or starts acting strangely, he or she is not inclined to get concerned about the machine's condition. However, it is only the operator — not the maintenance specialist — who sees how well the machine is operating from day to day. As a result of lapses in maintenance, such machines tend to experience frequent minor stoppages. These are small breakdowns or abnormalities that require the attention of maintenance staff; they are usually caused by chronically poor equipment conditions, such as accumulation of dirt or leakage of oil, steam, or air.

Changeover Loss Waste

Process-industry equipment generally entails a lot of changeover waste, due to the many vessels, hoses, conveyors, and other devices that require changeover. This changeover loss includes time loss, material loss, and other utility loss, all of which adds up to considerable financial loss for the company. The chief cause is the use of equipment designed for large-lot production. The loss-cutting response is to improve production planning and reach zero changeover.

Defect and Rework Waste

Perhaps the main cause of this kind of waste is the management attitude that a certain amount of defects and rework is to be expected and tolerated. At factories where the equipment has already been in use for several years, managers often assume it is only natural that the equipment should be dirty and rickety. In this sense, the managers have given up the battle against equipment deterioration even before it starts. No wonder such factories have so much defect and rework waste.

Yield Loss Waste

Specifically, this type of loss includes yield loss during start-up after a break and during changeover. In addition, the loss that occurs when optimum equipment conditions are not maintained can also be seen as yield loss. Too often, the optimum conditions so carefully discovered in the engineering laboratory are a far cry from the conditions actually maintained on the factory floor.

Handling Operation Waste

In many process-industry factories, the machining processes feature the latest, most advanced equipment but the final packaging and finishing processes still use old-fashioned methods that include a lot of manual handling. Sometimes, the line appears to be swamped with workers at these final processes. Some factories would like to change this, but their reliance upon subcontractors makes that impossible. The overstaffing of final processes can in many cases be traced to the production engineers who understand the processing equipment's technology but do not understand the production techniques that can boost efficiency at the final processes.

Another cause is the low level of skills training for the workers employed at the final processes. Factories try to keep costs down by hiring the least expensive workers, such as part-timers or subcontractor firms, but managers should realize how much loss from handling operation waste such a strategy invites.

CHANGEOVER IMPROVEMENT ON FILLING LINES

Figure 10-3 shows the layout of one of Company B's beverage filling lines. Although it is called a line, we can see that it is actually just a few stand-alone machines linked by a conveyor, much like the press lines described in earlier chapters. This filling line includes a 20-meter conveyor line and is operated by five to seven workers, who perform tasks such as inserting, sorting, inspecting, and reworking.

The changeover time is about one day for each line, and changeovers are therefore kept to a minimum — about three times per month. In other words, this is a strictly large-lot production line. As long as this emphasis on large lots continues, any manager's call for lower inventory levels is going to fall on deaf ears. As it stands, this factory's inventory level ranges from ten days' inventory for some products and up to two months' inventory for others. Their automatic warehousing system is filled to the brim with inventory.

Clearly, the way out of this mess is for the factory managers and workers to begin reducing changeover time, in increments such as 340 minutes to 170 minutes, 85 minutes, 30 minutes, 9 minutes and, finally, 3 minutes. To do this, they must master the steps and principles of changeover improvement.

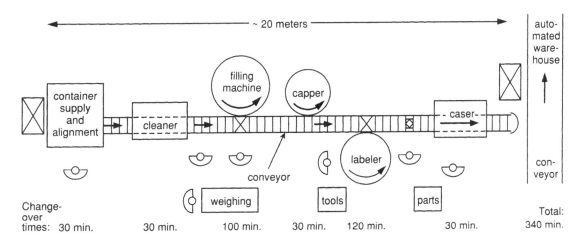

Figure 10-3. Filling Line at Company B

STEPS TO ZERO CHANGEOVER

Step 1: Study the zero changeover steps and principles

There is no point in starting changeover improvement until you have become familiar with the steps and principles involved. It is important that everyone share the same understanding of changeover improvement as they begin to work together to achieve zero changeover.

Step 2: Establish changeover improvement teams

It is best to have several changeover improvement teams, based on workshop groups, so that they can compete with one another. Since process-industry factories have long production lines, each team should start by eliminating waste from a particular process. After working out a set of improvement plans, the team members should hold a meeting to report on the improvement plans. Table 10-1 shows a process-specific waste-elimination chart used by one of the changeover improvement teams at Company B.

Table 10-1. Process-specific Waste Elimination Chart

Waste	Cause	Waste Elimination Plan
1. Overstaffing waste	Overdivision of labor	Cut personnel from seven to three; implement standard operation combination strategy
2. Waste due to oil leakage	Slack standards for oil caps	Improve changeover methods
3. Ill effects of break time on machines	Production of defects when operator is absent	Equipment maintenance
4. Line made up of widely spaced large equipment	Large-lot production approach	Shorten line, implement process razing
5. Line imbalance	Overdivision of labor	Implement standard operations
6. Changeover waste	Changeover (by one worker) takes 100 minutes	Reduce changeover time to 30 minutes by two changeover workers

In this chart, only the sixth instance of waste on the list is noted as changeover waste, but in fact all six types of waste are at least indirectly caused by poor changeover techniques.

For example, overstaffing is often caused by a need for extra workers to handle long and complicated changeover tasks. The second item, oil leakage waste, is often caused by improper use of screws and bolts during changeover. Longer changeover times also require more maintenance work and cleaning, which means extra labor costs. As for the third item on the list, when standards are not strict enough or are not strictly followed, repeated adjustments become necessary and equipment deteriorates more rapidly.

Step 3: Study current changeover conditions

Since process-industry production lines are actually nothing but stand-alone machines linked by conveyors, improvement teams should undertake changeover improvements on one machine at a time. The best machine to start at is the one where bottlenecks occur most. Often, changeover improvements there can be repeated at other similar machines along the line.

In the filling line shown in Figure 10-3, the improvement team chose the container filling machine, since that was the chief bottleneck point on the line. They began by studying the current changeover conditions for that machine. Table 10-2 shows the notes and measurements they took as part of their change-over operation analysis. As shown in the table, the most time-consuming part of the changeover is the cone attachment procedure.

Step 4: Reduce changeover waste

Each workshop's improvement team should work independently to reduce changeover waste. As Part I explained, changeover waste is divided into three main categories: setup waste, replacement waste, and adjustment waste. Table 10-3 shows the first two parts (setup waste and replacement waste) of an improvement team's changeover waste-elimination chart (see also Figures 10-4, 10-5, and 10-6).

Step 5: Train improvement team members

One of Company B's improvement teams was led by the manufacturing department manager and included both equipment operators and maintenance staff. It met once a week for two hours, and changeover demonstrations were held to train team members in waste-reduction techniques.

Step 6: Flag deployment

Next, the team members devised waste-elimination plans for the different types of equipment that they had been trained on, then gathered the improvement plans together and made a flag development schedule. (Flag deployment

Table 10-2. Changeover Operation Analysis

Work element	Time (decimal minutes)	Improvement notes
Remove wheel	60	Do not need to replace
Remove guide	80	Stop using screws for this
Remove screw	130	Do not need to replace
Prepare tools	140	Use specialized tool cart
Replace nozzle	670	
Remove cone	350	Do not change cone standards
Set up cleaning tub	100	
Remove nozzle	780	
Adjust stroke	490	
Clean	960	Rotate at high speed
Fill with new oil	1,020	Establish sequence
Remove cleaning tub	240	
Attach cone	2,980	No standards for attaching cone
Attach wheels and guide screws	440	
Adjust bolts	330	Adjustment waste
Adjust capacity	1,200	Devise measuring equipment
Clean up	180	
Total:	**10,150**	

Table 10-3. Changeover Waste Elimination Chart

Setup waste

1. Specialized carts	Make two specialized carts.
	Cart for conveyor section: make a flat cart.
	Attachment cart: make a tray that facilitates one-piece flow (see Figure 10-4).
2. Switch positions	Move switches to positions within easy reach.
3. Storage sites for tools	Store as close as possible (see Figure 10-5)
	Establish standardized, well-marked storage sites.
	Setup should be done by the line leader.

Replacement waste

1. Wheel	First try to find a way to eliminate changeover altogether. If some items are replaced very easily and quickly, their replacement should probably continue as is. Other replacement tasks can often be simplified and sped up by using wing nuts and C washers (see description of formula point 3 in Chapter 3).
2. Guide	Removing the guide takes a long time, so try to think of a way to avoid having to remove it. For example, the replacement can be restricted to just the part that needs adjustment. Or a five-point upper/lower pin set can be screwed in to enable simpler adjustment.
3. Screws	If replacement is unavoidable, save replacement time by finding a way to have the screws inserted and withdrawn from above.
4. Guide	Make the guide as cylindrical cover.
5. Cone	Find a way to do changeover without changing processing standards (see Figure 10-6).
6. Residual liquid	Assign two workers to this task; use a standard operation combination chart to develop task assignments. As with high-speed rotation, this helps reduce cleaning time. Next, plan a more rational standard sequence for cleaning and install specialized hoses for each kind of oil.

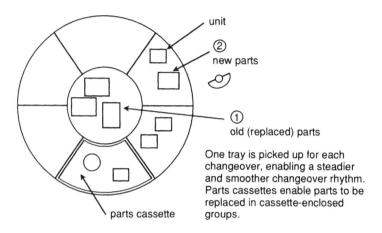

One tray is picked up for each changeover, enabling a steadier and smoother changeover rhythm. Parts cassettes enable parts to be replaced in cassette-enclosed groups.

Figure 10-4. Tray Section on Specialized Cart

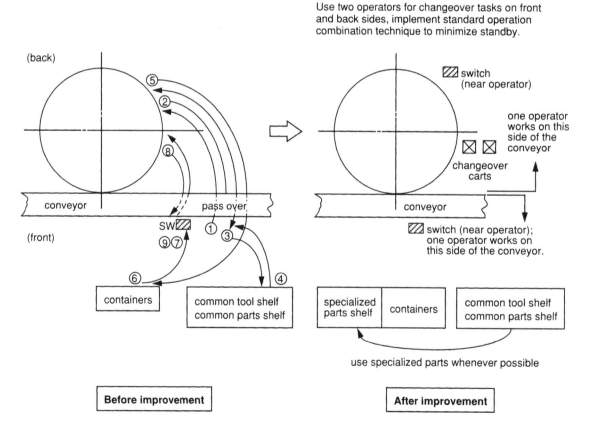

Figure 10-5. Switch Positions and Tool Storage Sites

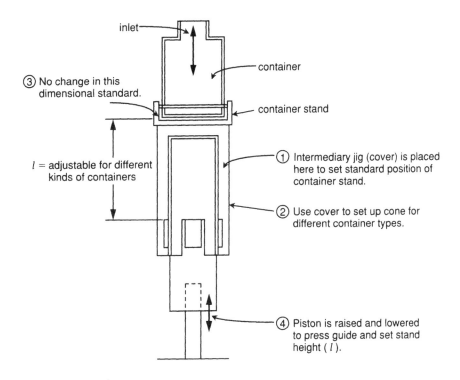

Figure 10-6. Remodeled Cone

is also discussed in Step 6 in Chapter 2 (there called red-tag strategy) and in Step 4 in Chapter 7.)

The team members should be committed to achieving a 95 percent success rate in their improvement plans. The other 5 percent includes plans not attempted and those that were attempted but did not have good results.

Often improvements involve devising new jigs or other devices, and these prototype devices must, of course, be tested. The testing process itself sometimes leads us to think of better devices.

Flag deployment is best carried out in small groups composed of people directly related to the target equipment; the schedule should be set for as short a period as possible. When the flag deployment schedule is stretched out over too long a period, enthusiasm may wane, at which point managers need to follow up with advice and encouragement. The leaders must prevent backsliding by ensuring that improvements become firmly established.

In process-industry factories, flag deployment requires a lot of perseverance due to the sheer quantity and variety of machines involved. This variety makes horizontal deployment challenging, too.

One key to successful flag deployment is willingness to explore the unknown. To do this, you must maintain an open, flexible attitude. Improvement plans are merely plans; if they appear to need revision, you should revise them until they are right. There is no point in pursuing an erroneous plan to the end, although many improvement teams do just that due to a lack of flexibility. In short, you must always be willing to improvise and make changes as you carry out your improvement plans.

The true cause of Company B's growing inventory is that it turns out products according to the production schedule. If the company practiced the PDCA (plan-do-check-action) cycle, it would change its production plans (P) to solve the inventory problem. The same goes for improvement plans: the point is to obtain the right results, not to stick to the plan at all costs.

Once the improvement teams finish making the small and medium-sized improvements, they should begin process razing. The large improvements should be saved until after the new line layout has been established. At Company B, the small and medium improvements alone were enough to reduce the labor requirements from seven workers to just three.

Step 7: Changeover demonstrations

Each time improvement team members succeed in cutting the changeover time by half, they should hold a changeover demonstration to teach their new changeover methods to others and help firmly establish the new methods. These instructive demonstrations have themselves reduced training time by half. They are valuable enough to be done for every improvement step that cuts changeover time in half.

CHANGEOVER POINTS FOR A PAPERMAKING MACHINE

One of the key points for process-industry changeovers is that, if possible, the changeover should be done without stopping the machine. Here are some examples that illustrate this important point.

In processes that use calenders, the goal is to change the calender width setting without stopping the machine, although you may have to slow it down. The same is true for papermaking machines. Most factories shut these machines off just to change their width settings.

When improvement team members at Company B were told it was possible and advisable to change the width settings without turning these machines off, their eyebrows went up in surprise and disbelief. Later, when they recognized that this was true, they came up with several improvement plans, such as:

- Make a width adjustment advice with an auto-return function
- Make a width adjustment device that uses pressurized water
- Make a width adjustment device that uses an elastic band

They developed prototypes of these devices over the next three months and later managed to achieve zero changeover for the width adjustment. Eventually, they followed the above steps and principles and achieved zero changeover for machines that had total changeover times ranging from 6 to 12 hours.

TEST YOUR SKILLS

The following seven principles apply to zero changeover in papermaking plants:

Principle 1: Try to enable width settings and other changeover settings to be done without shutting off the machine. It is OK to slow down the machine.

Principle 2: Find a way to change product types without having to change fluids in tanks.

Principle 3: Try to avoid having to rinse glue tanks when switching to a material with a different thickness.

Principle 4: Try to do model changeovers with minimal cleaning. Consider using a two-part line or a line with sharp turns.

Principle 5: Do not assign external changeover tasks to another section, since that would only increase labor needs there. Sending such work outside the workshop also slows the improvement process.

Principle 6: Use cassettes and one-touch operation devices whenever possible, especially for slitters.

Principle 7: Find a way to avoid frequent collar removals.

Figure 10-7 shows a paper tube collar that needs improvement. Try to apply some of the principles just described to plan an improvement for this device.

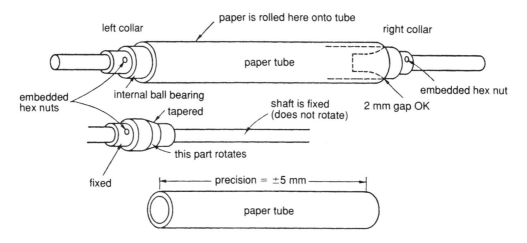

Figure 10-7. Paper Tube Collar

As the figure shows, a paper tube is used to roll up paper from the paper-making machine and slitter. Under current conditions, the worker adjusts the paper tube width by loosening the embedded hex nuts to reset the right and left collars. On the left side, only the hex nut must be loosened, but on the right side, the worker must loosen the hex nut, remove the collar, replace the paper tube, and then use an Allen wrench to retighten the right hex nut. There are commercially available automation devices for changing paper tubes, but this company cannot afford them. What kind of improvement can be made to solve this problem at little expense?

Hints:

1. The tapered part of the collar should have a diameter smaller than the paper tube's inner diameter.
2. The hex nuts should not have to be loosened and retightened.
3. Only the ball bearing part of the collar should have to turn.

11
Zero Changeover for PCB Auto-Inserters

Much of the electronics industry's manufacturing segment is strangely characterized by a combination of high-tech products and low-tech production methods. We will see some examples of this as we examine the improvement steps for changeover of auto-inserters.

Changeover improvement in machines used in the electronics industry falls into three categories that can be applied at any factory:

- Removing waste from setup and cleanup procedures
- Removing waste from replacement procedures
- Removing waste from adjustment procedures

Figure 11-1 shows changeover improvement trends over a five-month period at Company N. The next sections will describe the steps Company N followed to achieve zero changeover over this period.

Step 1: Establishing a Changeover Study Group

Figure 11-2 shows a parallel line of auto-inserter machines used to insert components on printed circuit boards (PCBs). One of the problems that arises when machines or other devices are arranged in such a line is the large amount of loss due to long changeover times. Nothing can be produced while changeover is being done. Most factory managers are painfully aware of this kind of problem and of the need for changeover improvement.

Company N began by establishing a changeover study group whose goal was to cut changeover time by half. At first, the study group had just four members, including the workshop foreman and the group leader. Whenever necessary, they also received assistance from the company's production engineering staff.

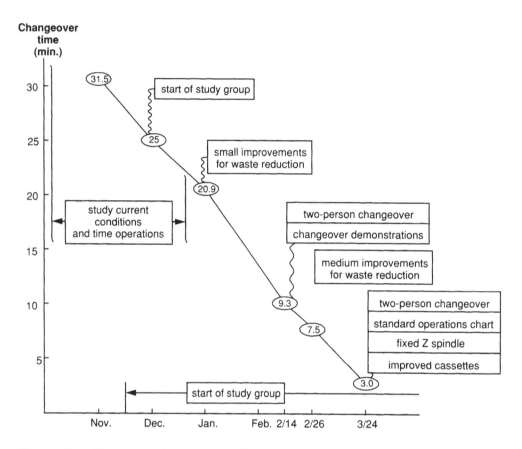

Figure 11-1. Changeover Improvement Trend

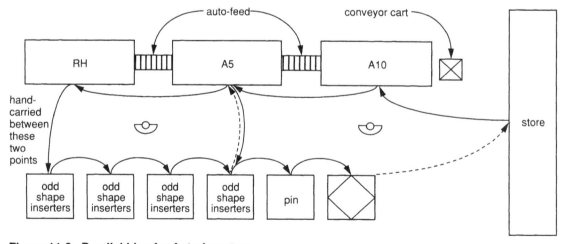

Figure 11-2. Parallel Line for Auto-Inserters

1. Their goal was to achieve zero changeover (3 minutes or less).
2. The study group met regularly for 2 hours a week.
3. Their meetings had three objectives:
   - study the fundamentals of changeover
   - make improvement plans to remove waste from changeover
   - carry out the improvement plans
4. Their initial goal was to reduce the changeover time to the single changeover range of 9 minutes or less. After reaching this goal, they pursued the second goal, which was to reach zero changeover.

Step 2: Studying Current Conditions (Operation Analysis)

Two people worked together in carrying out the operation analysis. One made the time measurements while the other watched closely to discover waste. Table 11-1 shows some of the results of their analysis.

Since the purpose of this analysis is to help eliminate waste, the analysis results should show where waste exists and suggest means of eliminating the waste. The time measurements should be in small, specific increments, preferably under 10 seconds.

The changeover work should be divided into categories such as: (1) setup, (2) external changeover, (3) attach, (4) set positions, (5) set standard dimensions, (6) trial operation, (7) inspection and measurement checks, (8) adjustment, and (9) other. The most important of these from the perspective of changeover work are positioning and setting standard dimensions. The analysis, however, showed little of either of these two types of changeover work. Instead, they found a lot of changeover time was spent on adjustments and on other operations, such as checking and measuring, the need for which was not clear. The observers also found that the machine was shut off for many operations that could be done while the machine was still on, such as die replacement, conveyance, walking to find tools, and cleaning up.

Step 3: Making the Changeover Waste-Elimination Chart

The analysis put waste into the three categories of setup waste (setup, cleanup, etc.), replacement waste (attaching and removing), and adjustment waste (positioning, setting standard dimensions, trial operation, inspection, and measurement checks). Table 11-2 shows the group's changeover waste-elimination chart.

Table 11-1. Changeover Operation Analysis

Factory XX's changeover improvement group

Process: Auto insert				Supervisor:			PCB/Part No.:		
Machine: M-1				Operator:			Changeover time:		
Machine No.:				Changeovers/month:			Measurements by:		

No.	Changeover steps	Current time	Changeover types			Waste elimination plan	Improved time	Achieved
			Int.	Ext.	Waste			
23	Peel off tape used to stabilize unloader width setting	3	√		○	Use clamp instead of tape	1	○
24	Tape used to hold PCB width setting belt	8	√		○	"	3	○
25	Machine power is switched off, then tape leader signal cable is unplugged	4	√		○	Do not unplug cable	4	○
26	Machine power switched back on	2	√					
27	Rewind tape leader signal cable	7	√		○	Do not unplug cable	7	○
28	Rewind PG tape	28	√		○	Make part of external changeover	28	○
29	Set PCB on loader	3	√					
30	Turn machine power ON	2	√					
31	Check contact of No. 1 device on coating head side	4	√					
32	Use satellite operation panel to adjust position	27	√					
33	Check contact of No. 1 device on mount head side	4	√		○	Adjust MHDH position	4	○
34	Use satellite operation panel to adjust position	13	√		○	Stop	13	○
35	Check for slippage after first contact	18	√		○	"	18	○
36								
37								
38								
39								
40								
41								
	Total	26.00					25.1"	

Table 11-2. Changeover Waste Elimination Chart

Type of waste	Process	Waste elimination plan	Person responsible	11	12	1	2/14	2/26	3/E
Setup	Waste in filling out item vouchers	Use kanban	See Figure 11-6	D	—					
	Changeover materials not ready	Use specialized change-over carts, establish changeover standard operations, and use specialized carts for Z spindles	Use NC tape (see Figure 11-6)	A			——	——		
	Tools not ready	Use gun belt	See Figure 11-8	B		—				
	Clean up NC tape	Make part of external changeover; automate NC tape rewind process	See Figure 11-5	B				——	——	
	Part replacement waste	Reduce variety of Z spindle parts	See Figures 11-9, 11-10, and 11-11	C	——	——	——	——	——	
	Waste in using hex bolts	Use butterfly bolts instead	See Figure 11-12	A		——	——	——		
Replacement	Waste in attaching and removing handle	Leave handle in fixed position	See Figure 11-13	A	—					
	Waste in reading data	Input data to data terminal		C	—					
	Waste in use of stopper bolts	Use clamps instead	See Figure 11-14	A	——	——	——	——	——	
	Stocker width adjustment	Make alignment jig	See Figure 11-15	B			—			
	Waste in adjusting suction cup position	Make alignment jig	See Figure 11-15	B			—			
Adjustment	Loader width adjustment	Use marker on sample board		A	—					
	Waste in adjusting position	Make a reference jig		D					——	——

Step 4: Doing Flag Development

Once all the changeover waste to be eliminated has been listed, the next step is to plan a flag development schedule such as the one shown in Figure 11-3 (pages 226-27). Divide improvement plans into large, medium, and small improvements, and begin with the smallest, least expensive improvements.

Step 5: Implementing Improvements

When two people are doing the changeover, a standard operation combination analysis should be done first to minimize standby waste, as shown in Figure 11-4 (page 228). For a description of the standard operation combination analysis method, please refer back to Chapter 6.

Once an improvement has been made, the flag should be erased and the completion date marked on the flag development schedule.

PRINCIPLES FOR AUTO-INSERTER CHANGEOVER IMPROVEMENT

Two of the 9-point formula for changeover improvement introduced in Chapter 3 apply especially to auto-inserter changeover. These are Principle 1 (prepare everything you need beforehand) and Principle 3 (avoid inserting and removing bolts).

Prepare Everything You Need Beforehand

The development of specialized changeover carts is an application of this principle. For more on this subject, refer to the Part I of this book describing the fundamentals of zero changeover.

Figure 11-5 (page 229) shows a specialized changeover cart in which the first level holds the NC tape machine and the second level holds the parts and tools needed for changeover. These carts are a good way to ensure that everything needed for changeover is ready beforehand.

To help maintain a clear indication of the production sequence, each changeover cart can carry a preprinted changeover kanban, as shown in Figure 11-6 (page 229).

Figure 11-7 (page 230) shows a specialized changeover cart that was developed for Z-spindle parts. Figure 11-8 (page 230) shows a tool belt designed to hold just the change-over tools that are needed (in this case, the L-wrench was not needed).

Avoid inserting and removing bolts

This is a basic principle for eliminating replacement waste that should be applied whenever possible. Always begin by trying to find a way to avoid each replacement operation. Figure 11-9 (page 231), for example, shows how one improvement team reduced the number of inserter parts replacement operations on their line via the following steps:

1. Make a table listing the inserter parts used for each product model.
2. Do a P-Q analysis to identify model-specific groups of parts.
3. Establish Group A as fixed parts, Group B as semi-fixed parts, and Group C as parts that require changeover every time.
4. Establish insert changeover program A for the fixed parts (Group A); switch to insert changeover programs B and C for the other parts (Groups B and C).

Figure 11-10 (page 232) shows an improvement that provides the changeover operator with pre-opened parts containers. Although this is a small improvement, the large quantity of containers makes it a valuable one.

Figure 11-11 (page 232) shows how adding a second person can reduce setup waste. In the figure, the front person is Worker A and the rear person is Worker B. Figure 11-12 (page 233) shows an improvement that replaces a hex bolt with a butterfly bolt.

Figure 11-13 (page 233) shows a situation where, perhaps out of stinginess, a company had made the worker carry one handle around to several cranks. Setting a handle into a fixed position at each crank was an improvement that eliminated waste in searching, finding, conveyance, and attachment.

Figure 11-14 (page 234) replaces a hex bolt that needed an L wrench with a butterfly bolt that can be easily hand-turned to enable adjustment of the slide stopper.

Figure 11-15 (page 234) shows a cassette method for reducing the number of part replacement operations during a changeover. These cassette cases have already been set up to contain parts categorized into Groups B and C.

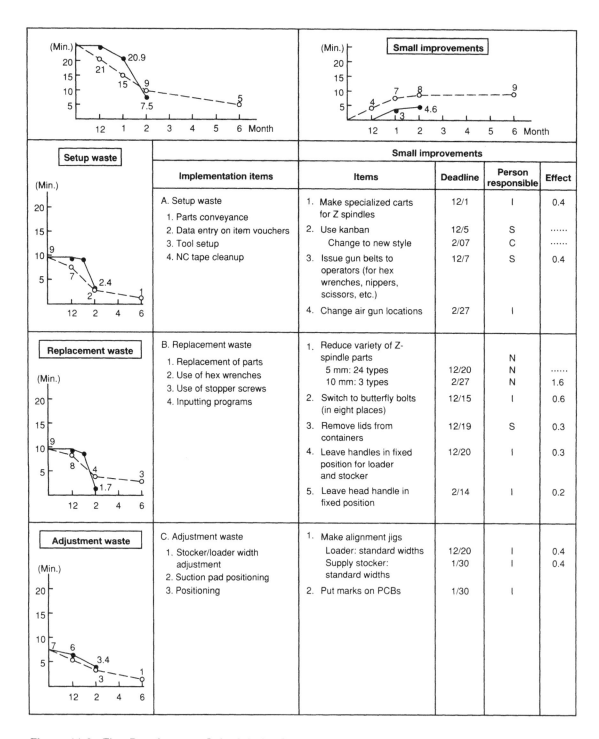

Figure 11-3. Flag Development Schedule for Auto-Inserter Improvements

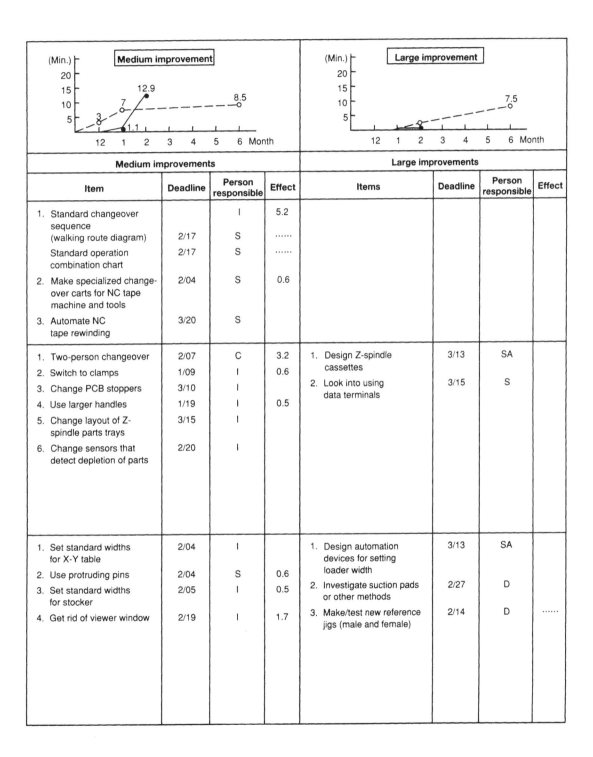

Medium improvements				Large improvements			
Item	**Deadline**	**Person responsible**	**Effect**	**Items**	**Deadline**	**Person responsible**	**Effect**
1. Standard changeover sequence		I	5.2				
(walking route diagram)	2/17	S	......				
Standard operation combination chart	2/17	S	......				
2. Make specialized change-over carts for NC tape machine and tools	2/04	S	0.6				
3. Automate NC tape rewinding	3/20	S					
1. Two-person changeover	2/07	C	3.2	1. Design Z-spindle cassettes	3/13	SA	
2. Switch to clamps	1/09	I	0.6	2. Look into using data terminals	3/15	S	
3. Change PCB stoppers	3/10	I					
4. Use larger handles	1/19	I	0.5				
5. Change layout of Z-spindle parts trays	3/15	I					
6. Change sensors that detect depletion of parts	2/20	I					
1. Set standard widths for X-Y table	2/04	I		1. Design automation devices for setting loader width	3/13	SA	
2. Use protruding pins	2/04	S	0.6	2. Investigate suction pads or other methods	2/27	D	
3. Set standard widths for stocker	2/05	I	0.5	3. Make/test new reference jigs (male and female)	2/14	D	......
4. Get rid of viewer window	2/19	I	1.7				

Part No./name:	Standard Operation		Chart creation date:		Required daily output:		27 units			Manual operation (HT)

Process:	Combination Chart		Section:		Time:					= Auto-feed (MT)

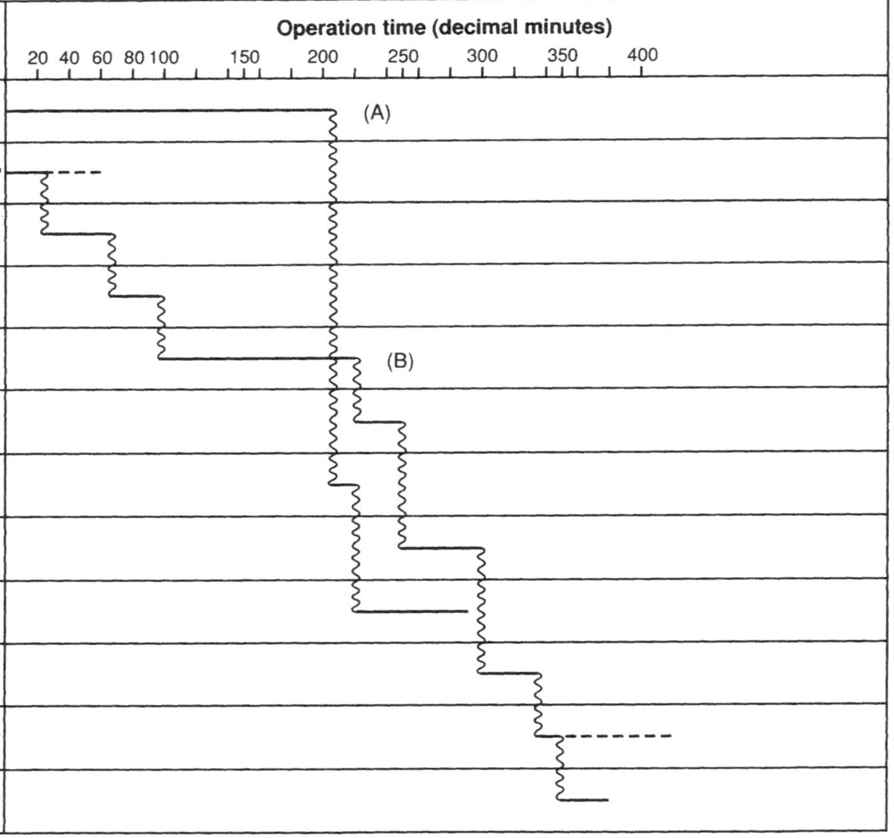

Note: (Front) indicates Worker A and (Back) indicates Worker B.

Figure 11-4. Standard Operation Combination Chart for Two-Person Changeover

The chart table:

Work sequence	Operation	Time HT	Time MT
(Rear) 1:	Remove parts	210"	
(Front) 1:	Input NC tape	26"	34"
(Front) 2:	Set X-Y table width	37"	
(Front) 3:	Set up pusher and stopper	25"	
(Front) 4:	Set up parts cassettes	129"	
(Front) 5:	Set loader width	23"	
(Rear) 2:	Set stocker width	15"	
(Front) 6:	Set position	50"	
(Rear) 3:	Set width and position of suction pads	66"	
(Front) 7:	Check clinch	30"	
(Front) 8:	Test operation	15"	75"
(Front) 9:	Remove parts	40"	

Operation time (decimal minutes): 20 40 60 80 100 150 200 250 300 350 400

= Walking

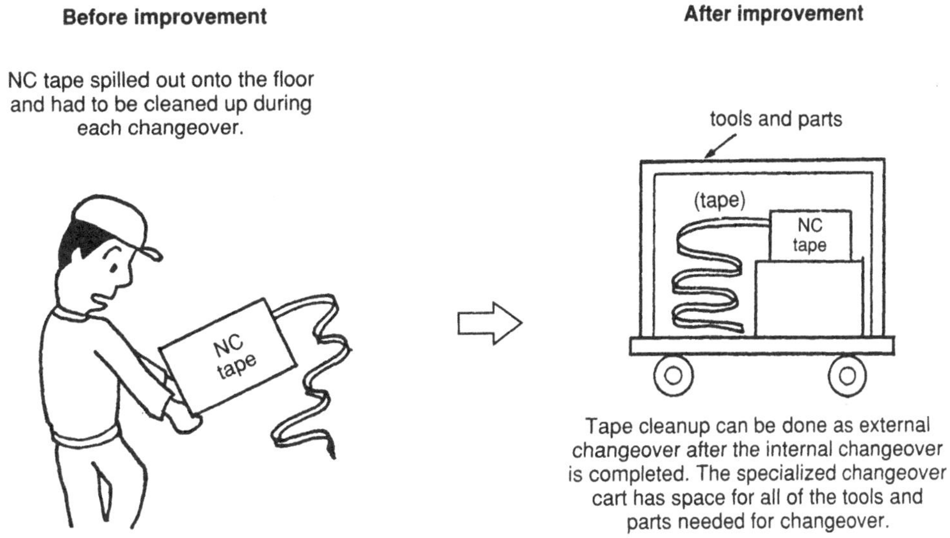
Before improvement
NC tape spilled out onto the floor and had to be cleaned up during each changeover.
NC tape
After improvement
tools and parts
(tape)
NC tape
Tape cleanup can be done as external changeover after the internal changeover is completed. The specialized changeover cart has space for all of the tools and parts needed for changeover.

Figure 11-5. Specialized Changeover Cart for NC Tape Machine

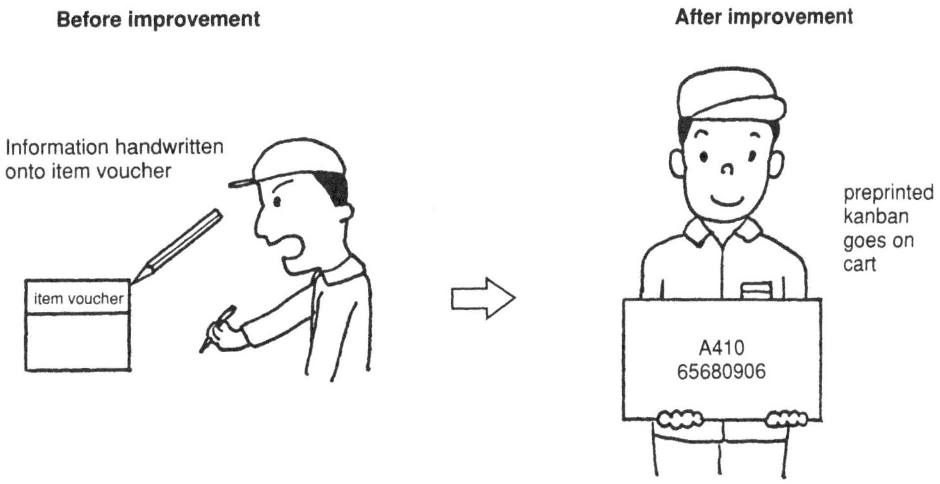
Before improvement
Information handwritten onto item voucher
item voucher
After improvement
preprinted kanban goes on cart
A410
65680906

Figure 11-6. Kanban

Before improvement

Workers had to search for, find, and
carry parts (searching waste, finding
waste, and walking waste).

After improvement

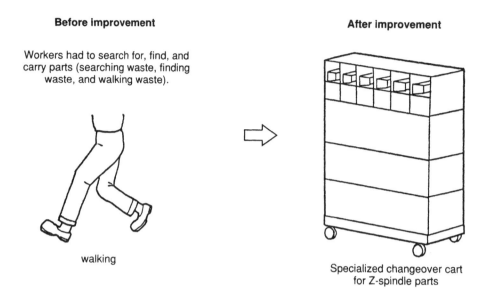

walking

Specialized changeover cart
for Z-spindle parts

Figure 11-7. Specialized Changeover Cart for Z-Spindle Parts

Before improvement

Preparation of tools
(searching, finding,
and conveyance waste)

After improvement

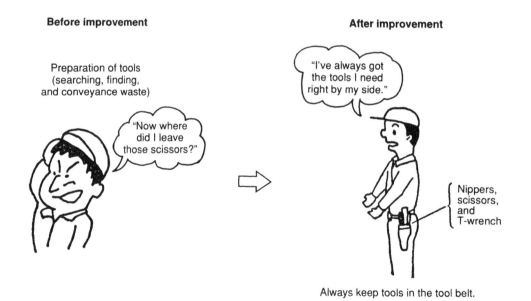

Always keep tools in the tool belt.

Figure 11-8. Tool Belt

Before improvement

After improvement

All Z-spindle parts had to be
replaced whenever the
product model was switched.

Auto-Inserter Parts List (Z-Spindle Parts)

PCB name:_____   H code: __F0__   Model: _____

Part No.	Qty.	Z No.	Polarity
200020		2	Left ($-$)
051011		3	
051511		4	
052211		5	
053311		6	
054711		7	
051021		8	
051521		9	
052221		10	
053321		11	
054721		12	
056821		13	
051031		14	
051531		15	
052231		16	
053331		17	
054731		18	
056831		19	
051041		20	
051541		21	
052241		22	
053341		23	
051051		24	
JW ( ).	R ( ).	HD ( )	TOTAL ( )

Comments:

Figure 11-9. Avoid Replacing Parts

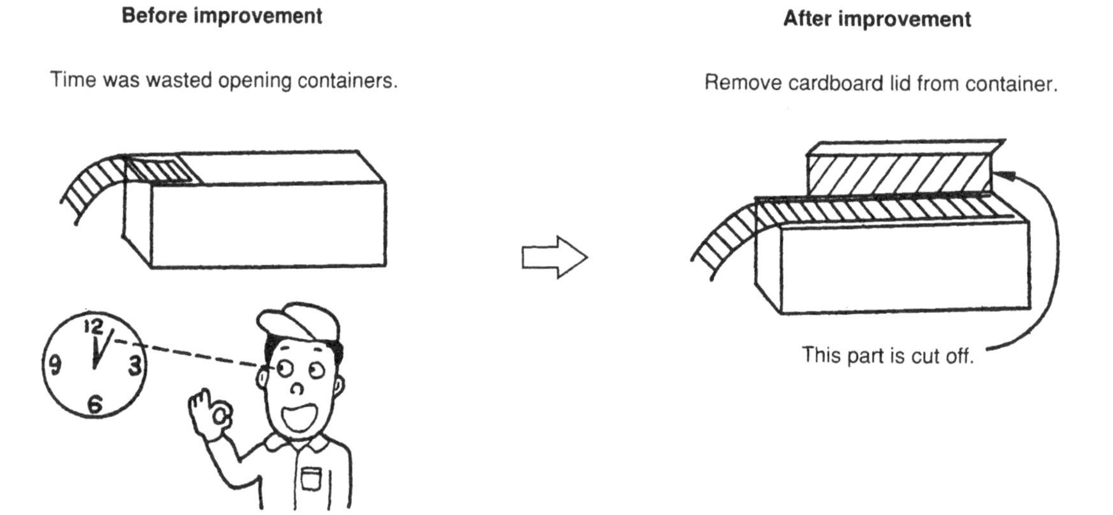

Before improvement

Time was wasted opening containers.

After improvement

Remove cardboard lid from container.

This part is cut off.

Figure 11-10. Pre-opened Containers

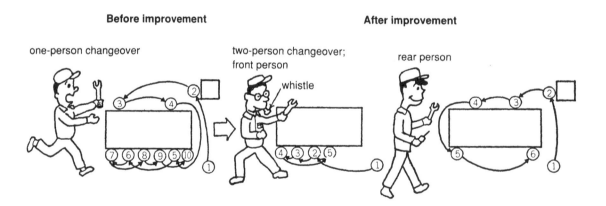

Before improvement

one-person changeover

After improvement

two-person changeover; front person

whistle

rear person

Figure 11-11. Two-Person Changeover

Before improvement   **After improvement**

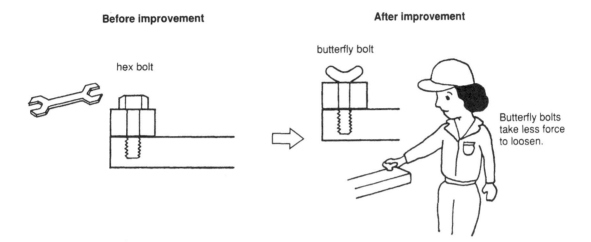

Figure 11-12. Butterfly Bolt

Before improvement   **After improvement**

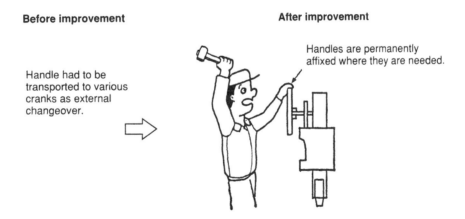

Figure 11-13. Handles Set in Fixed Locations

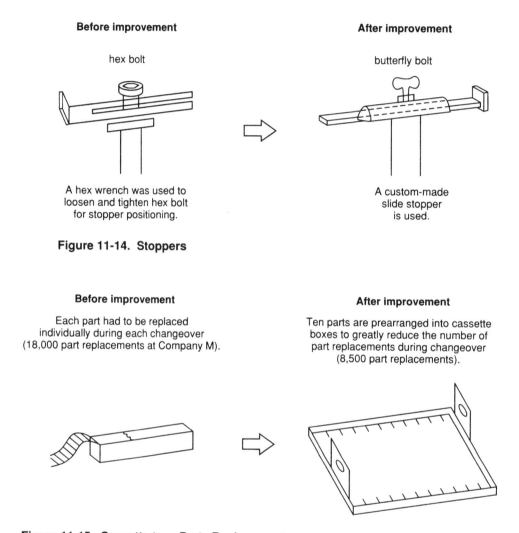

Before improvement

hex bolt

A hex wrench was used to
loosen and tighten hex bolt
for stopper positioning.

After improvement

butterfly bolt

A custom-made
slide stopper
is used.

Figure 11-14. Stoppers

Before improvement

Each part had to be replaced
individually during each changeover
(18,000 part replacements at Company M).

After improvement

Ten parts are prearranged into cassette
boxes to greatly reduce the number of
part replacements during changeover
(8,500 part replacements).

Figure 11-15. Cassette-type Parts Replacement

Other improvement examples include a standardized placement of small suction pads in seven sites. At least three pads are used at a time for various product models. This enabled zero changeover by eliminating the need to replace or position suction pads.

Company N's improvement teams carried out many other improvements and eventually they achieved zero changeover for all of the auto-inserter machines. With such improvements in place, any company that has its auto-inserters arranged in a U-shaped cell or a parallel line (as shown in Figure 11-2) should be able to achieve zero changeover, with staffing needs reduced to one operator per seven auto-inserter machines.

12

Zero Changeover for a
Sheet Metal Factory

Ishida Scale Co., Ltd. (hereafter abbreviated as Ishida) calls its new production system the Ishida Production System (IPS). This system emphasizes the formation of independent improvement groups that work mainly with supplier factories to use kanban for faster and more efficient delivery scheduling.

This chapter is adapted from an article appearing in *Factory Management* magazine, January 1987. The following excerpt includes a slightly edited and expanded version of Ishida's case study report concerning new line layout for the sheet metal processing line, with special attention given to the zero changeover improvements that accompanied this new line layout.

DOUBLING PRODUCTIVITY IN THE SHEET METAL FACTORY

Ishida's case study concerns improvement of a sheet metal processing line that produces hoppers for scales. Table 12-1 shows the "before" and "after" figures for this improvement.

Improvement steps

Step 1: P-Q analysis

The improvement group drew up a P-Q analysis chart (also known as an ABC chart), shown in Figure 12-1. This chart establishes three groups of product models on the sheet metal processing line.

Table 12-1. Sheet Metal Processing Line Improvement

Item	Before improvement	After improvement	Effect
Amount of in-process inventory	448 units	3 units	1/149
Lot size	224 units	14 units	1/16
Lead time	6 days	15 minutes	
Changeover time	30 minutes	10 minutes	1/3
In-process defect rate	5%	0.2%	1/25
Personnel	5 people	3 people	2-person reduction
Output per day	305 units	494 units	1.6 times
Output per worker per day	61 units	165 units	2.7 times
Transport distance	17.4m	4.0m	1/4
Required space	75.8m²	40m²	Approx. 1/2

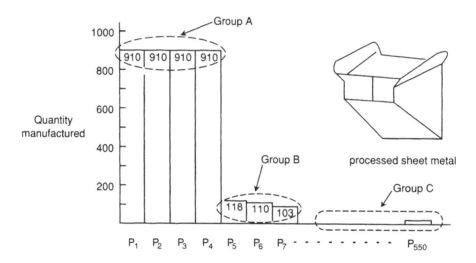

Figure 12-1. Identification of Improvement Targets via P-Q Analysis

Step 2: Finding causes of targeted waste items

Figure 12-2 shows the process-route diagram the improvement group made as their next step. Having identified waste in their processing line, the group was ready to begin planning improvements. Table 12-2 shows their list of waste items, along with the items' causes and the corresponding improvement plans.

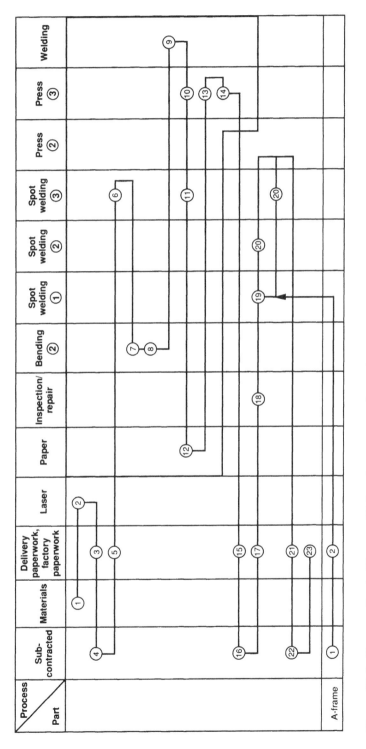

Figure 12-2. Process Route Diagram (Before Improvement)

Table 12-2. Waste Causes and Improvement Plans

Waste item	Cause	Improvement plan
1. Pick-up/set-down waste	Process-specific lot processing	Establish one-piece flow.
2. Conveyance waste	Process-specific lot processing	Establish one-piece flow.
3. Sitting while working	Specialized job assignments	Introduce standing while working.
4. Waste in subcontractor operations	Sending out simple work not the best way to save costs.	Bring it back into the line.
5. Processing waste	Specialized jigs	Design more versatile jigs.
6. Waste due to oversights	Tasks involving hand-positioning of workpieces	Devise mistake-proofing jigs.

Step 3: Value Analysis (VA) of sheet metal processing

Next, the improvement group used the VA method to study the value of the factory's sheet metal processing. They used the following checksheet, provided by their improvement adviser.

1. What is the objective?
2. Can the operation or part under study be safely eliminated?
3. Can custom-made items be replaced by commercial items?
4. Would a different processing method work better?
5. Would a different processing sequence work better?
6. Is processing precision unnecessarily strict?
7. Can alternative materials be used?
8. Can the rated values be relaxed a little?
9. Can slightly thinner sheet metal be used?
10. Can the process be made more compact?
11. Can two processing operations take place at the same time?
12. Can butt welding be done?

In short, the VA method looks at the objective of the target process and studies whether a more suitable material, size, or method can be used to better serve that objective.

Step 4: Process-razing proposals

After studying their process-route diagram and considering the types of waste they identified, the improvement group began looking for the best process-flow design. As a visual aid, they drew a flow diagram of the current layout, shown in Figure 12-3.

Next, they drew up another process-route diagram (Figure 12-4) and another layout diagram (Figure 12-5). This time, the diagrams showed the planned improvements.

Step 5: Completion of process-razing in the factory

The improvement group established the process-razing layout shown in Figure 12-5. Where additional equipment units were needed, they brought in new equipment without worrying about how high the capacity utilization would be. In buying new equipment and remodeling, they kept costs as low as possible while still serving the process-razing goals. Once the new layout was in place, they began trying out one-piece flow.

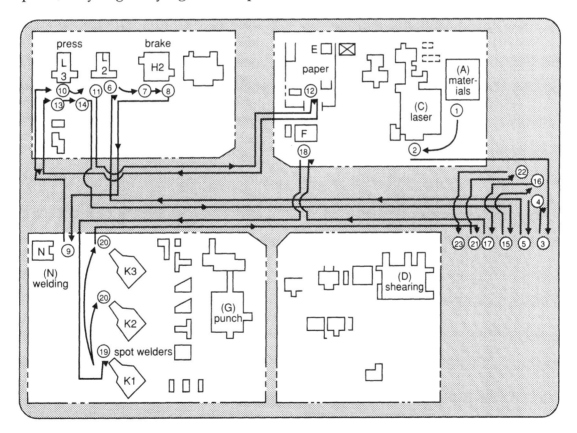

Figure 12-3. Flow Diagram (Before Improvement)

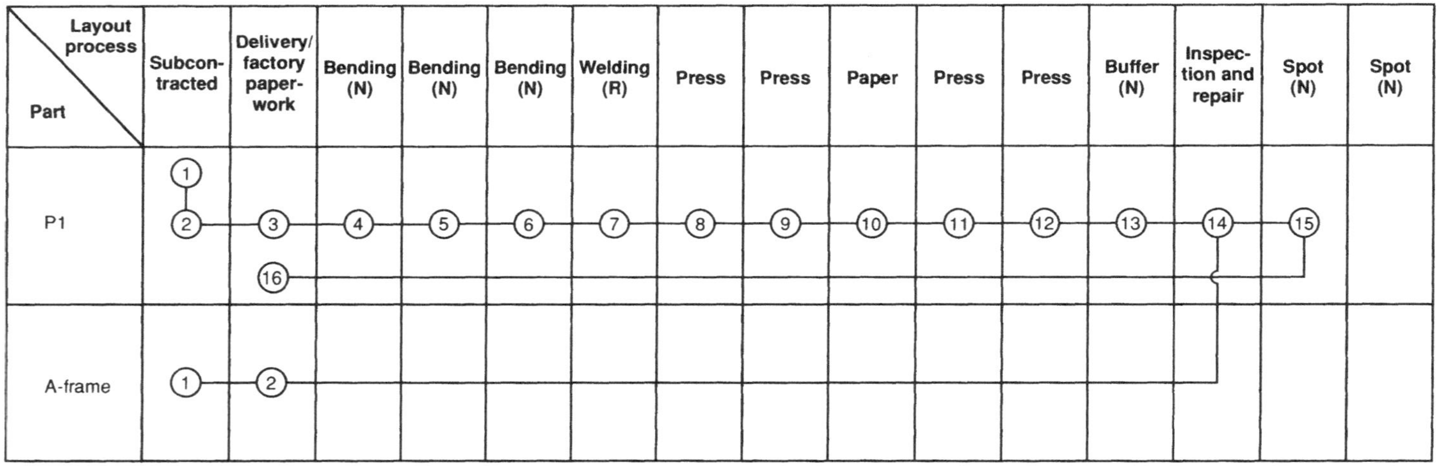

Layout process / Part	Subcontracted	Delivery/factory paperwork	Bending (N)	Bending (N)	Bending (N)	Welding (R)	Press	Press	Paper	Press	Press	Buffer (N)	Inspection and repair	Spot (N)	Spot (N)
P1	①—②	③ / ⑯	④	⑤	⑥	⑦	⑧	⑨	⑩	⑪	⑫	⑬	⑭	⑮	
A-frame	①	②													

Note: (N) indicates newly purchased equipment, (R) indicates remodeled equipment, and (F) indicates newly fabricated equipment.

Figure 12-4. Process Route Diagram (After Improvement)

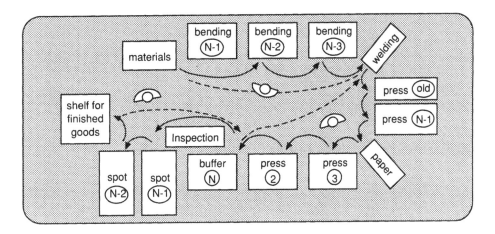

Figure 12-5. Flow Diagram (After Improvement)

The main hurdle to be cleared at this point was production of defects. The occurrence of defects meant that operators had to spend time making adjustments and repairs on the line; this made it impossible to meet the operating time required for one-piece flow. This problem was frustrating, and the group feared it had reached a dead end.

They learned that the answer to this problem lay in thoroughly investigating the causes of the defects and eliminating those causes. Two improvement group members made a careful study and found that the defects were due to imprecision in the angle of sheet metal bending. They managed to solve the problem.

This brought them to the next problem: changeover. They found changeover time adding up to over an hour; they responded by launching a changeover study group.

START OF CHANGEOVER IMPROVEMENT

The improvement group tried producing small lots consisting solely of product quantities that had been ordered. They then defined two changeover-related problems:

- Defects in changeover
- Loss due to long changeover time

The group went on to devise and implement the following measures to solve these two problems.

- *Formation of a changeover improvement team:* An improvement team was assembled. The following is just one of the improvement projects successfully undertaken by this team.
- *Design of specialized changeover carts:* The improvement team designed a specialized cart to hold changeover materials.
- *Standardization and simplified replacement of dies:* Using the principle of dead-end guide walls for standard settings (see point 5 in Chapter 3), the team was able to eliminate die adjustment during changeover.

After achieving the goal of single changeover, the team set a new goal of zero changeover. Although the improvement-making process held a few surprises, they managed to achieve the results shown in Table 12-1.

USE OF AUTO-FEED MECHANISMS (MT)

The improvement team's efforts included reducing manual operations (HT) by adding auto-feed mechanisms for automated operations (MT). This shift toward automation helped them establish a smoother flow of goods on their new line. For the future, the improvement team intended to continue finding ways to automate the line to reduce staffing needs.

In addition to the results described above, the improvement team noted several intangible results of their improvements:

1. The line had a steady rhythm that made the work less tiring.
2. Production scheduling became very reliable and consistent, so that they could basically tell by the clock how many products the line had turned out.
3. They found that having kanban on the carts that were brought to the first process was an effective way to integrate the flow of goods with the flow of information.
4. They also found that their new line layout was naturally conducive to mutual assistance among line operators.

Figure 12-6 shows some of the jig improvements made by the improvement team.

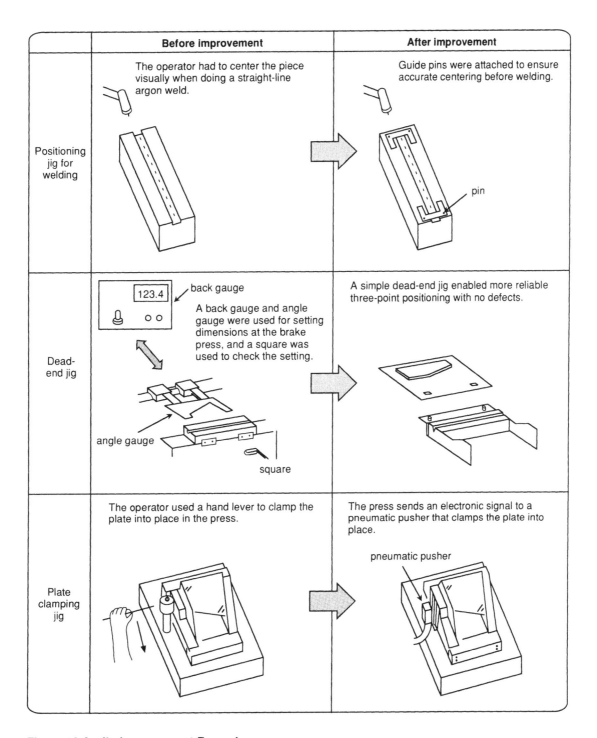

Figure 12-6. Jig Improvement Examples

13

Zero Changeover for Plastic-Molding Machines

Changeover for plastic-molding machines includes cleaning (such as cleaning out residual plastic colors or materials) as well as the physical change of parts. It is therefore a time-consuming process. After cleaning, the new die must be inserted at a steep angle, which also takes more time.

This chapter examines a case study from Company S, where an improvement group took on the difficult challenge of achieving zero changeover for plastic-molding machines.

OVERVIEW OF COMPANY S

Company S is a second-level subcontractor company that was founded in 1965; it has monthly sales of about ¥100 million ($800,000) and employs 53 persons. Its main product line consists of molded automotive parts supplied for its parent company.

The company has a total of 15 plastic-molding machines at its four factories. The plastic-molding machines include five types, ranging from 75-ton class to 240-ton class.

PROBLEMS AT COMPANY S

Company S sailed smoothly on the wave of rapid growth that occurred in the Japanese automotive industry during the 1970s. However, when the value of the yen climbed in the mid-1980s, Company S was obliged to cut costs twice in the same year, and soon found itself capsized in a sea of red ink.

The parent company, which had adopted the JIT approach, asked Company S to establish a 1-2-1 delivery system (delivery twice a day, one delivery time after receipt of kanban), which entailed handling product orders in quantities as small as one or two units.

Unfortunately, Company S had to experiment with many new dies and had to rework dies that had design flaws while striving to meet its customer's orders. As a subcontractor, Company S lacked the leverage to complain to the parent company about the latter's lack of manpower or its exceedingly short lead times for product development.

Meanwhile, Company S was trying to cut warehouse-related costs. The factory looked almost like a warehouse itself, though, with goods piled all among the processes. The company found itself unable to meet the payroll each month; it was sinking deeper and deeper into the red due mainly to its failure to respond to the cost-reduction needs of wide-variety small-lot production.

One of the key cost-reduction needs of wide-variety small-lot production is waste-eliminating changeover improvement.

SEVEN TYPES OF WASTE AT COMPANY S

The seven main types of waste at Company S are listed below in order of importance:

1. Inventory waste
2. Defect and rework (including trimming) waste
3. Waste due to poor flow
4. Conveyance waste
5. Changeover waste
6. Horizontal handling waste
7. Waste due to repeated development of prototypes

The primary problem was inventory waste, which could also be thought of as overproduction waste. The main cause of this kind of waste is time-consuming changeover. The changeover for each machine included three steps — color changing, die replacement, and condition setting; it easily took one or two hours to complete. Naturally, having spent that much time for the changeover, the factory managers were reluctant to have production runs any shorter than two days.

The managers of Company S could tolerate such overproduction as long as they knew that the parent company would order the products sooner or later; this often did not work out, however, because of frequent product model changes that shortened the average production life to about three months.

Other problems contributed to their steadily growing inventory. They were often surprised, for example, by orders for items that they had produced long ago and had lost track of. Sometimes they searched the entire warehouse, only to find that the products had gotten too dirty or were damaged during handling. This meant they had to rush through another large production run, which meant more surplus products for the warehouse.

Due to space considerations, we will not describe all of the seven types of waste at Company S, but will skip ahead to changeover waste, which is the focus of this book.

The most difficult part of changeover for plastic-molding machines is the color change procedure. To begin with, many different colors are used, ranging from red and white to black, gray, and ivory. The most troublesome and time-consuming color change is from black to white. Table 13-1 lists color-change time measurements at Company S before improvement.

Although the data in the table show time loss due to color changes as only about 5 percent of total losses, there are also other, non-time losses to consider,

Table 13-1. Color Change Times Before Improvement (rounded out to five-minute intervals)

Times (minutes) for 200-ton plastic molding machine

From \ To	Black	White	Red	Gray
Black		120	120	100
White	30		30	20
Red	30	120		30
Gray	20	120	30	

Times (minutes) for 100-ton plastic molding machine

From \ To	Black	White	Ivory	Gray
Black		20	15	10
White	5		5	5
Ivory	5	10		15
Gray	5	10	15	

Machine No.	1	2	3	4		Average
No. of color changes	6	2	5	0		31
Color change time (min.)	300	90	330	0		1,400
Average color change time (min.)	50	45	66	0		45

Actual time for color change at one machine ranges from 2.1 to 2.5 hours.

such as waste of materials and production of industrial refuse. These wastes are also significant losses.

When considering ways to minimize loss by eliminating waste, first ask: is there a way to avoid the color change entirely? If not, then look for the optimum (minimally wasteful) cleaning method and conditions.

The data in Table 13-2 were taken from direct observation of changeover procedures on a 100-ton plastic-molding machine, an operation that took 75 minutes to complete. This changeover time comes to more than 5 percent of the total operation time; the color change and related adjustment procedures accounted for 14 percent of the changeover time.

Obviously, a plastic-molding factory run like this will indeed find it hard to make a profit. The first goal of Company S's improvement group was to cut this changeover time by half.

Table 13-2. Data Based on Direct Observation of Die Replacement (Summary)

Measure-ments	Date/time:	March 11, 2:00 pm
	Machine:	No. 2
	Machine class:	100-ton
	Die weight:	400 kg (old) 600 kg (new)
	Product:	Holder
	Observer:	Factory superintendent

	Operation item	Time required (min.)	Improvement suggestions
Operation	Stop molding machine Remove old die	5	Try a two-person operation: second person brings new die to front of machine.
	Use crane to lift away old die	3	Do crane operation while machine is running.
			Make a platform to set dies on.
	Use crane to lift new die to machine	4	Make specialized cart for die.
	Attach and adjust new die	33	Two-person operation
			Eliminate bolts; use independent devices.
			Bundle hoses; set out tools along couplers.
			Use stoppers and guides.
	Preheat dies Set up correct conditions	10	Propane burner → preheating device
	Total	75	

IMPROVEMENT STEPS FOR CHANGEOVER OF PLASTIC-MOLDING MACHINES

After forming a changeover improvement team, Company S's president led them in an improvement campaign based on the basic principles for changeover improvement.

The basic steps for changeover improvement in this situation are similar to the changeover improvement steps explained in Part I. The only significant difference is that plastic-molding machine changeover includes the color-change operation.

Principle 1: Study Current Changeover Conditions

The first step is to conduct an operation analysis to help discover where changeover waste exists and where improvements are needed. Table 13-3 shows the results of Company S's operation analysis, arranged with a view toward making improvements. Improvement team members who had no experience in time study concentrated instead on observing current changeover conditions to find instances of waste.

Principle 2: Group Changeover Waste into Three Categories

The basic three categories of changeover waste are setup waste, replacement waste, and adjustment waste. A fourth category applies in the case of plastic-molding machines: cleaning waste, which includes color-change waste.

The Company S changeover improvement team figured that, on the average, a plastic-molding machine changeover performed by one person had the following time segments:

Die replacement (69 min.) + color change (45 min.) + condition setting (20 min.) = 134 min.

Of this, replacing the die and setting the conditions took 89 minutes.

The improvement team decided to try to achieve their goal of halving the overall changeover time by reducing the setup and replacement waste to one-quarter of previous levels. To do this, they devised the following improvement plans.

Table 13-3. Results of Die Changeover Operation Analysis

Factory XX   Date: Feb. 15

Process:		Person responsible:			Item: Holder		
Machine:		No. of operators: 1			Changeover time: 75 min.		
Machine No.: 2		Changeovers/month: 18			Observer:		

No.	Changeover steps	Time (sec.)		Changeover			Improvement ideas
		Cum.	Indiv.	Int.	Ext.	Waste	
1	Shut off molding machine						
2	Nozzle touch-back	5	5				Use two hoists
3	Attach old die to crane hook	2.10	2.05	○			Have new die ready
4	Loosen bolts on old die	2.50	40	○		○	Eliminate need for removing bolts
5	Move old die	3.40	50	○		○	
6	Remove bolts on old die	4.10	30	○			Try as a two-person task
7	Remove hoses	4.30	20	○		○	Use coupler for hoses
8	Move hoses	4.40	10	○		○	
9	Release die clamp	5.10	20	○			
10	Remove die	5.20	10	○			Find better alternative to using a crane
11	Move old die on storage platform	8.10	2.50	○	○	○	Do this step later

1. Setup: Target time = 20 minutes
   - *Eliminate waste in searching for, finding, and conveying new dies.* They developed specialized changeover carts for pre-changeover. They also used color-coding to improve the die storage system, which was organized according to corresponding parent-company factories.
   - *Eliminate waste in searching for, finding, and conveying tools, bolts, and nuts used in changeover.* They set up a tool rack featuring outlined storage places for the seven changeover tools.
   - *Eliminate waste in handling.* They attached permanent hooks on the dies to save time during changeover.

- *Eliminate standby waste during preheating.* They made preheating part of the pre-changeover operation. During pre-changeover, the dies are preheated to about 2° (centigrade) higher than the required temperature. They found that it took too much time to get the die preheated evenly using their propane burner. Therefore, they decided to develop a simpler preheating device that used electric heat.

2. Replacement: Target time = 30 minutes
    - *Eliminate waste from removal and attachment of pipes, hoses, and wires.* This is done by centralizing pipes and wires. Ideally, pipes, hoses, and wires should be gathered in one place, but this might require rebuilt dies. As an alternative to centralization, rubber bands can be used to bundle coolant hoses and can use couplers to enable quick and easy changeover. Similarly, wires can be bundled into multi-wire connectors to simplify and speed up changeover.
    - *Eliminate waste from removal and attachment of dies.* Part (a) of Figure 13-1 shows the components used in removing and attaching vertically inserted dies. Although there are positioning pins to aid standard-setting, removing and attaching this kind of die is still a troublesome task.

        Part (b) of Figure 13-1 shows an improvement in which positioning jigs were added at the bottom of the die and die holder. The guides fit together as the die is inserted to ensure correct die positioning. In this case, the die sizes are not based on the size of the products they make but instead on the size of the die holder frame on the plastic-molding machine. New plastic-molding machines should include a cassette system to provide universal die/holder fittings. For older machines, the dies can be modified as shown in part (c) of Figure 13-1.
    - *Ideally, the new die should be inserted as the old die is removed.* Figure 13-2 shows an example of a simultaneous die replacement method.
    - *Do not remove or attach bolts (Chapter 3, point 3).*
    - *Regard bolts as enemies; do whatever you can to get rid of them (point 4).* The fastening power of screws and bolts lies in the torque applied during the final turn. Turning them several times to reach that final turn is a waste of time.

        To eliminate such waste, insert washers that fill up the gap and enable the screw or bolt to be tightened and loosened in just one turn. More expensive alternatives to using bolts for fastening include the kind of auto-clamp device shown in Figure 13-3.

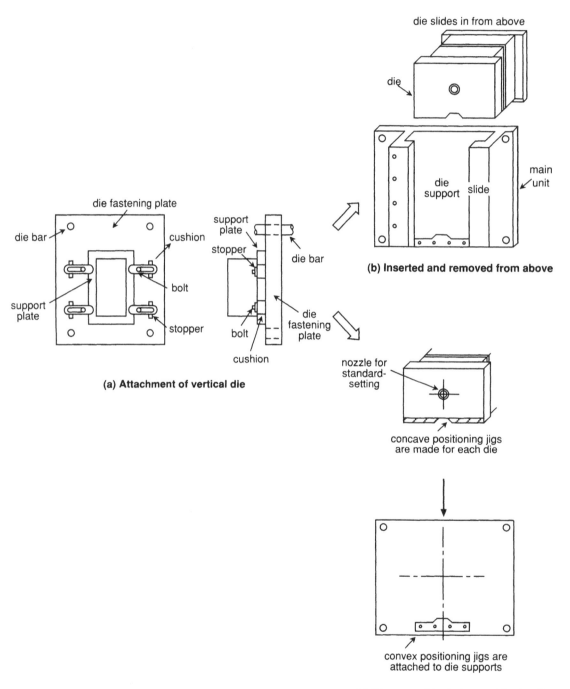

(a) Attachment of vertical die

(b) Inserted and removed from above

(c) Die support includes positioning jig

Figure 13-1. Die Improvement

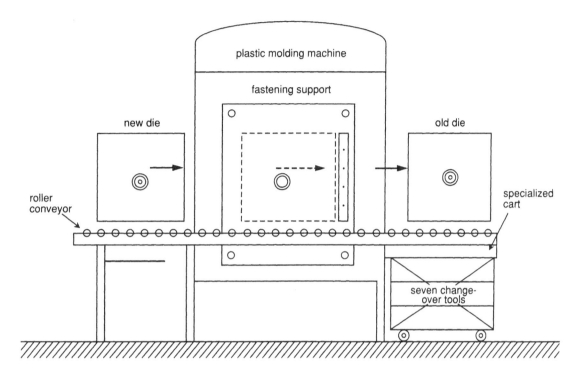

Figure 13-2. Transverse Slide Method for Simultaneous Removal and Attachment of Dies

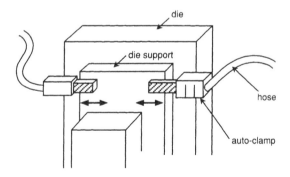

Figure 13-3. Auto-clamp Device

3. Adjustment: Target time = 20 minutes. If standard setting is done right to begin with, there will be little need for adjustments. Although the vast majority of plastic-molding machines use vertically inserted dies, the most efficient die changeover method is the transverse sliding method shown in Figure 13-2.

ANOTHER COMPANY S ACHIEVES SINGLE CHANGEOVER IN COLOR CHANGING

Another Company S (Starlight Co.) managed to achieve single changeover in its color-change operations.* Figure 13-4 shows a structural outline of the 800-ton plastic-molding machine targeted for color-change improvement.

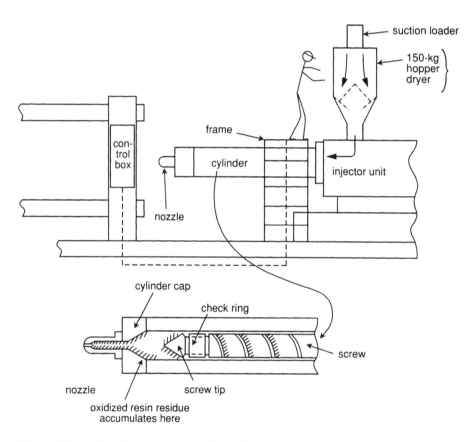

Figure 13-4. Why Color-changing Took So Long

Step 1: Study Current Conditions

The improvement group did an operation analysis while observing the current color-change procedures. They compiled their findings in the waste-

---

* This case study is treated in more depth in Chapter 11 of Kenichi Sekine, *One-Piece Flow* (Cambridge, Mass.: Productivity Press, 1992).

elimination chart shown in Table 13-4. Their improvement of the die change-over followed the steps already described in Part I. Therefore, we will focus instead on the steps they followed to eliminate cleaning waste.

Step 2: Criticize the Current Methods

The improvement group members studied each current operation, identified its purpose, and investigated whether the operation could be eliminated.

Step 3: Test Improvement Ideas in the Factory

At this step, the improvement team collects the methods and procedures that the study of current conditions has shown effective. It then experiments with different combinations of changeover conditions to find which combination results in the shortest total changeover time.

Company S's improvement group members had suggestions concerning the use of cleansers and operation conditions for the plastic-molding machines. They kept a chart of their results from condition combination tests to check into the cause-and-effect relations behind certain conditions (see Table 13-5).

To make the improvement effects clearer, the group leader kept a record of the number of die injection shots and the time required for changing the color from black to white. He also made other comments based on his observations and impressions, and noted the various processing conditions. Two operators were involved in the tests; they shared the tasks of operating the plastic-molding machine and supplying the cleanser.

Step 4: Determine Minimum Changeover Time Based on Current-condition Data

They selected the test No. 7 data in the chart shown in Table 13-5, which showed the shortest time of 18 minutes.

Step 5: Select the Starting Point for More Improvements

The improvement group studied current conditions and found a combination of conditions that would reduce total changeover time to 18 minutes.

Table 13-4. Waste Elimination Checklist for Plastic Molding Machine Color Change Procedures

Category	Time	Types of Waste	Waste Elimination Plans		
			a (small improvements)	b (medium improvements)	c (large improvements)
Setup waste	20 minutes	① Missing materials ② Tools ③ Antirust painting ④ Use pipe wrench ⑤ Layout (walking waste)	① Use kanban for changeover ② Set up 7 tool plates ③ Unify bolt sizes ④ Install ladders on the main unit and extractor unit	① Assign 1 person the job of inspecting mold repairs ② Use hoist or 2 cranes for changeover	① Double hopper ② Mold position ③ Temporary storage site for materials
Waste in removing and attaching items	25 minutes	⑥ Waste in removing and attaching hardware, bolts, nuts, and washers ⑦ Attach eject rod ⑧ Removing and inserting items from top of machine ⑨ Connecting and disconnecting hoses ⑩ Positioning hoses	⑤ Build and install spring-loaded mapper ⑥ Hang next to air hose hopper ⑦ Remove dirt (prevent foreign matter from accumulating)	③ Unify mold attachment thickness (on sides) ④ Centralize coolant hoses ⑤ Use right-angle design at exit ports for scraps	④ Use side-load, side-removal roller conveyor so that eject rods do not have to be removed ⑤ Perform changeover on front cap section only
Cleaning (color change) from black to white	90 minutes	⑪ Waste in excess screw turning ⑫ Cleaning sequence ⑬ Cleaning method ⑭ Method for using cleaning fluid ⑮ Scraps thrown on floor ⑯ Removal of grouped items	⑧ Prepare filter for external changeover ⑨ Cut off excess screw threads ⑩ Use labels to indicate proper cleaning sequence ⑪ Use 3 types of cleaning fluid (and get them ready beforehand) ⑫ Install scrap bins	⑥ Establish optimal conditions for cleaning method (a) Amounts of cleaning fluid (b) Types of cleaning fluid (c) Amount of materials (d) Types of materials (e) Insertion pressure (f) Extraction speed (g) Temperature of plastic resin	⎰ Cleaning fluid A for white to white changeover ⎰ Cleaning fluid C for white to black changeover ⎱ Cleaning fluid B for white to gray changeover ⑥ Introduce a right-angle design that does not stop at the front cap section
Adjustment waste (waste in adjustment for standards)	25 minutes	⑰ Adjustment in mold clamping ⑱ Adjustment in protrusion amount ⑲ Standard instructions are difficult to see ⑳ Limited-run samples are not checked	⑬ Use gauge to measure mold clamping (opening and closing) ⑭ Devise block gauges for protrusion amount and mold opening amount ⑮ Use cards to display mold standards	⑦ Inspect first of limited-run lot and stamp for approval	⑦ Use double device for material hopper to enable cassette method ⑧ Establish periodic changeover program for screw section
Total	160 minutes	㉑ Cleaning of filter ㉒ Straddling or climbing on the machine		⑧ Study feasibility of 2 lines (one black and one white with hopper and dryer)	⑨ Use conveyor instead of group item removal

Table 13-5. Condition Combination Tests to Determine Minimum Changeover Time

Test No. / Description	A Coarse cleanser brand	C Amount		B Sealing temperature (°C)	Finish cleanser brand	D Screw rotation speed (rpm)	E Amount of stroke (mm)	No. of shots Free shots	No. of shots Total shots	Time Free shots	Time Total	Overall impression	Ranking
1	S/ ABS	S	400 g	220	ABS	50	25	21	40	5'30"	22'55"	Not clean enough	8
2		ABS	2 kg	220	"	72	50	13	42	5'00"	27'40"	"	7
3		S	400 g	210	"	72	50	23	38	13'00"	20'40"	"	5
4		ABS	2 kg	210	"	50	25	41	65	10'00"	30'30"	"	6
5	H	H	500 g	220	"	50	50	22	42	4'05"	21'05"	OK	2
6		H	1 g	220	"	72	25	14	40	4'00"	25'50"	OK	4
7		H	500 g	210	"	72	25	8	27	2'15"	18'00"	OK	1
8		H	1 kg	210	"	50	50	16	43	3'40"	25'20"	Not quite clean enough	3

Comments (other conditions):

Injection pressure: primary pressure = 100 kg/cm²   secondary pressure = 80 kg/cm²   tertiary pressure = 5 kg/cm²

Cycle time: injection = 10 sec.   loading = 5 sec.   curing = 30 sec.

Injection speed: medium speed

ABS must go from black to clear

Note: A small plastic molding machine was used for the factory tests.

However, that was still twice the target time of 9 minutes, the single change-over time, so they needed a starting point for another round of improvements.

They narrowed down the starting points to two: improve the sequence of changeover operations and speed them up. To do this, they carried out more tests in the factory to improve the operation standards.

Step 6: Determine the Standard Changeover Sequence

Remembering that it's OK to move your hands but not your feet, they did a walking-route analysis to minimize walking waste. As a result, they moved all operation switches to a conveniently located control board.

After this step, they drew up a list of the new changeover procedures to formally and firmly establish the improved procedures.

Step 7: Training in Preparation for Changeover Demonstrations

Using the list of improved changeover procedures, the improvement group leader held training sessions. With practice, the operators became proficient enough at carrying out the new changeover procedure that they got the changeover time down to 10 minutes, just 1 minute shy of the single changeover target time. They decided this was close enough for them to move on to the next step: changeover demonstrations.

Step 8: Changeover Demonstrations for Horizontal Development

The improvement team recognized changeover demonstrations as a way of teaching improved changeover procedures by example. They drew up a standard operations chart for the changeover and, especially in heavily staffed workshops, they challenged the operators to get the changeover done within a certain number of minutes.

Eventually, they were able to reduce the color change time to just 5 minutes and 4 seconds. They are now striving toward the zero changeover target time of 3 minutes.

USING CASSETTES FOR CHANGEOVER ON INJECTION-MOLDING MACHINES

Do not replace the entire die. If possible, replace only the cavity section.

Figure 13-5 shows a changeover improvement that restricts changeover to the die's cavity section.* Cassette-type dies have been developed for many kinds of presses, but seldom have been developed for injection-molding machines.

General description of cassette-type dies

Cassette-type dies are dies whose cavity components have been remodeled as an easy-to-replace cassette. As Figure 13-5 showed, the die has two sections: the die set and the cassette (cavity). During changeover, we replace only the cassette section.

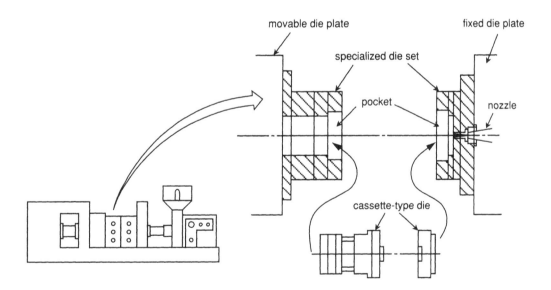

Figure 13-5. Cassette-type Die Structure

---

* This example was adapted from Yoshiaki Kanzaki, "Case Study from Tamura Electric Works," *Die Technology*, Vol. 1, No. 6, 1989.

In smaller injection-molding machines (100-ton class or below), the die set section is always kept attached to the machine while the cassette section is easily replaced. In larger injection-molding machines (150-ton class or above), several die sets are prepared as part of external changeover, and these are sometimes replaced also during changeover. The cassette sections are preheated by themselves, so that molding can begin as soon as they are loaded.

Advantages of the cassette method

1. *Enables a large reduction in die-fabrication costs.* Generally, adopting the cassette method enables a 30-percent reduction in die fabrication costs. The more cassettes that can be developed for a single specialized die set, the greater the cost savings.
2. *Shorter die fabrication lead times.* Adopting the cassette method can shorten the die fabrication lead time by as much as two-thirds. This is because it reduces both the variety and the quantity of die components by half.
3. *Facilitates and speeds up the die design process.* By using standardized die design sheets, dies can be designed more easily and in less time.
4. *Helps ensure high-quality products.* The cassette method uses a flexible temperature control circuit that directly controls the die temperature to ensure higher precision in the molding of products.
5. *Easier die assembly and maintenance.* Since the cassettes are only about one-seventh as large and one-sixth as heavy as conventional complete dies, they are easier to assemble and maintain.
6. *Generally reduces plastic-molding machine changeover time by half.*
7. *Greatly reduces die storage space requirements.*

14

Zero Changeover for Die-Cast Machines

Changeover improvement for die-cast machines has the following main points:

1. Preheat to at least 2 degrees (centigrade) higher than the optimum temperature for processing.
2. Install water-cooling devices.
3. Adopt transverse die removal and insertion.
4. Establish optimum processing conditions.
5. Design burr-free dies.

This chapter will examine two case studies on changeover of die-cast machines, one from Company O and the other from Company U.*

ZERO CHANGEOVER AT COMPANY O

Figure 14-1 diagrams the die-cast process at Company O, which is a vertical-handling process. Because of the furnace heat, the deburring press, drill, and other machining equipment are kept about five meters away from the die-cast machine.

The cycle time for this line ranges from 45 to 60 seconds. Workpieces that are removed from the die-cast machine are carried on a conveyor to a water-cooling process and then to an air-cooling process, after which they go to the deburring press.

---

* The case studies in this chapter were adapted from Kenichi Sekine, *Zero Changeover Techniques* (Tokyo: Nikkan Kogyo Shimbunsha, 1986), Chapter 5.

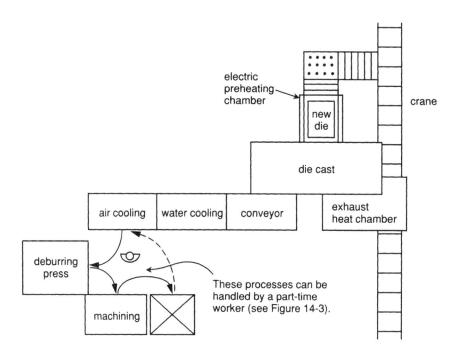

Figure 14-1. Vertical Handling Die Cast Line

Figure 14-2 illustrates the electric heating chamber that was devised for preheating workpieces and also shows the die replacement method. The new die is taken out of this preheating chamber and pushed into position. Since it takes about seven hours to preheat a die using the exhaust heat from the furnace, it is better to use the exhaust heat to some extent and then move the die to a preheating chamber.

This amount of equipment improvement was enough to enable Company O to achieve zero changeover. Their hose layout improvement is shown in Figure 14-3.

COMPANY U'S APPROACH TO ZERO CHANGEOVER

Company U, a supplier to Company O, has a factory that specializes in die casting. Naturally, this factory also includes a machining line. It uses kanban to control delivery. Company U achieved zero changeover in two main phases.

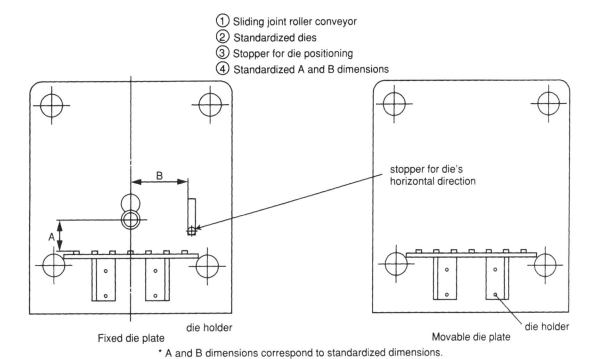

1. Sliding joint roller conveyor
2. Standardized dies
3. Stopper for die positioning
4. Standardized A and B dimensions

stopper for die's
horizontal direction

B

A

die holder

Fixed die plate

die holder

Movable die plate

* A and B dimensions correspond to standardized dimensions.

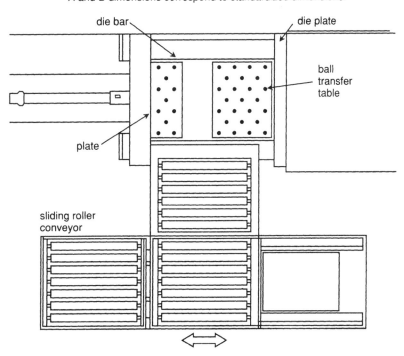

die bar   die plate

ball
transfer
table

plate

sliding roller
conveyor

Figure 14-2. Transverse Replacement Method

Improvement hint: Use couplers to simplify hose connections

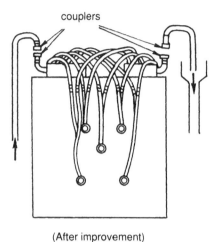

(After improvement)

Figure 14-3. Hose Centralization

Step 1: Study current conditions

Figure 14-4 shows an improvement trend chart that ends with a change-over time of 22 minutes: still a long way from the single-changeover level of 9 minutes, let alone the ultimate goal of zero changeover (3 minutes). Figure 14-5 shows a rough estimate of the changeover times for various changeover steps after the first round of improvements. Table 14-1 shows the results of the improvement group's operation analysis.

The following items require improvement to help further reduce the changeover time:

1. Very little is done in the way of changeover setup. The changeover setup procedures are left to the changeover workers to decide. The factory managers do not understand the current conditions very well and are thus unable to provide guidance for improvement.

2. There is too much standby waste caused by searching, thinking, and other unnecessary activities during changeover. As was the case with vertical presses, they need to emphasize weeding out wasteful operations from external changeover. There is no reason why external changeover should include troublesome and time-consuming tasks such as searching and deliberating.

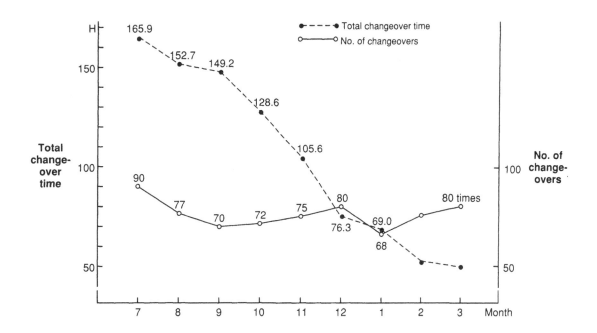

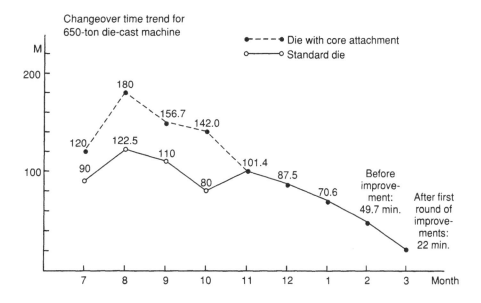

Figure 14-4. Improvement in Changeover Time on 650-Ton Die-cast Machine

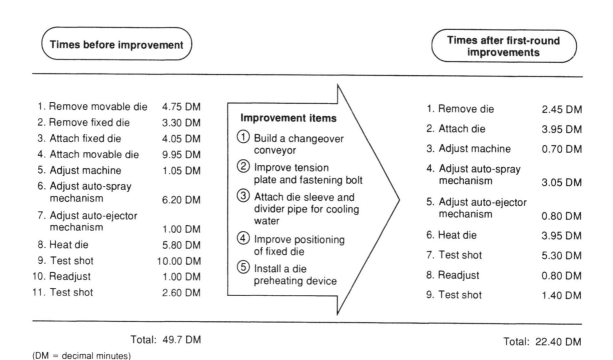

Figure 14-5. Comparison of Changeover Times Before and After First Round of Improvements

3. There is no standardized sequence of operations. Setup work is sometimes mixed in with replacement work, and there are many other instances where the operation sequence is not rational.

4. The variety of dies makes die centering difficult. The operators waste a lot of time in making adjustments. If the dies were standardized, they could simply be slid up against centering jigs to eliminate position adjustment after attachment. Many factory managers automatically reject this idea simply because their assortment of dies are made by more than one manufacturer.

5. The coolant-hose layout is hard to understand. The hoses should be color-coded to make them easier to recognize. As is, it takes an expert to figure out which hoses go where.

6. The dies are not preheated. Even though preheating of dies and nozzles is becoming common practice at die-cast factories, this factory has yet to make this improvement.

7. The tension plate uses a screw, which makes it hard to remove and replace; it also makes it hard to adjust the ejector rod.

Table 14-1. Main Points of Operation Analysis for Die-cast Machine Changeover

Category	Operation	Improvement item	Sequence	Improvement plan	Sequence
Setup	① Convey from die storage site ② Remove die from hook and wire ③ Return to extruder ④ Prepare pallet 13.3 min.	① Improve layout ② Set up die storage address system ③ Improve hook position ④ Eliminate conveyance waste	C	Design a layout for multi-process handling Improve balance of hook position Centralize pipes and wires Improve coolant pipes	C A B A
Coolant pipes	① Attach and remove hydraulic hoses ② Attach and remove coolant hoses ③ Wiring 33.4 min.	① Install easy-to-change coupler joints ② Centralize pipes and wires ③ Find a way to keep hydraulic valves from closing	A B C		
Replace-ment — Dies	① Remove and attach extruder joints ② Open and close dies ③ Attach and remove dies ④ Adjust position ⑤ Move hoist ⑥ Remove and attach die cover 25.1 min.	① Install die support ② Install stopper wire for hoist ③ Use boltless fasteners ④ Standardize die thickness and size ⑤ Switch to transverse die replacement ⑥ Use ratchet wrenches	C A	Switch to transverse die replacement Use auto-clamp mechanism Use independent fasteners Use ratchet wrenches Standardize dies Improve ejector rod Taper nozzle	C B A A C A A
Sleeves	① Adjust sleeve alignment ② Remove fastening bolts ③ Preliminary attachment ④ Final attachment 34.2 min.	① Install a centering guide ② Standardize bolt sizes ③ Use independent fasteners ④ Do not use screws for ejector rod	C B A		
Adjust-ment — Pro-cessing conditions	① Check die fastening tightness ② Set conditions ③ Test operation ④ Start operation	① Build a die preheating device ② Install a conveyor to remove products from line ③ Switch from multi-machine handling to multi-process handling ④ Taper nozzle	B B C A		

8. It takes too much time to align the plunger sleeve and die. This adjustment would not be necessary if the die sizes were standardized.

9. It is wasteful to have to change the die hook for each die, and the hook's position is not good. The hook should be in the center of the die for better balance.

10. After installing the die, a level gauge should used to check the die position.

11. Dies cannot be replaced unless the coolant hoses are first removed.

The improvement group's operation analysis helped bring these points to light. The steps for devising improvements are the same as those described in earlier chapters that discussed press changeover improvements.

Step 2: Devise improvement plans

First, the improvement group recognized the need to have all setup items in place to avoid waste during the setup phase of changeover. As in the case of presses, the improvements for doing this included:

- Development of specialized changeover carts
- Establishment of changeover kanban
- Grouping of changeover items

To these three improvements, we might add a fourth: development of a die preheating device.

Because die-cast machines are die-forging machines, to avoid defects the dies must be forged at a specified temperature. To reduce waste involved in spending time to warm up the dies, someone suggested that a die preheater be built on top of the furnace, so that it can use the furnace's exhaust heat.

However, this exhaust-heat furnace also proved too slow in warming up dies, so the group developed a simple electric preheating chamber.

The team also found ways to reduce waste during the replacement phase of changeover. If possible, it is best to use two hoists or cranes, so that one can bring in new dies from the side while the other takes out old dies from the top. Alternatively, one could bring in new dies from the top and take out old ones from the side. Bringing in dies from the side requires sliding joints and a roller conveyor, and the dies should ride on free ball bearings till they reach a positioning stopper. Old dies can be lifted from above by hoists or cranes.

Another key issue is the layout of hoses. When operators must search for, find, select, line up, and position a variety of hoses, the work can be complicated and confusing. When a die has several holes where coolant water goes, it is not easy to tell which hoses go where. Sometimes there are up to 20 hoses to connect. To make such connections easy for even less experienced operators, we should develop jigs and couplers that centralize hoses for easier identification and connection, as shown in Figure 14-3. This kind of hose layout improvement can cut a 20-minute hose connection operation down to 1 minute or less.

IMPROVEMENT IDEAS

1. Establish group organization for removing and attaching dies.
2. Practice the group organization plan until it becomes second nature.
3. Combine lateral die insertion with vertical die removal or vice-versa. This should eliminate the need for horizontal plates.
4. Centralize water-coolant hoses so they do not have to be individually removed when replacing dies.
5. Install stopper wires for hoists or cranes.
6. When dies cannot be inserted laterally, attach a permanent hook in a well-balanced position on the die, such as shown in Figure 14-6.

① Position hook so that die hangs straight and is well-balanced.
② Try to use a permanent hook.
③ Experiment with locating pins or centering jigs to facilitate die loading.

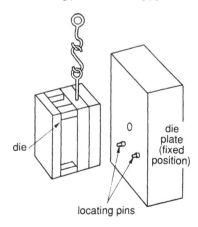

Figure 14-6. Die Hook Position

Figure 14-7 shows an example of independent fastening tools that improve die fastening, and Figure 14-8 describes the kind of die standardization needed to enable use of the independent fastening tools. If the factory can afford it, auto-clamp mechanisms, such as shown in Figure 14-9, are a valuable means of improving die replacement.

Adjustment waste is largely the product of insufficient adherence to standards. Standards for die casting are centered on the die inlet port. When attaching a die, the inlet port standard setting determines whether the nozzle and die will match correctly. Therefore, die standardization should also be based on the inlet port.

Conventionally, die sizes have been based on the size of the product. This method has produced a wide variety of die dimensions. To improve this situation, new dies should be made in dimensions based on the group of die-cast machines in which they will be used. In other words, each die must be capable of use in any die-cast machine that belongs within a certain group of machines.

This approach differs only slightly from the improvement approach for presses, discussed in earlier chapters. Basically, the two approaches are the same.

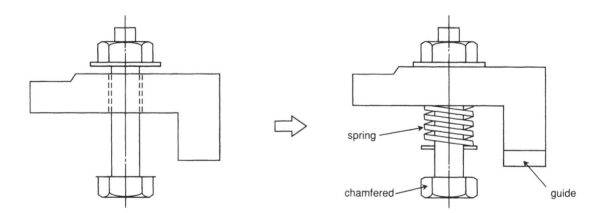

① Do not remove bolt completely. Bolt is only tightened and loosened.
② Bolt and nut sizes are standardized.

Figure 14-7. Independent Fastening Tool

① die thickness ④ die extrusion groove dimension
② height of die center ⑤ length
③ inlet hole ⑥ width

Try to establish groups of dimensions and standard sizes

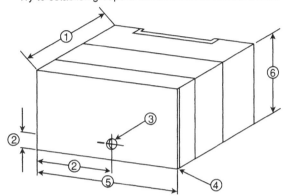

The inlet hole should be the basis for determining all other size standards.

Figure 14-8. Die Standardization

① Can the die be fastened without using bolts?
② If bolts must be used, can they be turned just once to tighten or loosen them?

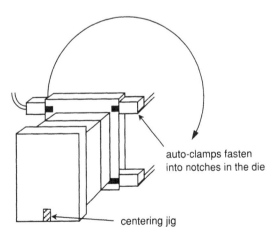

auto-clamps fasten
into notches in the die

centering jig

Figure 14-9. Boltless Fastener

1. Make the die's inlet port the basis for standardization.
2. Establish standard outer dimensions for dies based on the largest dies that can be handled by the target group of die-cast machines, as shown in Figure 14-8.
3. Attach die-plate stoppers that have protruding centering jigs, as shown in Figure 14-10. Or, it may be better to attach locating pins instead. Experiment to find out which is better in each case.
4. Eliminate the use of screws for ejector rods. Insert a spring to make the rod return automatically, as is done in most new ejector rod devices. Do not use screws or bolts to fasten ejector rods; instead, use a device that does not make direct contact.
5. This is a minor matter, but it is better that the tongue in the tongue and groove be tapered for a better fit.

To summarize, Company U achieved its zero changeover goal by implementing four improvements:

1. Remodeling machines to enable transverse loading and unloading of dies.
2. Installing an electric die preheater.
3. Building a centralized group of water-coolant pipes or hoses.
4. Using two hoists for loading and unloading dies.

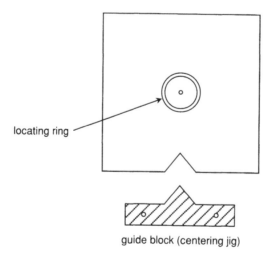

Figure 14-10. Centering Jig

15

Zero Changeover for Assembly Lines

Company O has more than 60 assembly lines in its assembly plant, and conducts model changeovers on each of these lines after each production run of about 10 product units. Company O has established zero changeover on all its lines. The assembly workers have grown well accustomed to this way of doing things, and think nothing of having to do about 20 changeovers per day as part of their normal routine.

Company M, a clothing manufacturer, has been trying to do the same thing, but with little success. Its "custom-made" approach to small-lot production is plagued by long cycle times, overstaffing of lines, and close to 100-percent manual operations.

In this chapter, we will examine the problems affecting Company M and see how it overcame these problems to establish zero changeover on its assembly lines.

WHICH IS BETTER: MIXED-FLOW OR REDUCED STAFFING ON ASSEMBLY LINES?

Without going into detail in describing mixed assembly, let us consider an example of a mixed-flow assembly type of conveyor line, shown in Figure 15-1. This line assembles a mixed flow of the following six product models in the following total quantities.

Product A   50 units
Product B   20 units
Product C   14 units

> Product D   3 units
> Product E   18 units
> Product F   21 units

Generally, this kind of mixed-flow arrangement is adopted for conveyor lines that are expensive and that are designed for large-lot production, such as automobile or bulldozer assembly lines.

The method of building assembly lines that have only a few workers handling a large number of assembly processes is too complex to describe here in detail; suffice it to say that this method has been widely used for building one-person U-shaped assembly cells.

Such reduced-staff assembly cells are increasingly common in factories that assemble motors or electronic components. The objectives of such cells are shown in the just-in-time (JIT) production system outlined in Figure 15-2.

The reduced-staff approach is better, even in economic terms, because of today's market needs for wide-variety small-lot production. In deciding how many U-shaped assembly cells to build, consider such factors as the investment costs, inventory-related loss, and loss due to changeover. If possible, it is always good to avoid changeover — even zero changeover.

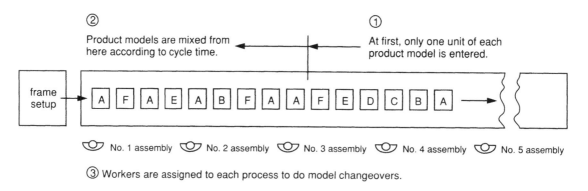

Figure 15-1. Mixed-flow Assembly on a Single Conveyor Line

SHORTENING PRODUCTION DESIGN LEAD TIME IS EVEN MORE IMPORTANT THAN IMPROVING CHANGEOVER

Table 15-1 describes the design process for stitching embroidery onto women's clothing. Note that it takes five days to get the preliminary samples made, and eight days to get the multicolored samples made.

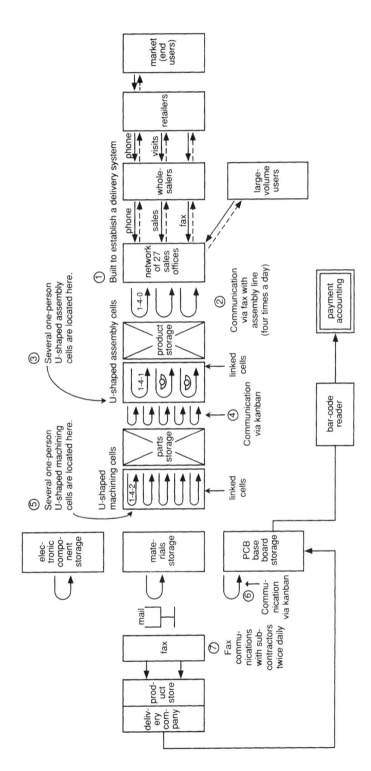

Figure 15-2. Just-in-Time Production System

Table 15-1. Embroidery Design Process for Women's Apparel

Category	Sequence	Process name	Time
Preliminary sample	1	Develop embroidery pattern concept	3 to 4 days
	2	Outline drawing of design	6 hours
	3	Color design	2 hours
	4	Plan production sequence (draw charts, determine material quantities, write stitching instructions, plan changeovers, etc.)	2 hours
	5	Make preliminary samples (inside and outside)	5 days
	6	Evaluate samples	30 minutes
Multicolor samples	7	Make revisions (repeat 2 to 6 times)	3 hours
	8	Plan production of color design	3 hours
	9	Plan sequence (same as step 4 above)	30 minutes
	10	Make color samples (in each color)	8 days
	11	Check and revise color design	1 hour
Set standards for final samples	12	Make final exhibit samples	8 hours
	13	Draw production schedule and diagrams	3 hours

Obviously, the production lead time includes the processing time and the retention time. In this assembly factory, retention time accounted for over 90 percent of the production lead time. If the company can eliminate the causes of all that retention, it can establish a quick delivery system even without improving its changeover methods.

If the design process for seasonal products takes too much time, the pressure to deliver the products in time for the season falls on the shoulders of downstream stages, such as the assembly lines. All too often, the design and procurement departments adopt a leisurely pace in bringing out a new product, and the production department then finds itself having to make sample production and mass production almost simultaneous, since there is no time left for a normal production setup period. Naturally, when production setup is diminished, defects abound and custom jigs to reduce production costs are developed late, if at all.

Take another look at Table 15-1 and try to estimate the total amount of time between steps 1 and 13. If you estimated 27 days, you are very close. One might well wonder how an apparel factory that needs 27 days just for the embroidery can ever hope to establish a quick delivery system. Obviously, they cannot, but this embroidery process can be expected to pass a lot of pressure on to downstream processes in the factory. What can this factory do to improve its situation?

1. Bring the sample production process into an integrated line. Figure 15-3 shows an outline of how this can be done. Refer to Part II of this book for a detailed description of how this kind of line is developed.
2. Establish a daily delivery system for subcontracted work and in-house work, and try to make it a 1-1-1 system (items delivered once a day, one delivery time after they are ordered). An address system should also be used for stored items.

Company M established a goal of reducing the embroidery design process from 27 days to just 9 days, renaming the target period "single design" (after "single changeover").

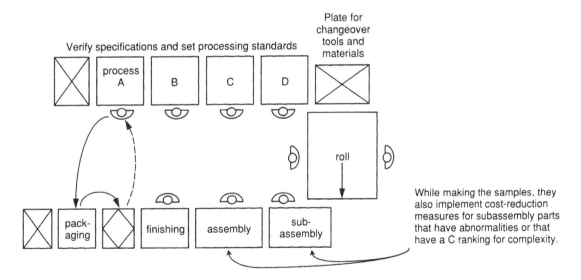

Figure 15-3. Line Integration of Sample Production

ON ASSEMBLY LINES, CHANGEOVER HAPPENS AT THE PREVIOUS PROCESS

At Company M's apparel factory, after the patterns are designed and produced, they are sent to the production setup department. Figure 15-4 gives a general idea of this process flow.

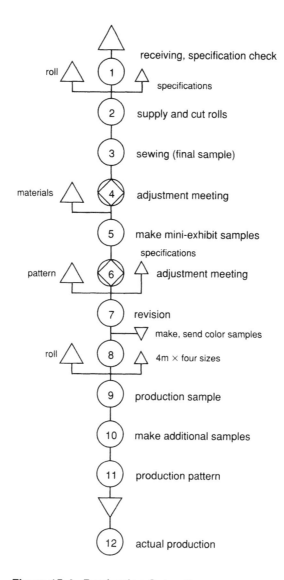

Figure 15-4. Production Setup Process

Note that processes 3, 5, 7, 9, and 10 all have to do with producing samples. Although Company M cannot eliminate sample production (its wholesale customers demand it), it can at least reduce the sample production processes through line integration, as shown in Figure 15-3.

This means improving the flow of the sample production process. In the old days, samples were usually produced slowly and manually by one person.

In today's era of wide-variety small-lot production, samples should be made using flow production, like mass production.

Once the sample production line is in place, it needs to be integrated into the pre-changeover stage for mass production in the following steps.

1. The people who establish the production standards (i.e., those who make and approve the patterns, processing standards, and specifications) should provide standards and specifications that are easy for the operators to understand. For example, if they show the assembly diagram and the parts list on the same piece of paper or signboard, it is easier for operators to see when there are missing parts, parts selection errors, assembly errors, or misplaced items.

2. Each process must be provided with a list of all items that concern that particular process, so that the operators and supervisors will have only one document to consult.

3. Prepare a list of the value analysis target items for the sample production line and give it to the operators. Such items may include:
   • blind stitching to meet reverse-side standards
   • subassembly work that takes too much time
   • parts that take a lot of time to prepare
   • clear indication of C-grade items on the process table

4. As they assemble parts to make samples, assembly workers (along with the person in charge of setting manufacturing standards and the line supervisor) should give a C rank to all abnormalities, hard-to-assemble items, and time-consuming operations. They can then concentrate their cost-reduction efforts on these C-ranked items. This step is a very important part of pre-changeover.
   If for some reason they are unable to find a way of reducing these costs, the line supervisor should make one sample by hand to see if the problem can be resolved by a skills-based approach.

5. Whenever possible, all samples should be strictly inspected and evaluated. Try to look at things with a fresh perspective, as if you were a disinterested third party. Then recheck the list of important items.

6. Check whether changeover is following the sequence indicated by the changeover kanban (in-process kanban). Pay special attention to the reliability of equipment adjustment, jig attachment, and other changeover tasks.

7. Make sure all setup items have been prepared beforehand. At Company M, these would include the following:

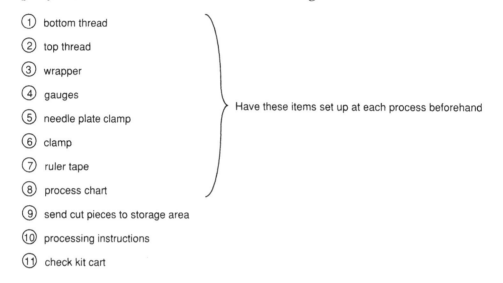

   ① bottom thread

   ② top thread

   ③ wrapper

   ④ gauges

   ⑤ needle plate clamp   Have these items set up at each process beforehand

   ⑥ clamp

   ⑦ ruler tape

   ⑧ process chart

   ⑨ send cut pieces to storage area

   ⑩ processing instructions

   ⑪ check kit cart

8. Implement sequential changeover. Explain the purpose and method of each changeover operation to the operators. Make sure the processing standards are clearly explained and understood.
   - Work sequentially beginning with the operators at the first process.
   - Make sure that any sewing machines moved are moved sequentially.
   - If possible, form the lines first, then transfer the people to them.
9. Observe the actions of the operators for deviations from the processing standards. Pay especially close attention to:
   - right-angle stitching
   - two-sided standards (blind stitching)
   - stitching on very thick or very thin materials
10. Find ways to prevent deviation from standards.
   - Try to pre-align the wrapper and gauge for stitching
   - Develop mistake-proofing jigs (*poka-yoke*)
   - Be careful to confirm the precision of stretchable materials after they are cut from the pattern
   - Establish standards for three stages of positioning: start, middle, and end

11. If the cycle time varies a lot, have operators check the cycle time by giving vocal signals of their work progress. If necessary, redistribute the work load or establish a set of mutual assistance instructions.

12. If defects or rework occur right after a changeover, consult with the line leader and consider having the assistant leader do a full-lot inspection. This will help keep the operators from developing bad habits.

13. Check for missing items immediately after changeover. Check the changeover time and the number of kit carts on hand. Also check the weekly schedule to see which model change is next.

This list is a kind of "à la carte" approach to zero changeover. Of these steps, number 4 is the most significant.

About the Authors

Kenichi Sekine was a 1944 graduate of the Navy Air Force Academy and completed Kurume Industrial Special School in 1948. He joined Bridgestone in 1948 and remained until 1972. As chief QC inspector at Bridgestone, he introduced TQC and led the company's application for the Deming Prize. From 1968 to 1972, he worked for an affiliate of Toyota Motor Company, where he promoted the Toyota production system (TPS).

In 1973, he left to found the TPS Consulting Group. Under his direction the group:

- provided consulting on worksite IE to Toyota-affiliated companies
- built U-shaped lines in an assembly department at Oriental Motors
- built U-shaped line at Nuinac
- built load-load lines in an assembly department at T Company
- minimized automatic assembly personnel at Uni Charm and provided consulting on the JIT production system
- built assembly lines with minimal personnel at TDK
- provided consulting on the high-diversified small-lot production systems in Nagano Prefecture
- provided consulting on worksite IE to Komatsu
- provided consulting on TPS to Danden
- improved the assembly lines at Japan Maranz
- provided consulting to Ishida
- provided consulting on setup improvement to Tateishi Electric
- provided consulting on inventory reduction and setup improvement to Kunimitsu Paper

- provided consulting on worksite IE to a Komatsu affiliate
- provided consulting on setup improvement of the packaging line at Ajinomoto
- provided consulting on TPS to a Yanma Diesel affiliate
- improved processing lines at Fuyo Industry
- introduced and promoted TPS to Facom (France)

In 1985, Mr. Sekine founded the Added Value Management Institute (TPS Consulting Company, Ltd.). Among its achievements, the company:

- built U-shaped lines in a motor department at Mitsubishi Electric in Korea (productivity improved by 50 percent)
- built U-shaped lines in a electronics assembly department at Toyo Precision Industry (OPC) in Korea (productivity improved by 30 percent)
- built U-shaped lines in an electronics assembly department at Modern Electronics in Korea (productivity improved by 30 percent)
- converted conveyor lines into U-shaped lines in an air conditioner plant at Daiu Career in Korea (productivity improved 30 percent). Cut setup time in half. Cut shaft processing personnel from eleven to five.
- built U-shaped line in an assembly department at Mikuni Industry (productivity improved by 100 percent)

Mr. Sekine's expertise lies in the specific areas of implementing TPS, zero setup, cutting assembly/processing personnel in half, cutting the designing period and personnel in half, innovative Total Productive Maintenance (TPM), and inventory reduction.

Mr. Sekine has published many books on manufacturing process improvement. Other titles available in English include *One-Piece Flow, One-Piece Flow Video*, and *Design Team Revolution*.

Keisuke Arai graduated from Osaka State University with a degree in engineering. From 1957 to 1982 he worked for Mitsui Shipbuilding, Inc., where he advanced to product manager, responsible for design, construction, quality control, process control, and cost control of nuclear power-related projects. While at Mitsui, he produced the *Index of Project Documentation* for the Engineering Association.

Mr. Arai became an independent consultant in 1982, serving as an advisor to a number of manufacturing companies. He has been with TPS Consulting Company since 1986, serving as a chief consultant. He also lectures at SANNO University.

Index

9 781563 273414

*For Product Safety Concerns and Information please contact
our EU representative GPSR@taylorandfrancis.com Taylor & Francis
Verlag GmbH, Kaufingerstraße 24, 80331 München, Germany*

T - #0112 - 230425 - C0 - 280/208/17 - PB - 9781563273414 - Gloss Lamination